Social Exclusion and Discrimination with Weaker Sections of Society: An Inclusive Policy

Emanual Nahar

KALPAZ

Reprint in India, 2024

First Published, 2016

Published by

Kalpaz Publications
C-30, Satyawati Nagar,
Delhi – 110052
E-mail: kalpaz@hotmail.com
Ph.: 9212142040

Printed at: G. Print Process, Delhi

Cataloging in Publication Data—DK
Courtesy: D.K. Agencies (P) Ltd. <docinfo@dkagencies.com>

Nahar, Emanual, author.
Social exclusion and discrimination with weaker sections of society : an inclusive policy / Professor Emanual Nahar, Dr Kanchan Chandan, Ms Manjinder Kaur, Dr Sucheta Singh.
pages cm
ISBN 9789351281979 (HB)

1. Marginality, Social—Government policy—India. 2. Discrimination—Government policy—India. I. Chandan, Kanchan, author. II. Manjinder Kaur, editor. III. Singh, Sucheta, editor. IV. Title.

HN690.Z9M26 2016 DDC 307.14120954 23

Contents

Foreword

India Post-Independence continues to develop while excluding certain groups like the Dalits, Backward classes, women and religious minorities who are yet to taste the fruits of development. Constitutional Rights hardly seem to have touched these groups. While India has made terrific progress in the fields of science, agriculture, information technology etc., these groups continue to reel under poverty, destitution and exploitation, being almost out of the mainstream population. Statistics clearly indicate that all the benefits of economic growth, information technology, legislation and even protective discrimination have eluded those at the bottom of social hierarchy. This scenario has been explained in terms of 'social exclusion', signifying persistent and systematic discrimination suffered by marginalised groups. Though the concept of social exclusion is borrowed from the West yet it signifies the ground reality prevailing in Indian society. With no trickle-down effect of economic growth in sight so far, the gap between the rich and the poor has widened disproportionately, creating a volatile situation. Despite numerous policies and welfare measures, development has failed to reach out to the poorest of the poor. Further, women and children in poverty happen to bear multiple disabilities due to poverty, gender and patriarchal ethos.

India in its development plans has placed special stress upon 'Inclusive Policy' with the objective of accomplishing an equitable growth/development. Interestingly, it is not individuals but groups, viz. lowest rung among Scheduled Castes and Tribes, women, street children, the disabled population etc., who have so far remained totally excluded from the project of development, most probably due to the cultural, social and political deterrents. It is important to note here that merely prioritizing an 'Inclusive Policy' cannot bring sudden and abrupt changes on desirable lines. Instead, the process is likely to be thwarted by a number of factors such as cultural factors including religion, caste, patriarchy, etc. apart from the politics of social exclusion.

It is in this backdrop that a one-day Seminar was organized by the Centre for the Study of Social Exclusion and Inclusive policy. It is an effort to provide the social scientists, State officials and NGO representatives with a platform for brainstorming on the issues and deterrents confronting the agenda of inclusive policy. While some of the issues confronting social scientists in the region are general in nature, having parallels in other parts of the country, there is need to identify specific issues and deterrents in the pursuit of an Inclusive Policy in the North-Western region. Papers presented by various faculty and research Scholars from Panjab University and Various other Academic institutions were really good piece of research. There was a well attempted effort to illustrate social discrepancies' present in today's society. This book is an endeavour to help the research students from Sociology, Social Anthropology, Political Science, Dalit, Minority and Women Studies.

Professor Surinder K. Shukla
Department of Political Science,
USOL, Panjab University,
Chandigarh

List of Contributors

1. **Ms Priyanka,** Assistant Professor, Rayat Bahra College, Ropar (Punjab)
2. **Dr Emanual Nahar,** Professor-Department of Political Science, USOL, Punjab University, Chandigarh.
3. **Dr Suman,** Assistant Professor, Department of Laws, Delhi University, New Delhi.
4. **Dr Sipra Sagarika**, Assistant Professor, Department of Sociology, Panjab University, Chandigarh.
5. **Amrit Pal Kaur,** Assistant Professor, University Institute of Legal Studies, Panjab University, Chandigarh.
6. **Dr Kamla,** Assistant Professor, University School of Open Learning, Department of Political Science, Panjab University, Chandigarh.
7. **Dr Nirmal Singh,** Assistant Professor, University Institute of Legal Studies, Panjab University, Chandigarh.
8. **Dr Kanchan Chandan**, Research Associate, Centre for the Study of Social Exclusion and Inclusive Policy, Punjab University, Chandigarh.
9. **Manjinder Kaur,** Research Assistant, Centre for the Study of Social Exclusion and Inclusive Policy, Punjab University, Chandigarh.
10. **Dr Sucheta Singh,** Research Assistant, Centre for the Study of Social Exclusion and Inclusive Policy, Punjab University, Chandigarh.
11. **Dr Ranjay Vardhan**, Senior Assistant Professor in Sociology, Post Graduate Government College for Girls, Sector 42, Chandigarh.

12. **Dr Sunakar Patra**, Assistant Professor in Sociology, Post Graduate Government College for Girls, Sector 42, Chandigarh.
13. **Dr Gobind Chandra Sethi**, Assistant Professor in Political Science, Post Graduate Government College, Sector-46, Chandigarh.
14. **Dr Mona Arora**, Assistant Professor in Sociology, SD College, Sector 32, Chandigarh.
15. **Amrit Kaur,** Assistant Professor, Post Graduate Government College for Girls, Sector 42, Chandigarh.
16. **Poonam Sharma**, Assistant Professor, Government Home Science College, Sector 10, Chandigarh.
17. **Tejinder Pal Singh**, Assistant Professor, SGGS College, Sector 26, Chandigarh.
18. **Gunjan Setia**, Assistant Professor, Department of Sociology, Panjab University Constituent College, Shikhwala.
19. **Parminder Kaur**, Research Scholar, Department of Sociology, Panjab University, Chandigarh.
20. **Nirat Pandey**, Research Scholar, Department of Political Science, Panjab University, Chandigarh.
21. **Kanwar Deep Singh**, Research Scholar, Department of Political Science, Panjab University, Chandigarh.
22. **Rupinder Aulakh,** Research Scholar, Department cum Centre for the Women's Studies and Development, Panjab University, Chandigarh.
23. **Dr Manish Kumar,** Assistant Professor in Political Science, Rayat College of Law, SBS Nagar (Punjab).

Towards Inclusive Policy: Cultural, Political and Economic Deterrents

An Introduction

The Indian constitution in its Preamble proclaims that India to be Sovereign, Democratic, Secular, Socialist, Republic and ensures to secure all its citizens, Justice, Liberty, Equality and Fraternity. The Directive Principles are the directives to Parliament for the improvement of social, economic and political status of the weaker sections of the society which are continuously exploiting by the majority. These Constitutional Rights and Provisions hardly seem to have touched these groups. India has made a terrific progress in the field of science, information technology and so many other spheres. Despite of India's record of economic growth and development forms of poverty remains a major challenge to a large majority of its citizens. Statistics and Census report clearly indicates that all the benefits of economic growth, information technology and even protective discrimination have eluded those at the bottom of social hierarchy. This scenario has been explained in terms of 'social exclusion', signifies persistent and systematic discrimination suffered by marginalised groups. Social exclusion concept was borrowed from western countries and defined as 'The process through which individuals or groups are entirely or partially excluded from full participation in the society within which they live'. It occurs when some groups of people due to colour, caste, races and religious bases denied access to opportunities and resources which are necessary for survival. Social exclusion is deep-rooted a process in India. It hampers the growth of development and social integration. The removal of social exclusion is the top agenda of our democratic society of India. Therefore, removal of forms of discrimination is the most important task to be performed before an inclusive society is reconstructed. This is also the most democratic task of all since it is call to establish a society based on equality: social, political and perhaps economic too. If discrimination is a problem for democracy, which it is indeed, democracy could also be a destabilising factor for a society based on discrimination. Democracy for a discriminatory society is a great challenge since it upholds the principle of equality, and therefore proposes radical changes in the existing patterns of distribution of social and economic powers. Democracy's task is not finished with the simple decelerations of the principle of equality.

In India and its development plans placed special stress upon 'Inclusive Policy' with the objective to achieve an equitable growth. Central government of India also set the goal for 'Inclusive Development' in different plans. The focus area of twelvefth five year plan is elimination of all types of discrimination, awareness creation and change in the mindset of the people. Convergence of various programmes to improve educational, health, social security, livelihood, working and living environment for all deprived sections of the society. To achieve these objectives of inclusive growth in a democratic set-up, government adopted strategy with formulation and implementation a numbers of welfare programmes so that the benefits and outcomes of the economic growth and development read the needy ones. Only plans and laws on paper are not enough, government must show serious concern and work with more commitment to address the suffering of these people.

On this grounding, Centre for Study of Social Exclusion and Inclusive Policy, Panjab University, Chandigarh organised a National Level One-day Seminar. The Seminar was held under the sponsorship of ***ICSSR-NWRC Panjab University, Chandigarh***.

Following sub-themes were taken up in various sessions during the Seminar:

- Mainstreaming the Scheduled Caste: Issues and Strategies.
- Strategising Gender Equality
- Inclusion of the Socially Excluded: Poor, Disabled, Street Children, etc.

- Politics of Marginality with special reference of Minority Communities of India.

Many Eminent scholars from various universities and colleges participated in the deliberations during the Seminar. Various issues related to Inclusive policy in India were discussed during the three technical of the National Seminar.

The Seminar began with the Welcome Address by Dr Emanual Nahar, he briefed the audience about the motive of the Seminar. In the Inaugural address, Professor M.M. Puri, former Vice-Chancellor, Panjab University, Chandigarh, expressed that policies are not static and cannot serve the purpose years to come. Social fabric of society is also bound to resist various changing climate. Change is the law of nature to deal with the changing situation. New policies should need to be framed with the involvement of different sections of society. No group should be excluded.

In the Keynote address, Professor Karori Singh, Director, South-Asian Studies, University of Rajasthan, Jaipur, pointed out that India has a society which aspired to have a neo-liberal economic, electoral, democratic polity and assertion of neo-conservative social orientation. Such a model of society is self-destructive in it and cannot be a model of society is self-destructive in it and cannot be model of inclusive society. He suggests technology, management and innovativeness have potential to envisage inclusive. India wherein everyone will be enable to exercise full freedom and equality, ensured justice, prosperity and security and thereby ensuring dignified life to each and every citizen will be real social inclusion.

In the presidential remark Professor Ronki Ram, Dean, Faculty of Art, Honorary Director, ICSSR, Panjab University, Chandigarh, explained that exclusion does not mean ex-communication. Excluded group continue to be a measure of society but not to allow enjoys the wealth of society. They generate the wealth for society and very active in production set up. He emphasised on the dire need to relook and reframe the present framework of the society.

The Seminar was divided into four technical sessions; third and fourth technical session of the seminar was run parallel. First technical session of seminar was chaired by Professor Manvinder Kaur and Dr Ameer Sultana and ten papers were presented in this session. Second session of the seminar was chaired by Professor Pampa and Dr Suman Gupta and eleven papers were read out in this session by various professors and research scholars. Third session was coordinated by ProfessorDhian Kaur and Professor Ravinder Kaur while the fourth one was coordinated by Professor Surinder Kler Shukla.

Dr Sipra, Assistant Professor, Department of Sociology, Panjab University, Chandigarh in her paper "Religion and its Interactional Dynamics: A Study of Changing Contours of Tribal Community" discussed the alteration in the colonial approaches of isolation with the tribal population opened the doors of integration for the indigenous group. The wave was meant for strengthening tribal identity but with its expose to several multilayer factors such as globalisation, migration, intrusion of middle men and contractors, modernisation, multiple religious faiths etc, there were major lapses marked in the identities of the tribal people.

Amritpal Kaur, Assistant Professor, University Institute of Legal Studies, Panjab University, Chandigarh, in the paper "The Policy Approach in Disability Sector: The Core Issues" argued that India is one of the world's fastest growing economies and claims to be the largest democratic republic. According to a World Bank estimate in 2011 it has a population of 1.241 billion and the census of the Government of India reveals that 2.13 per cent of this population have disabilities. During this period of Indian economic growth, policy support for human rights of persons with disabilities is essential, to ensure the equity gap is decreased and that the voices of these persons are heard. In India, there can be physical, social, psychological, rehabilitation, accessibility and economical barriers to access and inclusion of services related to the disabled persons.

Dr Kamla, Assistant Professor, USOL, Department of Political Science, Panjab University, Chandigarh, in her paper "Political Marginalisation of Scheduled Castes in Elections to General Constituencies of Punjab Vidhan Sabha - A Case Study of 2007 and 2012 Elections" highlighted that even hundred years after Guru Ravidas began preaching the oneness of God's creation, Scheduled

Castes in Punjab and rest of India continue to be marginalised in socio-cultural and political arenas. They lay at the bottom of the Hindu caste hierarchy, of which Dr B.R. Ambedkar, wanted complete annihilation, to usher in an egalitarian society in India. The rigid and socially maligned social hierarchies of Indian society meant that a commitment to equality and social justice was hardly a "natural" sentiment. The same phenomenon continue to stall political advancement of Scheduled Castes - also called Dalits - in so called liberalised democratic set-up. Though Punjab has the highest concentration of Dalits (31.9 per cent) in the country, reservation in education, employment and political decision making bodies (Panchayats and Legislatures) has not enhanced their political fortunes.

Dr Nirmal Singh, Assistant Professor, University Institute of Legal Studies, Panjab University, Chandigarh in his paper "Dalits Inclusion in a Democratic System: Ambedkar Prospect" discussed about various ideologies of dealing with the oppression of the poor and discriminated sections of society protecting their freedom and dignity, their sheer survival as human being and communities, have proved not just inadequate but by and large irrelevant. There is no exclusive model available for the development of Dalits. The development of Dalits has historically been articulated in emancipatory terms: emancipation from caste oppression, bondage, social exclusion, humiliation and so on. It is true that caste is an anathema in a secular democracy and must be abolished. And our Constitution rightly abolished it.

Dr Kanchan Chandan, Research Associate, Centre for the Study of Social Exclusion and Inclusive Policy, Panjab University, Chandigarh, in her paper "Women with Disabilities: A Politics of Exclusion" made an effort to illustrate plight of women who are not equal physically or psychologically with other section of the society, and are subjected to several kind of discrimination, and violence against them. Many initiatives have taken to bring social inclusion in the society, still women are facing social exclusion in different walks of life, be it social, political, economic, social exclusion of women who are disabled or differently able is no exception in terms of social exclusion of women in society. Women with disability are more marginalised and discriminated; attitude of the society is precarious towards them.

Ms Manjinder Kaur, Research Assistant, Centre for the Study of Social Exclusion and Inclusive Policy, Panjab University, Chandigarh in "Sex Preference and the Value of Sons and Daughters in India" argued that it is rather recently that it has been somewhat recognised that today's woman and tomorrow's mother is yesterday's girl-child and that it is her all rounded healthy development-socio-economical, physical, mental, emotional, intellectual-which will determine not only the status of today's girl-child and tomorrow's woman and mother but also the quality of life of the families and of the generations to come. As such, it is girl child's abuse and exploitation violating her right to life and unhealthy development that presents one of the greatest hurdles in improving the women's status and nation's real progress.

Dr Sucheta Singh, Research Assistant, Centre for the Study of Social Exclusion and Inclusive Policy, Panjab University, Chandigarh in her paper "Violation of Human Rights in Unorganised Sector: A study of excluded group of Migrant Labour in Punjab" highlighted the good governance government keeps on making policies or acts but no conscious action has been witnessed on ground to verify the fact that these policies have been effectively implemented or benefitted the mass or not. It can be safely said that after contributing their labour in the upliftment of the economy of Punjab. Migrants are quite far off from the benefits like social security, protection of the right to health, housing, education, water and access to sanitation. Beside this, they are kept isolated to the access to the right to identity, including birth registration.

Dr Ranjay Vardhan, Senior Assistant Professor in Sociology, P.G. Government College for Girls, Sector 42, Chandigarh, in the paper "IT and Gender: From Social Exclusion to Social Inclusion" highlighted that women have been traditionally socially excluded from development process and they could not reap the benefit of development due to patriarchal attitude and prevalent orthodoxies. However, among other factors, Information Technology has a deep impact on the society and has been playing an important role in bringing social change. The digital divide that existed in the usage of ICT by gender is minimising between male and female users. Women are being empowered with the spread and usage of as ICT as it is enabling them in education, jobs, income, improvement in family and social status, etc. IT is helping women from social exclusion to social inclusion especially in urban areas.

Dr Sunakar Patra, Assistant Professor, Department of Sociology, P. G. Govt. College for Girls, Sector- 42, Chandigarh, in the paper "Development Projects at Odisha's Coast and the Silent Spiriting away of Fishing Communities" discussed the State's new strategy of ensuring development through the philosophy of liberalisation, privatisation and globalisation seems to have counter-productive results. The fact is that most of the development projects and policies for ports, industrialisation, mining, trade, and transport have deleterious effects on the marginalised and deprived sections. These policies have not only failed to benefit them, but have also increasingly threatened their source of livelihood.

Dr Gobinda Chandra Sethi, Assistant Professor in Political Science, Post Graduate Government. College, Sector-46, Chandigarh in the paper "Government Initiative in mainstreaming Dalit: Issues and Challenges" discussed that the sense of feeling the word Dalit, nowadays, is to remind not only age-old oppression/deprivation and the victims of such oppression deprivation but also to the hardship of their condition of life. This further symbolises a struggle for recognition of self-identity, expression of historical reality of oppression due to caste-based untouchability and occupations and a determination for creation of egalitarian society. Social Inclusion is the removal of institutional barriers and the enhancement of incentives to increase the access of diverse individuals and groups to development opportunities.

Dr Mona Arora, Assistant Professor, Department of Sociology, SD College, Sector-32, Chandigarh, in her paper "Gender Discrimination: The Status of Girl Child" discussed that it is gender and culture that determines the position of a child, especially the girl child in the Indian social structure. Experience has shown, over and over again, that investment in girls' education translate directly into better nutrition for the whole family, better heathcare, declining fertility, poverty reduction and better overall economic performance. Unfortunately, gender bias continues to manifest itself in Indian society and at every stage of life she is discriminated and neglected for basic nutrition, education and living standard. In spite of the right to equality enshrined in the Constitution and the various laws, due to socio-economic factors, the incidence of neglect, abuse and deprivation, particularly in case of girl child, has gradually increased.

Amrit Kaur, Assistant Professor, PGGCG, Sector 42, Chandigarh, in her paper titled "Social Mobility among Scheduled Castes: A Study of Village Mugalmagri in Rupnagar District of Punjab", highlighted caste as a powerful organisation in Indian society. It provided a structure for arranging and organising social groups in terms of their statuses and positions in the social and economic system. The 'Untouchables' considered to be outside of the varna system and named as "untouchables" or ati-sudras or avarna. They were considered to be inferior in all respects by the higher castes and were placed at the bottom of ritual and social hierarchies and had been subjected to varieties of disabilities.

Poonam Sharma, Assistant Professor, Department of Sociology, Government Home Science College, Sector-10, Chandigarh in her paper "Political Empowerment and Participation of Dalit Women" highlighted that the women empowerment in India has largely been contextualised within the homogeneous understanding of women's reality. As a result, the multiple realities of women's oppression with respect to their caste and religious position is often undermined both in academic and bureaucratic explanations of women's subordination. Dalit women are particularly vulnerable and marginalised as they suffer from multiple discriminations as women, as poor and as dalits. While some governments have enacted Constitutional safeguards and affirmative action to promote access and opportunities, reservation policies in public sector employment of such laws and programmes remains weak and insufficient.

Tejinder Pal Singh, Assistant Professor, Department of Sociology, Shri Guru Gobind Singh College, Sector 26, Chandigarh, in his paper titled "Between Exclusion" And "Unfavourable Inclusion": Realising the Right to Food for Dalits made an attempt to analyse various meanings and dimensions of "social exclusion" given by Amartya Sen, and also explores the inextricable linkage between the condition of food security, the Right to Food in India, as well as the 'hidden apartheid' (in terms of prevalence of hunger and malnutrition) to realise an equitable, inclusive and sustainable path to development. The causes of hunger and under nutrition are often not a scarcity of food but an inability to access available food in a caste stratified society. The "paradoxical" situation is such that while being a Welfare State, Indian Constitutional and democratic ethos guarantee justice, liberty and equality, yet various forms of discrimination and exclusion still persist. The principles of free-market laissez-fairism, based on high economic growth rates, have failed to 'trickle down' and improve the food security situation of rural India, especially for this most vulnerable and marginalised sections.

Ms Gunjan Setia, Assistant Professor, Department of Sociology, Panjab University Constituent College, Shikhwala in her paper "Political Marginalisation in Punjab villages: A nexus of Corruption, Factionalism and political distrust." In her paper she puts forward the changing attitudes, experiences and beliefs of the rural folk after the green revolution in Punjab. It tries to deal with the issue of political marginalisation and political reality as perceived by the inhabitants at village level.

Parminder Kaur, Research Scholar, Department of Sociology, Panjab University, Chandigarh in her paper "Crime against Dalit Women" highlighted that dalit women are in a worse position than dalits in general in terms of sex ratio, wages, employment, occupation, assets, health, social mobility. The impunity enjoyed by both dominant caste community and the state officiates continues largely due to the insensitiveness and the continuous failure of the criminal justice administrative system. The higher degree of deprivation among dalit women is reflected in other indicators of well being-under nutrition and health.

Nirat Pandey, Research Scholar, Department of Political Science, Panjab University, Chandigarh in his paper "Revisiting Delhi Gang Rape: Strategising gender empowerment at linguistic level" highlighted that today the literature on the issues like social inclusion and exclusion is second to none in social sciences. These are the most discussed issues in academic in last two decades especially after the rise of 'Subaltern school'. But the literature which ponders over the idea that how media's narration perpetuates and reproduces stereotypes, which further nurtures the processes of exclusion and hierarchy in society, is subdued, especially in the context of India. The paramount reason for it is the dominance of sociological and ethnographic approach of the former literature. But the fact which cannot be denied is that media is one of the prominent tool which has been playing an important role in maintaining existing patterns of power and hierarchies. The nature and the role of Indian media in disseminating gender stereotypes is an under researched area.

Kanwar Deep Singh, Research Scholar, Department of Political Science, Panjab University, Chandigarh in his paper "Politics of Religious Exclusion: Status of Sehajdari Sikhs in the Sikh Panth" attempted to examine and analyse the contemporary status of Sehajdhari Sikhs in the Sikh 'Panth', on the basis of their historical origin and evolution. The paper will focus of the political dynamics behind the resulting explorations in context to the religious status of 'Sehajdhari Sikhs', which form a significant part of Sikh Community.

Dr Kanchan Chandan,
Ms Manjinder Kaur and
Dr Sucheta Singh

1

Politics of Social Exclusion: A Study of Dalit Christians in the State of Punjab

—*Ms Priyanka and Emanual Nahar*

Abstract

Christian Community in Punjab has not gained either politically nor socially and their development has remained stunted. They are also ignored by the political parties, and administrative set up. They are suffering from what is called ***'Structural Violence'.*** *The Community stands nowhere in the Jat Sikh dominated society; they have been neglected throughout on the basis of religion and suffer from what is called* ***"Symbolic Violence".*** *Although their conversion to Christianity was a protest against the* ***'Obnoxious Caste'*** *system but a change of religion as not cleared their scar. Christians do not enjoy state patronage which is given to other scheduled caste and backward classes. After conversion to Christianity, they have lost the right to reservation in government jobs. Christians of Punjab stand at the lowest rural rung of the society among the dalit classes especially in the border areas.* ***This paper explores and analyse that how the poor socio-economic conditions of Christians of Punjab have excluded them from the rest of the society. The paper also highlights that due to vulnerable conditions of Christians in rural area of Punjab, they are treated merely as 'object' instead of as 'subject'.***

Introduction

This study paper is confined to the study of politics of social exclusion of Christians in Punjab. Although, the issue of exclusion in India has been widely discussed by various scholars. Very few have attempted to offer a systematic analysis of the issue through a theoretical or conceptual basis. This study examines the socio-economic conditions of Christian Community of Punjab. In the State of Punjab, they have been socio-economically oppressed, culturally subjugated and politically marginalized for decades. It is fact that backwardness of dalits have certainty altered their political aspirations and often denied them opportunities of entering into an active political life. Neither the centre nor the state government paid any special attention toward marginalised and neglected community i.e. Dalit Christians. They are not only ignored in the socio-economic spheres but also in political field by the centre and state government. Today, a section of Christians have now begun to identify them as **'Dalit Christians'**. They are strongly raising their voices to get the benefits of reservation as have been given to Hindu Scheduled Castes.

The dalit Christians issues cannot be seen in an isolated manner from the rest of the dalits of India. These issues are relating to religious change and leading to socio-economic mobility, identify, differentiation stratification, urge for self determination and participation, movements toward viable and sustainable communities, reservation and discrimination as well as issue relating to dalit Women, official church and its personnel. **Lancy Lobo** rightly observed that the problems of Dalit Christians are not only social and religious but also economic and Political.

In Punjab, they are constituted about two percent of the total population of the state. In the Majha region (borderland of state) percentage of dalit Christian's population is highest amongst all districts of Punjab. A large numbers of people of this community are converted from the downtrodden class and adopted the Christianity religion. They joined the Church seeking *liberation and Solace* in the *'New Community'*. But the Churches failed to fulfill their expectations. There is cultural distance between the upper caste Christian's clergy and Dalit Christians (**Ghanshyan Shah, 2001**, p29). In fact, the upper caste Christians has separate identity from other Dalit Christian families. A tussle between the upper and lower caste Christians is evidence in many churches particular in Kerala State. **(M.N. Srinivas (ed.) 1996.p272).** But in Punjab, rural Christians (99 percent) in Punjab are landless marginal, backward, and poor along with low status and illiteracy are considered by Christian leaders to be the major problems. **"They are socially depressed, economically backward and need and politically powerless community in Punjab." (Emanual Nahar, 2007, pp153-154)**

Socio-Economic Profile: A Study of Christians

Education

Education is the catalyst that helps to form creativity, attitude, capacity, value and confers status. It is also an important variable which constitutes to the socio-economic status of a person or a group. Education is also a means which enabled them to break the physical distance in inter-personal relations imposed by castes differences. It is also a key for social mobility and providing a new opportunity life. So for the general literacy rate of Punjab is concerned that 69.95 percent (for males is 75.63 percent, for females it is 63.65 percent) Literacy among the Dalit Christians is Punjab on the whole is still low.

Majority of the population of this community is residing in rural area of the Punjab's. This study shows that 49.58 percent illiterate and 17.96 under metric 22.5 percent metric, and 10.41percent graduates. The borderland state of the Punjab has only less than 10 percent Christians are educated rest of the illiterate The literacy rate among Dalit Christians specially in border area is far below comparatively than scheduled caste of Punjab.

Occupation

The survey of this study shows that 72.41 percent of the working population of Christians is engaged in agriculture sector in overall Punjab. About 14.17 percent Christians are employed in various professions. In Punjab only 3.75 percent Christian possess agricultural land and more than 95 percent Christians are landless.

The majority of the Dalit Christian working as helper, ***Plaee, Paledri,*** roads and building labour, casual labour night soil labour, ***Bratha Labour*** and unskilled agricultural labours. They depend on the landowner for their daily bread. The system of ***Athri*** is in fact bounded labour system in which the person is bonded o his ***Sepi*** (Landowner) for the lifeline. The poor, illiterate and dalit people of this community specially in Majha or border area of the Punjab belonging to this category.

The state of Punjab, has given a lot of benefits to SC's/ST's but these benefits are not meant for economically weaker section i.e. Dalit Christians of Punjab and overall position of this community in Punjab as Community is marginal, poor and backward comparatively than other sections.

Income

There are lot of differences between the annual Income of dalit Christians and other sections of the society. They are landless and have no resource of income. Most of the dalit Christians are unskilled labours and agriculture labours. 90 percent are working in agriculture sector in rural area of Punjab and so majority of the Dalit Christians belonged to lower income group.

Socio-Economic Exclusion

Dalit Christians in Punjab were largely converted from the down trodden people of the society by missionary and adopted Christian religion. Actually their socio-economic marginality and social degradation in society compelled them to follow the Christian religion. Very few Christians who are educated, employed and urban respondents claimed there is change of the socio-economic status of the Christians but majority of the respondents refused to accept there is any type of change after adoption of Christianity in the Punjab. They have the same socio-economic conditions like other dalits of the society. Today, various denominations have failed to solve their socio-economic problems. Even they are unable to bring a big changes in their status. The following table shows:-

• **High status 19.45 percent** • **Moderate status 30.14 percent** • **Low status 50.41 percent**	**Both urban and Rural Dalit/Christians of Punjab**

Christians do not enjoy state patronage which is given to other scheduled caste and backward classes. After conversion to Christianity, they have lost the right to reservation in government jobs. They stand at the lowest rural rung of the society among the dalit classes specially in the border area of the Punjab. In this area, they remained socially separate and were forced to live in separate residential localities called ***Thathi.*** Due to poor conditions in rural area of Punjab they are also treated merely as ***'object'*** instead of as ***'subject'.***

After 1947, Christian Community in Punjab has not gained either political or social and their development has remained stunted. They are also ignored by the political parties, and administrative set up. They are suffering from what is called **'Structural Violence'.** They stand no where in the Jat Sikh dominated society; they have been neglected throughout on the basis of religion and suffer from what is called **"Symbolic Violence".** Although their conversion to Christianity was a protest against the **'Obnoxious Caste System'** but a change of religion has not cleared their scar.

Along with Dalits, Dalit Christians are also exploited by the richman/landlord in various parts of the Punjab State. They are engaged by landlord at lower wages or to make them work without wages against their will. They could not organized themselves to raise a voice against the low wages. Actually the economic condition of the dalits including dalit Christians is aggravated by social disabilities and back of political influence.

In the agrarian society of the Punjab state, the status, conditions, prestige and power of any community caste or groups is determined by the possession of land and the land holders maintained their economic power and social superiority over the dalits by keeping them at a low economic level. So for the Christians are concerned they are landless and have worse conditions still connected with their previous castes and treated ***'untouchable'***. Even today, they are humiliated by higher castes because of their lower socio-economic status. They do not have their own separate identity, traditions and cultural values. Actually the dominant majority either Sikhs or Hindus are generally powerful, are attempting to impose its own culture values on weaker sections in the Punjabi Society. So that is why they are also suffering from the **stigmatized identity** in the State of Punjab. (**Emanual Nahar, 2007, pp-240-241**).

Politics of Exclusion and Dalit Christians

In India, dalit Christians have similar conditions like dalits of society. They are ***'harmless creature'*** they has been targeted & harassed by landlords, police, fanatic and powerful person of the society and state has failed to punish and provide security to dalit Christians. The following Acts and Rules are enacted only for SC/ST in Indian society.

- **Protection Civil Right Act, 1955**
- **Protection Civil Rule, 1977**
- **SC/ST prevention of Atrocities Act 1989**

These are supposed to give the SC/ST dalits special protection against various kinds of atrocities but not applicable to the dalit Christians of SC origin. The fanatic and communal groups are playing dirty politics with this community to keep distance and to make discrimination on the basis of religion by debarring from these acts.

The third paragraph of the Presidential order of 1950 was amended by the Parliament to extend the constitution benefits to the 'Sikhs' and the 'Buddhists' along with the 'Hindus'. Regarding the criteria of amendment, the point made by Ram Vilas Paswan in 1990 needs to be noted. Paswan, who was the then Union Minister of Welfare and Labour, while stating the objects and reasons for proposing to include Buddhists of Scheduled Caste origin in the list of Scheduled Castes, said that the change of religion does not alter social and economic conditions. But above all the third paragraph of the 1950 Presidential order is a direct contradiction of Article 15 and 25 of our Constitution since it had used religion as the criterion to describe who will be a scheduled caste. This needs to be deleted completely (Massey, 2002:72-73).

In India the opportunities for employment are very scanty and the state is the greatest employer. The principle of non discrimination and equality is also upheld in matter of public employment in the Constitution Art 16 say "No citizen shall, on grounds of religion, race or caste, be ineligible for, or discriminated against in respect of, any employment or office under the State. The Constitution of our country in Article 16, gives equality of opportunity in matters of public employment. But, again, because of the Presidential order, of 1950 and the refusal of Shanker Dyal Sharma to issue ordinance (The Tribune March 29: 1996) for reservation for Christians during the regime of

Narashima Rao, and the two amendments thereto after, referred to above, *Dalit* this fundamental right Christians have been deprived of rights. This has been made available to the Dalits in the fold of Hinduism, Sikhism and Buddhism. This also amounts to discrimination on grounds of religion which the 'state' is forbidden to do under Article 15.

The denial of Justice to the *Dalit* Christians is also against the letter and spirit of Articles 14, 15, 16 and 25 of the Constitution of India on equal justice, equal opportunities and freedom of religion. If a Scheduled Caste becomes a Christian he loses all the reservation facilities, and if he produces a certificate of Scheduled Caste he gets back all the benefits. Even the children of the same scheduled caste parents, living under the same roof, sharing the same meals are discriminated against or the basis of religion. Sohan Singh gets all the reservation facilities. While his own brother Mohan Masih is denied all the benefits just because "Masih" happens to be a Christian. It is a bad luck, if any Christian symbol is noticed with him/her or at his/her residence. He/she loses all the service benefits. It is also violation of the constitutional rights. Despite of 57 years of independence, the *Dalit* Christians continued to be the victims of all kinds of treatment. The history of independent India is both pathetic and shameful on the treatment meted out to *Dalits*.

The Mandal Commission's report has unambiguously stated that state assistance should be given to all genuinely backward sections of people irrespective of religion or caste which many thought would end the discrimination against the poor among the minorities. But the 'soft' communists or secularists or religious fanatics in the majority community are now said to have found another excuse to deprive the Christians of these facilities. The argument advanced is that the backwards having un-Indian sounding or Anglo-Saxon" names cannot claim such benefits. (Sarto, Esteves 1996: 190).They can afford to discriminate against Christians in this manner because they are a negligible "vote bank". This is the way our rulers create divisions, frictions and differences in our country. (Ibid)

The other serious implication of the Presidential order of 1950 is that it has also affected another fundamental right of the *Dalit*

Christians, which is meant to protect their personal life as well as liberty. In the last 67 years of India's independence, the country's three largest minorities. Muslims, Christians and Sikhs – have been targeted by fanatics of the majority community and other vested interests, on the basis of their religious identity alone, resulting in a serious assault on their basic rights, including the right of life itself Article 21 of the Indian constitution clearly stipulates". "No person shall be deprived of his right of personal liberty except according to procedure established by law". The example of the *Dalit* Christians not getting protection of life and personal liberty are the various govt. acts and rules passed by the Parliament to give special protection to the scheduled castes which are not applicable to the Christians of Scheduled Caste origin during atrocities. These acts and rules include protection of civil rights Act 1955, Protection of Civil Rights Rule, 1977 and Scheduled Castes and Scheduled Tribes (Prevention of Atrocities) Act 1989. All these acts and rules are supposed to give the SC *(Dalits)* special protection and rights against various kinds of atrocities and oppressions, meted out to them by the people of so-called upper castes or forward classes. But this protection is not made available to *Dalit* Christians.

Although under Article 21, the State is bound to protect the life and liberty of every human being, but it has failed to protect this right. There are a lot of violations. Such type of violations threatens the very right to life, physical integrity and health of citizens. Here are some of the headlines in the national media. "Persecution – Christians are now being systematically targeted. Saffron Brigade striked again in various states of India. Christian missionary schools were attacked and copies of New Testament were burnt at various places.

Article 25 of Indian constitution gives full right to all citizens the "freedom of conscience and to right freely to profess practice and propagate religion". The Christians have almost always faced problems with this fundamental right especially with the last part of propagating its faith. A number of states such as Orissa, Arunachal Pradesh and Madhya Pradesh have passed acts through their legislature severely curbing this right. In many states like Punjab, the concerned authorities refused to allow any venue and date for religious conversions or religious conventions for preaching the teaching of Jesus Christ. It is entirely a violation of Article 25. Father T.K. John also expressed the feeling that the basic rights of the religious minorities are violated in a number of ways. (Sumanta Banerjee, 1999:177)

(a) Although some Indian State Government did enact legislations entitled 'Freedom of Religion Bill'; they were full of ambiguities which were utilized by the state machinery to practice discrimination against religious minorities.

(b) Refusal to grant official recognition, to certain religious groups and religious communities.

(c) Legal bias against certain religion groups and religious communities

(d) Restriction on public information about religious groups by descriptions only a preferred religion in official text books and ignoring the others. In Gujarat, state BJP government is also trying to impose some limitation on freedom of conscience and free profession.

Although the Article 25 of the Indian constitution gives a wide opportunity to profess, practice and propagate any religion, but from time to time it has been misinterpreted by the various Hon'ble Courts of law which have imposed many limitations. As the Supreme Court held in the case of stainless vs. Madhya Pradesh (1977), the right to propagate does not mean the right to convert others forcibly. However, he is entitled to accept or adopt another religion by his own choice and free will. (Nirmalendu Bikash 2000: 3565.).

Article 29 offers protection of cultural rights of minorities and Article 30 (1) gives them the right to establish and administer education institutions of their choice. Clause 31(2) states that the state "shall not, in granting aid to educational institutions, discriminate against any education institution on the ground that 'it is under the management of a minority, whether based on religion or language." But with regard to the rights provided in Articles 29 and 30 also, the Christians continue to face problems throughout the country. The first major problem which the Christian educational institutions are facing is the intervention of State Education Department and Universities at different levels. Questions are being raised whether a special place can be offered to the members of the Christian community as students or trainees. Government not only discriminate against minority schools, colleges, nursing colleges, and hospitals in granting aid, but also impose many rules and restriction to prevent minority institutions from appointing their own candidates. When a vacancy comes up schools and other institutions they are forced to accept the State's choice and on many occasions the Christian educational institutions have had to go to court to get justice.

Some of fanatics groups are not in favour of separate and distinct culture for minorities. They want that all minorities in India must group up their separate culture as India is one country and one culture Prof. Madhok suggested that: "That the minorities must adopt Indian (Hindu) names. In short they must adopt the Indian culture – the national culture – in their religion. Their religion should bend its loyalty, towards the Indian Nationalism". The suggestion made by Madhok is totally against the rights guaranteed under Article 29 of the Constitution which says.

"*Any section of citizens, residing in the territory of India, or any part thereof, having distinct language or culture of its own, shall have the right to conserve the same all persons are equally entitled to freedom of conscience and the right to profess, practice and propagate their religion.*" In fact the Muslims, the Christians and the Sikhs each have their own separate and distinct cultures. The above guarantee given by the Constitution negates the right to conserve the culture of the minorities. Such utterances have been in vogue for many decades. It is a shame that the leaders of the largest democracy, with large number of religions allow the propagation of such mindless thoughts (which are clearly against the constitutional rights) against such minuscule position of the population as the Christians. (Mathew & Bakshi 1995: 3-4).

Christians in the State of Punjab

Since 1952, there was the provision of legislative council in which every section of society had the provision for representation to which the community's interest. This facility was also enjoyed by the Christian community from 1952 to 1967. When the Akali party came to power they moved a resolution to abolish legislature council with the help of Congress MLA's. After this not a single Christian was nominated or elected in the state of Punjab.

The Congress Government of Punjab (2007) has increased the reservation quota for **Balmiki and Mazhbi Sikhs** through Amendment, but refused to give this benefit to Dalit Christians which was promised by the Congress party during election time. Punjab Assembly also recommended reservation for **Rai Sikhs** to the centre government and Parliament resolved to include **Rai Sikhs** in scheduled caste list in Punjab, but refused to Dalit Christians. It is totally discriminates with their community on the basis of religion.

The Dalit Christians is Punjab politically marginalized and powerless community in India. In the 2009 Lok Sabha Elections, out of 543 members there were only 8 Christians and 36 Muslims and 11 Sikhs in the Lok Sabha. All the Christians came from south. Not a single Christian was from Northern India. Even, in the 2012 Legislature Assembly elections of Punjab there are about 30 Schedule Caste, One Muslim. Since 1952, not a single Christian has been elected as a member of Legislature Assembly of Punjab so far. Actually economic backwardness and lower social background of the community and dominated Sikh society has given them little or no scope in the Political arena especially in the state of Punjab.

Conclusion

In Punjab, the Dalit Christians is in microscopic minority, economically poor, political powerless, socially depressed. A change of religions has not cleaned their scar and not brought big changes. Both Congress and Akali both are playing politics with this community. There is a need to educate and create awareness among the Dalit Christians for social justice. The Christian leader should shoulder the responsibility and make sincere efforts to organize Christian community on one platform. They should join with all other Dalit liberation organizations for socio-economic justice. On the other side, government should pay special attention for marginal community. It is also a moral duty of community that they should organize themselves and start a social movement for their rights.

References

Pande, B.B. (2007) Criminality of the Marginalized Sections or the lumpen-Proletariat Criminality See in C. Raj Kumar and K Chockalingam, (ed) Human Rights, Justice and Constitutional Empowerment Oxford University Press, New Delhi, pp 392-394.

Robinson, Rowena (2007), Indian Muslims: The varied dimensions of marginality, Economic and Political weekly Vol. 42, No.10, pp. 839-843.

Tharamangalm J. (1996) Caste among Christians in India see in M.N. Srinivas (Ed) Caste its Twentieth century Avatar" Vivking by Penguin Books India, New Delhi, p. 272.

Nahar, Emanual (2007) Minority Politics in India: Role and Impact of Christians in Punjab Politics, Aurn Publisher, Chandigarh.

Darden, J. (1989) Blacks and other Racial Minorities: The Significance of Colour in Inequality. Urban Geography, Vol. 10.

Davis, B. (2003a) Marginality in a Pluralistic Society. Eye On Psi Chi 2(1):1-4.

Davis, B. (2003b). What is Marginality?

IGU (International Geographical Union) (2003) Homepage.

Kirkby, J. (2000) Land Degradation and Development, Optimism of Pessimism? Sam Moyo, SAPES Trust, Zimbabwe.

Larsen, J. E. (2002a) Spatialization and Culturalization of Social Policy: Conducting Marginal People in Local Communities. Paper presented at the conference Area-Based initiatives in contemporary urban policy, Danish Building and Urban Research and European Urban Research Association. Copenhagen 17-19 May 2001.

Larsen, J. E. (2002b) Who Cares about and for Marginal People? Danish Social Sci-ence Reaserach Council, Copenhagen.

Sommers, LawrenceM., Mehretu, A. and Pigizzi, Bruce W.**M.** (1999): Towards typologies of socio-economic marginality: North/South /Comparisons. in: Jussila, H., Majoral, R. and Mutambriwa, C.C. (eds) Marginality in Space-Past, Present and Future: Theoretical and methodological aspects of cultural, social and economical parameters of marginal and critical regions. Ashgate Publishing Ltd, England, pp.7-24.

Ghanshyam Shah (2001) Dalit Identify and Politics (ed.), New Delhi: Saga Publication.

M.N. Srinivas (1966) Social Change Modern India, Orient Longmans.

Ghaha S, Gurung and Michal Kollmir (2005) Marginality: Concepts and their Limitations, University of Zurich, Winter Thurerster, Zurich pp. 10-11.

Laitin, D., (1996) A formal Model Marginality and Security, In S. Nolatshungu, (ed.) Margins of Insecurity: Minorities and International Security; New York University of Rochester.

Sommers, LawrenceM., Mehretu, A. and Pigizzi, Bruce W.M. (1999): Towards typologies of socio-economic marginality: North/South /Comparisons. in: Jussila, H., Majoral, R. and Mutambriwa, C.C. (eds) Marginality in Space-Past, Present and Future: Theoretical and methodological aspects of cultural, social and economical parameters of marginal and critical regions. Ashgate Publishing Ltd, England, pp.7-24.

2

Return of Kashmiri Pandits: Problems of Perceptional Divergence and Trust Deficit

—***Dr Suman***

The violence unleashed by militants in the late 1980's and the consequent combating exercises by state forces in Jammu and Kashmir have not only frequently violated the basic rights of life and liberty of the people but also undermined the age-old tradition of tolerance and communal amity built over a period of centuries in the Valley. The escalation of insurgent violence, which developed into an "invisible war" by 1990, had created panic among the minority Kashmiri Pandits comprising only around three per cent of the total population in Kashmir. The militants also targeted and killed some prominent Kashmiri Pandits like Tikka Lal Taploo (a BJP leader), N.K. Ganjoo (Sessions judge), Satish Tikku, B.L. Kaul, B.L. Zutshi, M.L. Raina, Sarvanand Kaul Premji, (a poet, advocate and social worker) etc. According to government report of March 2010, 219 Kashmiri Pandits were targeted by militants from 1989 to 2004. Among these 122 casualities were witnessed between 1 January 1989 and 1 December 1990.[1] In addition, the Pandits were provoked "through the use of posters, asking them to either quit or get converted to Islam." Some temples were attacked and idols were stolen.[2] Consequently, the Kashmiri Pandits, who had lived in peace along with their Muslim compatriots in the humanistic and pluralistic context of Kashmir[3], felt insecure and sensed a heavy dose of Islamic card in the militant upsurge. According to some, a glimpse of an exclusive religion based fervour "manifested itself on the night of 19 January 1990, when the air and atmosphere of Srinagar incessantly reverberated with the orchestrated chant of highly inflammatory *jihadi* exhortations...from the loudspeakers of hundreds of mosques in the city and its suburbs...It was that terrifying night which set the exodus in motion."[4] Ever since the day has been observed as 'exodus day' by the Kashmiri Pandits. Barring a small number of families, most Kashmiri Pandits had left their hearths and homes behind and crossed over the Pir Panjal mountain range through the Jawahar Tunnel. It was estimated that about 2,50,000 Kashmiri Pandits moved out of the valley and many of them languished in migrant camps and borrowed shelters in abject conditions in different towns such as Jammu, Udhampur, Pathankot, Chandigarh, Delhi and beyond etc. Initially, lots of people were crammed into one or two halls and suffered inhuman conditions. Some even lacked money to fulfil their daily requirements including food. According to a migrant Pandit family, "It was very hard after we left Kashmir. There were days when we had no money to buy food."[5] The young generation that has lived its life in the squalid camps of Jammu has highlighted their plight through books, blogs and films to make the world aware about their problems.[6] It was a mass migration of Pandits. The number of their families in Kashmir shrank from 140,000 in 1980s to 19,865 in 1998.[7] Bulk of the migrant families were provided shelters in Jammu and the remaining in other states/Union Territories including Delhi.

While narrating their woes, the migrant Pandits lamented, "January 19 got etched in our hearts with an ink of fear and terror. The world needs to be made aware about the circumstances which led to our migration from the valley."[8] However, the efforts made by various organisations, including theNational Human Rights Commission (NHRC), have brought about some improvement in their living conditions. Incidentally, the Pandits in the Valley used to constitute a relatively privileged group (traders, professionals, service class etc.) before their exodus.The *jihadi* upsurge in Kashmir rendered them homeless and forced to "live in wretched exile." According to some "It was not only about losing one's home but the loss of one's history and culture."[9] In other words their wholesale migration from the valley was a big blow to "Kashmiriyat" or the common cultural heritage of a tolerant tradition and peaceful co-existence.

Besides the insurgent violence and *Jihadi* upsurge which dissipated the tolerant tradition in Kashmir, some controversial matters, particularly the role of the then Governor of the state, Mr Jagmohan, was allegedly considered to be a potent factor which encouraged the mass migration of the minority Pandits.[10] As a matter of fact, a section of people in the valley saw the Governor's hand in the exodus of Pandits.[11] Some have also questioned the role of Abdullah's who shot back that exodus of Pandits took place under the Presidents' rule with Jagmohan, a BJP hand, as the Governor of Jammu and Kashmir. At that time it was the V.P. Singh Government at the Centre which was being supported by BJP from outside.[12] The Ex-Chief Minister, Mr Omar Abdullah, however, admitted that none in the valley made any serious attempt to stop the exodus of Pandits. According to him, "Not a single voice was heard on loudspeakers at the mosques asking the Pandits not to leave."[13]

Presently, the militant violence has declined in the state, yet a large number of Kashmiri Pandits are reluctant to go back to Kashmir.Their return will indeed restore the plural character and the diversity for which the Kashmir was known all over the country. It may be mentioned here that even the 1947 communal holocaust which raged through Bengal, Punjab etc. "failed to have any echo" in Kashmir where minority Pandits remained safe and protected. Sheikh Mohammad Abdullah used to say that Kashmir without Pandits is inconceivable. Even Mahatma Gandhi during his visit to Kashmir said "Kashmir is a ray of light in the all pervasive darkness." The present Chief Minister, Mufti Mohammad Sayeed, also emphasised "If we have to keep our multi-religious society intact and end political uncertainty, Kashmiri Pandits have to return to the Valley with dignity and honour."[14] The group of interlocutors appointed by the government of India also recommended that the government should facilitate the return of communities displaced from their homes.[15]

Recently the issue of their return has snowballed into a major controversy due to mixed messages from both the Centre and the state government. The present Union Home Minister, Mr. Rajnath Singh, asked the state government to allocate land for 'composite townships' to accommodate Pandits who wished to return to the Valley. In response, the Chief Minister, Mufti Mohammad Sayeed, assured that the land would be allocated for the townships.[16] But his assurance inadvertently created a political storm in the region as the separatist groups outrightly opposed the idea of a separate township in the Kashmir Valley. In fact, both the hardliners and the moderate faction of the "Hurriyat Conference" as well as the "Jammu and Kashmir Liberation Front" (JKLF) called for a shutdown against the decision of setting up of isolated settlements for the Kashmiri Pandits in the valley. They described the isolated townships as an attempt to make "another Palestine out of Jammu and Kashmir."[17] Accusing the government of "Israeli-type settlements", the chairman of the hardline Hurriyat Conference, Syed Ali Shah Geelani, said "In the garb of the return of the Kashmiri Pandits, a state within a state is being created." Hence he opposed the idea of creating separate colonies for Kashmiri Pandits in the valley. Likewise, the chairman of the moderate group of All-Parties Hurriyat Conference, Mirwaiz Umar Farooq, termed it as an attempt to "divide the Valley along religious lines." Mr Yasin Malik, chairman of the JKLF, also "drew parallels between the proposed zones and Israeli settlements in Palestine."[18] According to him, the "isolated settlements would create walls of hatred between the communities."[19] More than that, he said, "It is an RSS ploy inspired by the Israeli settlements and land-grab in Palestine." He also sat on a 30-hour fast to protest the proposed separate settlements. Swami Agnivesh, a social activist from Delhi who advocated dialogue between the two communities, also joined Yasin Malik in fast.The members of minority groups, including non-migrant Kashmiri Pandits, Sikhs and Christians from the Valley also participated in the protest. Swami Agnivesh said that the protest for which members of the various religious communities had gathered, was a "clear message that they want to live together in a composite way and no one can stop them from doing so."[20] While the separatists sounded the protest bungle against the plan, the issue also rocked the State Assembly. One of the MLA, while saying that the settlement plan was unacceptable, warned to launch an agitation against any move to set up township for Hindus in the Kashmir valley.[21] However, some, while criticising the views of separatist groups on the issue, said:

"Comparison of townships for Pandits with Israeli settlements is repugnant. Pandits are no Israeli settlers. They are the rightful settlers, the original aborigines of the Kashmir valley who have a history of 5,000 years. The separatist leaders who are talking about secularism and composite culture, are the same people who were responsible for the forced migration."[22]

The Kashmiri Pandit Sangharsh Samiti (KPSS) also flayed the separatists for calling a shutdown and accused them of "being the prime offenders of the crimes done against this miniscule community." In fact, the President of the KPSS questioned the separatists as to why todate not a single report or demand of inquiry was made from the separatists' camp over the killing of Pandits in Kashmir.[23] The issue among others has also acquired space outside the country. For example, the All Party Parliamentary Group (APPG) of British Hindus, led by lawmaker Bob Blackman and supported by four other MPs tabled the first-ever motion in the British Parliament to commemorate the displacement of Kashmiri Pandits.[24] The motion sought justice for the atrocities committed against Kashmiri Pandits and demanded to take effective measures to prevent the commission of genocide and crimes against humanity as was seen against the Kashmiri Hindu community.[25]

However, among the Kashmir based political parties, the National Conference has also opposed separate settlements for Kashmiri Pandits.The leader of the party and former Chief Minister, Mr Omar Abdullah, called it a process of "ghettoisation" of Kashmiri Pandits.[26] He doubted that many Kashmiri Pandits would like to return to the Valley just to be housed in ghettos, segregated and isolated."[27] Even the Shiv Sena, an ally of BJP, in an editorial in *Saamna* questioned the plan saying" is this some big slum redevelopment project for the sons-of-the-soil?[28] The Congress Party also believed that separate townships would not be a solution for the plight of Pandits. The Congress spokesperson, said, "We believe that Pandits should be encouraged to resettle in their original places of residence so that they can again be a part of the composite culture."[29] This apart, the civil society groups have also accused the government of "creating a divide among Kashmiri Muslims and Pandits by its proposed move." According to them" Kashmiri Pandits are part of the Valley and society. To return to their homes is their right which no one can take away from them."[30]

Keeping the dissenting voices in view, the Chief Minister, Mr Mufti Mohammad Sayeed, clarified that there would be no separate townships for Pandits as the government was not in favour of any "Israel-type clusters for pandits" and wants "every community to stay together."[31] He blamed the media for misquoting and emphasised that "he was not in favour of separate clusters but wanted return of Kashmiri Pandits with full honours to complete the composite culture of the valley." He also ensured the state Assembly that his government would "create an atmosphere…to facilitate the return of Kashmiri Pandits."[32] Furthermore, the state government clarified that it was "awaiting the return of the Pandit migrants and they will be settled at their original places of habitation with honour and dignity." However, the Union Home Minister, Mr Rajnath Singh, said that there was no going back on the plans for separate settlements for the displaced community and the Centre would stick to whatever decision it had taken.[33] Doubting the assurance given by the Union Home Minister, the Chairman of All Party Migrant Coordination Committee said "the BJP has not been able to take stance on several key issues and surrendered the township plan."[34]

In the existing conditions, the Kashmiri Pandits have rather favoured a "separate homeland" than "composite townships."[35] While observing the World Refugee Day on 20 June 2015, for the first time, they submitted a memorandum to the present Prime Minister Mr Narendera Modi seeking status of "internally displaced persons" for the Pandit community.[36] According to them, the successive state and Central governments, including the present NDA regime, have continued to call us migrants.[37] Therefore, according to the Panun Kashmir, an organisation representing displaced Kashmiri Pandits, homeland was the only way that could pave the way for their return. It also urged the centre to talk directly to the Pandits and take them into confidence.[38] Further, it demanded a "separate homeland" with a Union Territory status outside the ambit of Article 370. Some Pandits also perceived "It is impossible for us to reside in settlements with the members of the community that was responsible for our exodus and ethnic cleansing." While protesting in Delhi against the proposal of composite townships, Pandits said "they would return but on their own terms, not on those who led to their exodus.[39] The terms mainly included improvement in the communal atmosphere, grant of separate homeland at a place north and east of the Jhelum in close proximity to their religious sites and a Union Territory status."[40] In addition, they demanded a probe into the circumstances that led to their exodus and reopening of prosecution cases against all those involved in the killing of Kashmiri Pandits in the Valley.[41] This speaks about the trust deficit and fear psychosis which haunts the Pandits on the matter of their return to the Kashmir Valley. The Vice Chairman of the Panun Kashmir even said that the proposed composite township was a conspiracy to mislead the people by ensuring a token return of Pandits to the valley." According to him, "the communally charged atmosphere in the Valley which forced the Pandits to migrate had worsened." Further he questioned, "How can we return without confidence that things on the ground have improved? The state and its institutions have now been infiltrated by communal elements."[42] According to the chairman of the All Party Migrant Coordination Committee, "Displacement was not an outcome of a natural calamity but the minority community was a victim of religio-ethnic cleansing carried out by terror groups in a planned manner. Out of sheer nostalgia we cannot afford to put our progeny to the risk of another migration and need constitutional rights."[43] This makes it evident that the idea of "composite townships" to resettle the displaced Pandits in the valley has neither drawn any favour from the Kashmiri Muslims nor convinced the affected Pandits who have yet to overcome the ghost of insurgent violence and propaganda they had witnessed on the eve of their exodus in 1990-91.

Apart from this, the new generation of Muslims in Kashmir has hardly experienced living with Pandits who fled the Valley in 1990. Similarly, a generation of Pandits brought up in various migrant camps has little interaction with the Kashmiri Muslims. More than that, majority of residential properties belonging to Pandits have been either encroached or burnt down or sold in distress,which leaves little prospect of resettling them in their original houses in the villages and towns of Kashmir.[44] In addition much has changed in a span of 25 years in the villages and towns where they lived prior to mass migration. Some, while suggesting that the government should give land and compensation to the displaced, have felt that separate townships won't work as it would intensify the mental and physical barriers between the two communities.[45]

The efforts towards their return to Kashmir have been made earlier too. But the shocking incidents of early 1990s and security fears have doused such attempts. The UPA government under the Prime Minister's Package for Jammu and Kashmir had announced that Pandits would be rehabilitated with dignity in Kashmir. In fact, on April 25, 2008, the then Prime Minister, Manmohan Singh, announced "Rs 1,618-crore package for the relief and rehabilitation of Kashmiri Pandits. It also included an employment package for the displaced community. Close to 3,000 Kashmiri Pandit youth were recruited and later posted in different districts of the valley in various government departments under the PM's employment package."[46] In addition the package also included money for the purchase or construction of houses and schooling of children. The relief package, however, failed to enthuse most of the migrant families to return and avail benefits of the scheme. Subsequently, in 2012, the Jammu and Kashmir government had sought revision of the Prime Minister's package, which included an enhanced cash assistance of Rs 20 lakh to each Pandit family for reconstruction of a house which was Rs 7.5 lakh in the earlier package.

A renewed attempt to encourage their return with 'dignity, security and assured livelihood' has also been made by the present NDA government. In the Union Budget of 2015-16, Rs 320 crore has been earmarked for the rehabilitation of Kashmiri Pandits. This apart, the Union Home Minister has acceded approval for enhancement of cash relief for Kashmiri migrants from the present level of Rs 1,650 per person per month to Rs 2,500 per person per month subject to the ceiling of Rs 10,000 per month for each family.[47] The number of registered Kashmiri migrant families at present is about 62,000. The Union Home Minister has also given in principle approval for additional 3,000 government jobs to Kashmiri migrants.[48] However, security concerns, fear of insurgent violence and lack of proper execution of the plan has hampered the process of their return.[49] Ironically enough, killings of Kashmiri Pandits have had also taken place when the government planned to rehabilitate them in the Valley." The first of such massacre took place in 1997 in the Sangrama village of Badgam district. Seven Kashmiri Pandits were killed at that time. This was repeated in 1998 when 26 Pandits were killed in Wandhama on the eve of India's Republic Day. In 2003, 24 Pandits were killed in

Nandimarg....most of these killings took place when the government was planning to rehabilitate the displaced Pandits back to the valley."[50] The harrowing incidents of this nature, obviously, further deepened the distrust among the migrant Pandits. Moreover, the recent terror attacks on the telecom companies in Kashmir in May 2015 created a scare among the Kashmiri Pandits, particularly the youths recruited under the PM's employment package. According to one of the youths posted in the northern town of Sopore:

"We saw a ray of hope in the jobs provided under the PM's employment package. We thought that our miseries would end, but condition in the valley is visibly changing. We are in a dilemma, and wonder whether our decision to move to the Valley in 2011 was right or wrong. Though we have not been targeted so far, fear is visible among the girls working in the Education Department."[51]

The terror attacks on mobile services apart, the experiences of those Kashmiri Pandits who had returned at different points of time in the last 25 years appeared to be hardly encouraging on account of one factor or the other. Some among the youths, who returned to the Valley for jobs under the PM's rehabilitation package say "No one is staying here in a proper way...most want to go back...our parents are in Jammu and we are here for a job, so the families are broken and almost everyone is disturbed." Moreover, having spent entire childhood and youthful days in Udhampur, he said "I was a migrant in Jammu and after spending so much time and setting our lives there; we came here because of the government job. Now we are migrant here."[52] Likewise a woman living in a "transit camp", said her husband was working in Delhi and kids were living with their grandparents elsewhere.[53] Living away from their families is compounded by the colony's poor infrastructure like the long walk uphill to fetch water from a spring, lack of drinking water and frequent power cuts. This apart, sometimes they bear "anti-India" sentiment.[54] However, inspite of these problems the Pandits in the transit camps and temple complexes have received full support of the local people. The temple complex in Baramulla district has small rooms for each family, a common toilet and bathroom, and a security post. A Pandit family which migrated to Jammu in 1990 decided to come back for the chemist shop it owned in Baramulla. On return, this family found that their house had been taken over by the CRPF, but the shop was intact. The local people helped them to restart the business. In Jammu the family has got a flat in the Jagti township for migrants. It wants to have one like that in Baramulla to "feel more secure."[55] Another Kashmiri Pandit resident of the temple complex said that he had come back for business and felt safe with the support of the local people. However, he said that "many who came back with them have returned to Jammu. According to him, "those who wish to return now can no longer go back to their original houses…as those properties are too expensive now. A new township might be good."[56]

Conclusion

The mass exodus of Kashmiri Pandits in January 1990 could be regarded as the most traumatic event which jolted and jettisoned the age-old tradition of tolerance and brotherhood in the Kashmir Valley. Communal amity and "blending of cultures at once tolerant to beliefs of others"[57] have been integral to the life of people in the Valley. The sudden outburst of violence combined with fanaticism and divisive politics forced the Pandits to fled away leaving their homes and homeland behind. The factors such as their being away for over 25 years, continuity of intermittent violence, divergent views and trust deficit have resulted in multiple problems and complexities blocking the process of their normal return. The issue of composite townships or, for that matter, settling them in their original houses have failed to generate a consensus on the issue. Likewise, the idea of separate townships has rather led to dissenting voices. Though the Kashmiri Pandits are indigenous people of Kashmir and have every right to be settled in the Valley, yet the issue of their return has snowballed into a major controversy as the Pandits suffer from a fear psychosis and the separatists see "Israel like situation" in the composite townships as proposed by the authorities. Some organisations of Pandits have also asked for a separate homeland with the status of a Union Territory.

Since the element of fear among the Kashmiri Pandits and their staying away for over 25 years have complicated the problem. Attempts must be made to quell the fear through talks with the Pandits, local Muslims, separatists groups and party organisations to build confidence and restore the traditional amity and tolerance. An intense debate is also required over how to make the homecoming and Hindu reintegration into the now Muslim but once a common Kashmiri milieu.[58] The issue of Separate Township does not address the security fears of Pandits. An unfolding of trust alone might pave the way for the two communities, to begin to hear each other.[59]

References

1. Shujaat Bukhari, "219 Kashmiri Pandits killed by militants since 1989", The Hindu, 24 March 2010. Quoted in Sheikh Abdul Hamid, "Migration, Return and Rehabilitation : State response", International Research Journal of Social Sciences, Vol. 2(10), 7-10, October 2013, p. 8.
2. Hari Jaisingh, *Kashmir – A Tale of Shame,* New Delhi, UBS Publishers, Distributors Ltd., 1996, p. 111.
3. Shyam Kaul, "Identity Politics of Kashmiri Pandits", in Rekha Chowdhary (Ed.) *Identity Politics in Jammu and Kashmir*, New Delhi, Vitasta Publishing Pvt. Ltd., 2010, p. 264.
4. *Ibid.* p. 265.
5. Namita Kohli, "Back Home in The Valley", *The Hindustan Times*, April 19, 2015.
6. Sumit Hakhoo, "25 yrs on, Kashmiri Pandits' fate caught in time warp", *The Tribune*, 20 January 2015.
7. See, Sheikh Abdul Hamid, "Migration, Return and Rehabilitation of Kashmiri Pandits : State Response", *International Research Journal of Social Sciences,* Vol. 2(10), 7-10, October, 2013, p. 9.
8. Sumit Hakhoo, "25 yrs on, Kashmiri Pandits' fate caught in time warp", opcit.
9. *Ibid.*
10. Manash Bhattacharjee "Returning without solutions: Kashmir and the Pandits" *Economic and Political Weekly*, Vol. XLIX, No. 46, November 15, 2014, p. 14.
11. Available at http://www.indiainfoline.com/article/print/news-top-story/politicising-the-plight-of-Kashmiri-Pandits-114060200249.
12. *Ibid.*
13. See, Kuldip Nayar, "Getting used to encounters", *The Tribune*, 22 April 2015
14. "Due attention will be given to flood victims of Jammu", *The Tribune,* 11 April 2015
15. Government of India, Ministry of Home Affairs, "Decisions Taken by CCS Regarding Jammu and Kashmir on Saturday", 25 September 2010. Available at http://pib.nic.in/newsite/release.aspx?reid=65989, accessed on 9 April

2015. Quoted in Amnesty International Report, "Denied" Failures in accountability for human rights violations by security force personnel in Jammu and Kashmir. Released in July 2015.

16. *The Hindustan Times,* New Delhi, Editorial.
17. Azhar Qadri, "Valley shuts over Pandits' townships", *The Sunday Tribune*, 12 April 2015.
18. Zahid Rafiq, "Zones for Pandits will turn Valley into Palestine : Hurriyat", *The Hindu*, 9 April 2015.
19. Azhar Qadri, "JKLF begins protest against township plan", *The Tribune*, April 19, 2015.
20. *Ibid.*
21. Sumit Hakhoo, "Pandits feeling dejected", *The Tribune*, 8 June 2015.
22. "Why return to Valley does not enthuse migrants", *The Sunday Tribune*, 12 April 2015.
23. *The Tribune*, 10 April 2015.
24. "Motion on Kashmiri Pandits tabled in UK Parliament", *The Tribune*, January 23, 2015.
25. *Ibid.*
26. Azhar Qadri, "Valley shuts over Pandits' townships", *The Sunday Tribune*, 12 April 2015.
27 "Govt clears the air, says Pandits to be settled in native places" *The Tribune*, 9 April 2015.
28. Shiv Kumar, "Sena demands Kashmiri Pandits' 'ghar wapsi', *The Tribune*, 15 April 2015.
29. *The Tribune*, 9 April 2015.
30. "Pandits welcome in homeland to live among us", *The Tribune*, 11 April 2015.
31. Azhar Qadri, "Valley shuts over Pandits' townships", *The Tribune*, 12 April 2015.
32. *The Tribune*, April 10, 2015.
33. *The Hindustan Times*, New Delhi, April 10, 2015, Also see, *The Tribune*, 9 April 2015.
34. Sumit Hakhoo, "Pandits feeling dejected", *The Tribune*, 8 June 2015.
35. Ravi S Singh, "Want separate homeland, not townships: Kashmiri Pandits", *The Tribune*, 5 May 2015.
36. *The Tribune*, "Pandits seek 'internally displaced persons' status, submit memo to PM", 21 June 2015.
37. *Ibid.*
38. *The Tribune*, 12 April 2015.

39. See, Ravi S Singh, "Want separate homeland, not townships: Kashmiri Pandits, *The Tribune*, 5 May 2015.
40. Ravi S Singh, "Community rejects plan for composite township", *The Tribune*, 9 April 2015.
41. Ravi S Singh, "Want separate homeland, not townships: Kashmiri Pandits, *op cit.*
42. Ravi S Singh, "Community rejects plan for composite township", *op cit.*
43. "Why return to Valley does not enthuse migrants", *The Sunday Tribune*, 12 April 2015.
44. *Ibid.*
45. *Ibid.*
46. Sumit Hakhoo, "Pandits in N-Kashmir fear another exodus" *The Tribune,* 3 June 2015. Also see, "Why return to Valley does not enthuse migrants", *op cit.*
47. Mohammed Iqbal, "Ministry okays cash relief hike for Kashmiri Pandits", *The Hindu*, July 21, 2015.
48. *Ibid.*
49. Majid Jahangir, "1 family home, 5,000 await cash like", *The Sunday Tribune*, 12 April 2015.
50. Rekha Chowdhary, "Religion and Conflict in Jammu and Kashmir", in Rekha Chowdhary (Ed.) *op cit*. p. 167.
51. Sumit Hakhoo, "Pandits in N-Kashmir fear another exodus", *op cit.*
52. Azhar Qadri, "Outside in Jammu, now one in Kashmir", *The Sunday Tribune*, 12 April 2015.
53. Namita Kohli, "Back Home In the Valley", *op cit.*
54. *Ibid.*
55. *Ibid.*
56. *Ibid.*
57. P.N.K. Bamjai, *Socio-Economic History of Kashmir (1846-1925)*, New Delhi, Metropolitan, 1987, p. 18.
58. *The Hindustan Times*, New Delhi, Editorial, *op cit.*
59. Manash Bhattacharjee "Returning without solutions: Kashmir and the Pandits", *op cit,* pp. 15-16.

3

Religion and its Interactional Dynamics: A Study of Changing Contours of Tribal Community

—*Dr Sipra Sagarika*

Abstract

The alteration in the colonial approaches of isolation with the tribal population opened the doors of integration for the indigenous group. The wave was meant for strengthening tribal identity but with its expose to several multilayer factors such as globalisation, migration, intrusion of middle men and contractors, modernisation, multiple religious faiths etc, there were major lapses marked in the identities of the tribal people.

Key Words: *Tribal identity, modernisation, migration, globalisation.*

Introduction

There have been radical changes in a few decades in the ideas concerning the religion of the tribal community. Religion is said to be the human response to the apprehension of something, power which is supernatural and supra-sensory. It had been regarded as a product of civilisation until Tylor convincingly proved that the primitive societies have their own versions of religious activity not very different from that of civilised societies. Tylor considers religion as the belief in supernatural beings and called this belief as animism. By animism it was implied that exceedingly crude form of religion in which magic is the predominant element. Marett defined it as a feeling compounded of awe; fear and wonder aroused by supernatural beings and called this as preanimism. HL Menchen explains religious function is to give man access to power which seems to control his destiny and its sole purpose is to induce those powers to be friendly to him. Several primitive forms of religion from which Anthropologists believed that other religions have developed are as- magic (J.H. King), fetishism (de Brosses, A. Comte), totemism (J.F. Mc'Lennan, J.G. Frager), manism (H. Spencer), Pre animism (R.R. Marett), animism (E.B. Tylor) and cult of society (Emile Durkheim).

In the context of globalisation it is changing in a very fast manner again. Because of influence of global secular culture the response of tribal communities are varying from region to region.

Sociology of Religion

Religion for Marx was essentially the product of class society. His ideas on religion are part of his general theory of alienation in class divided societies. Religion is seen as the opium of the masses. Religion is seen as the both a product of alienation and as an expression of class interests. It is at one and the same time tool for the manipulation and oppression of the subordinate class in society, an expression of protest against oppression and a form of resignation are consolation in the face of oppression. Religion for Marx is ideological. It is reversed world consciousness because it is a product of reversed world. It is a form of thought in which men and their circumstances appear upside down as in 'camera obscure'. He explains 'Religion is nothing but the fantastic reflection in men's' minds of those external forces which control their daily life, a reflection in which the terrestrial forces assume the form of supernatural force. Marx on his theses on Feurbach makes his standpoint on religion more evidently. Emile Durkheim in his work "Elementary Forms of Religious Life" provides a detailed account of religion existing in the then societies. Religion then for Durkheim is nothing other than the collective force of society over the individuals represent to themselves the society of which they have with it. Religion then is not illusion, it is not false consciousness. When believers believe they depend upon and are subject to moral power from which they receive all that is best in themselves, they are not declined, this power exists, it is society's "Protestant Ethics and Spirit of Capitalism" attaches the reason of rational capitalism to the religious ground. The spirit of capitalism is derived from Calvinist teaching and was characteristic of the outlook of the Calvinist and Calvinistic Protestant. In his section on religion in Economy in Society (1978) translated and published separately as 'The Sociology of Religion' (1965).Weber begins his analysis by looking at which he considers to be the most elementary forms of religious belief and behaviour, namely the religions of tribal societies. He explains that religious and magical thought and behaviour are not set apart from every day purpose and are oriented primarily towards economic ends. Thus, a kind of intrinsic relationship between the economy and religion is reflected here.

Anthropology of Religion

Functionalist such as Bronislaw Malinowski (1884-1942) opened the doors of modern fieldwork. In his first great monograph 'Argonauts of the Western Pacific (1922), he explained religion and science in terms of his functionalist theory of human needs. In late work he crafted seven spheres within which society must satisfy basic human needs i.e. Metabolism, reproduction, bodily comforts, safety, movement, growth, health. Religion he argued, several to bind a community together. Magician on the other provides psychological assurance. All his life he wrote against the Western stereotype of irrational savage. His study on the Trobriand Island was substantive in this field.

Radclife Brown (British Structural functionalist) (1881-1955), viewed religion as the cement of society. It analysed religion and depicted how it is acting to contribute and maintain the social structure of the group. John Middletons' Lugbara Religion mainly captured the incidence of witchcraft and explained that as structures of society were changing, social relationships were strained and so witchcraft attacks were increasing.

Further, in this field of Structuralism, French Anthropologist, Claude Levi Strauss, analysed religion in terms of binary opposition, revealing the inner logic. Some basic opposition was supposed to be universal, to be found in myths, symbols and cultural practices all over the world, for example, opposition between males and females, raw and cooked, nature and culture etc. This was also influenced by the Structuralism linguistics. Further in USA a wave of interpretative Anthropology emerged on which Clifford Geertz in his work 'Interpretation of Culture' (1973) moved away from structural functionalist. He introduced the term and concept of 'thick description'. Greetz (1973:91) in his famous essay 'Religion as cultural system' defined religion as-

> "a system of symbols which acts to establish powerful pervasive and long lasting moods and motivations in men by formulating conceptions of a general order of existence and clothing these conceptions with such as aura of factuality that the moods motivations seems uniquely realistic."

Evans- Pritchard's' new way of doing Anthropology "Witchcraft, Oracles and Magic among the Azande" raised several classic questions of rationality and translation reality to religion, and beliefs of the Azande people. Victor Turners' first work was a classic structural functionalist analysis of the dynamics of matrilineal kinship among the Nedembu of Zambia . Thereafter he produced a series of analysis of the symbolism of Nedembu rituals which were unraveled in their richness and details. Turner draw particularly on Arnold Van Genneps' work on rites of passage- any ritual which marks a change of state, but especially life crisis rites. Van Gennep had posted three stages through which participants in such rituals must pass; separation, marginality or liminality and aggregation. Louis Dumont's Homo Hierarchicus in India attempted to explain caste system in terms of pure and impure.

Tribal Religion: In Anthropological Lensing

- A concern with godline beings and mens' relations with them.
- A dichotomisation of elements of the world into sacred and profane and a central concern with the sacredness.
- An orientation towards salvation from the ordinary conditions of worldly existence.
- Ritual practices.
- Beliefs which are neither logically nor empirically demonstrable nor highly probable, but must be held on the basis of faith.
- An ethical code, supported by such beliefs.
- A mythology.
- A body of scriptures or exalted oral tradition.

Demography of Tribal Population in India

The demographic account of the tribal population shows that India has total 72,738,360 tribal forming 8.08 per cent of the total population of the country (2001 census). Further 16.73 per cent are scheduled castes. The country has 4635 communities including 3742 castes and 427 Scheduled Tribes to the harmony in the 26 States and six Union Territories. Odisha has 10.38 per cent of the total tribal. Some of these tribal are quite large in number such as the Gond, Bhil, Santal, Oraon, Munda, while some others have very low population i.e. Onge, Great Andamanese, Toto, Ragi etc.

Tribal Religious Identity Issues

Accounting the tribal religion, Risley explains Hinduism and Animism as an amalgamation of magic and worshipping. Dr Hutton opines that the tribal religion represents the material not yet built into the temple of HINDUISM, while Erwin advices to group all the aboriginal tribe of India with an exception to those of Assam as Hinduism as they are the part and parcel of Hindu religion. For instance particularly in case of Munda religion an attitude towards the supernatural being is that of reverential fear. A marked degree of dependence on propitiation and conciliation of being along with magic is marked.

Mr P.C. Tallents the then superintendent of census, Bihar and Orissa, is very pessimistic in drawing a satisfactory boundary like between Hinduism and Animism and acknowledges the difficulties of distinguishing one from the other. Some elementary features of tribal religious identity includes animism (belief in spirit), Bongaism (Bonga is conceived by Hos as a power of 'Mana' that pervades everywhere (Majumdar, 1950:278), Naturalism (worship of nature is another form of belief which prevails among the tribal's sun, moon, earth etc.). Totemism (the mysterious relation of sacred belief of tribal attached to same plants, animals or objects. Taboo (is a rather negative custom of any belief, which is regarded as "holy dread" by Majumdar (1961: 357, 62), Magic is the integral part of tribal dimension which further works as weapon to tackle dangerous and uncertainty of situation. Ancestor worship (It is the worship of ancestors and it widens the reach of the worshipper and it plays a vital role in the tribal life, Dube 919700 and Vidyarthi (1963:144). The tribes of Chhattisgarh like the Amat, Bhuyian, Dhur, Karm and Oriya Gond have ancestor worship. Polytheism (The divine powers have been identified with a group of powerful forces and duties which control and influence the happenings in the community. Further tribal belief in four categories of spirits i.e. protective spirit, benevolent spirit, evil or malevolent spirits and ancestral spirit, along with some sacred geography, such as sacred areas, sacred centres, sacred specialists and sacred performances.

Identity Issue

The alteration in the colonial approaches of isolation with the tribal population opened the doors of 'integration' for the indigenous group. The wave was meant for strengthening tribal identity but with its expose to several multilayered factors such as globalisation, migration, intrusion of middle men and contractors, modernisation, multiple religious faiths etc, there were major lapses marked in the identities of the tribal people. The tribal cultural transformations were in a sense detrimental for the community. To further expand it, tribal group have undergone a metamorphosis from a singular or particularistic identity to multiple identity. Even in some cases their identity are overlapped by some identity imposed on them. In simpler terms, "ascribed identities" are absorbing additional identities thus creating horizons of artificial identities. There are instances of the identity being assigned to groups or individuals by some extraneous agencies like authority in power. Such identity may or may not agree to the people "self ascription" of the same. (Danda, 1991:51-52). But there are frequent observation where within identities are ultimately conforming with imposed identities.

Basu Mullick rightly asserts that the "identity does not become a problem in the history of a people until their identity is being questioned or threatened by others." (1953: 5-6). Agitation develops when identity of any group is threatened as with the identity of any group some ideology always works. Therefore, ideology as an expression of "Identity always contains a criticism of how power is disturbed, and advocates a redistribution of powers, Ideology and identity are always a political reality." (Basu, Mullick, 1993:12)

"Concern for protection of language, culture and identity and resistance against oppression has been always marked as an evident mark of invariably every tribal movement." (Danda, 19991: 176-177). It is thus seen that search for the identity of the people. Sometimes implies a demand for a redistribution of political power. Several typologies of identities are marked. For instance, ascribed identity, achieved identity, self imposed identity, imposed identity etc.

TRIBAL AND HINDU INTERACTIONS

- **Tribalisation with reference to Samleiswari Devi in Sambalpur, Orissa**

Through the empirical study of Chitrasen Pasayat it is marked that several cultural and religious trajectories of the tribals and Hindu caste go hand in hand. He makes that there are every possibility of tribal and Hindu elements co-existing in a given cultural item. In case of Sambalpur analysis of transformation of a tribal deity into a Hindu one is marked. It is traced that admission of a tribal deity into the local Hindu society may come about without any drastic change in the core elements of the tribal deity. The transformed deity may be placed with a distinct position in the existing religious structure in the regional Hindu society. Such transformation may occur without any structural change in the social status of either the tribal people or the caste Hindu s worshipping the deity within the existing social structure of the region as a whole. The relation between the caste Hindus and tribal people may remain unchanged despite the fact that caste-Hindus worship the tribal deity and vice-versa.

It can be suggested that the Hindu religio-cultural structure is a device by which deities other than that of caste Hindus are accepted into the Hindu religion. In case of Sambalpur tribal Devi Samleiswari, the caste Hindus have accepted her as their God and have attached Hindu status by pouring Sanskritic elements. So tribalisation is followed by Sanskritisation. Even though both appear contradictory but here these are complementing. Although Hindus accept and worship her but they do not attach it with desanskritisation, neither do they look at this in a degraded manner. The second assumption is that transformation does not necessary means addition of Sanskritic elements and replacement of tribal element or vice-versa rather this means a harmonious co-existence of both tribal as well as Sanskritic elements in an empirical situation. The incorporation of the tribal deity into Hindu fold may be viewed as tribalisation. But the degree of incorporation is directly linked with the amount of Sanskritic element in a particular deity. It may be viewed that Hinduism in its codified form is different from the tribal religion in many respects. For our purpose, there are mainly two distinctive ideal levels of religious systems of tribal people and caste Hindus are crafted out. Such as-

In case of tribal the uniconical image is marked where within deities do not have definite shape and size or anthropomorphic icons but Hindus worship their deities in such shapes. Moreover it is constructed on the rules of the 'Silpa Sastra'. Tribal religion appeared in human sensitive whereas Hindu appeared in knowledge of tradition. In case of tribal regular worship according to rules and regulations are not compulsory but in case of Hindus there are attachment of the deities with living person's therefore timely offerings and prayers are offered. In case of the tribal gods and goddesses it is believed that the gods have limited power but Hindus believe in unlimited power and potentiality both to create and destroy. In case of tribal the deity is worshipped by a tribal or a non-Brahmin, but in case of Hindu it's always a Brahmin. Tribal is not universal but Hindu is universal in nature. In case of tribal most Gods are cruel and dangerous, but for Hindus majority are soft hearted and their blessings can make ones life more prosperous, except few such as Shiva Shambhu is considered to be destructive in his 'rudra rupa.'

Further certain remarkable changes are marked in Samlei Devi which marks the alteration in the traditional means of worshipping of her. For instance-

1. The image of Samlei is found in the form of a large head like stone, and now there are attempts to reshape it as in photographs with a physical anatomy kind of an appearance.
2. Earlier the Devi was descending through spirit possessors of lower caste people, but nowadays these practices are reduced just as similar to the Hindu god's functional belief patterns.

3. Earlier the Devi was worshipped under a seme (Bomax malabaricum) tree. Later the deity is enshrined into a temple, as Hindu people do...
4. Earlier both vegetarian and non-vegetarian offerings were accepted by the Devi but now due to the reflections of the Hindu purity and pollution concepts now there is a rethinking of the non-vegetarian offerings are undertaken.

Historical account shows that the CHAUHAN rulers in Sambalpur areas accepted tribal deities as the State goddesses or 'Esta Devi'. First they accepted the tribal deities and then they started the sanskritising rituals and constructing temples. The present temple of Samleiswari Devi is the example of such development. Bose (1967:202) opinion seems to be accurate when he says that "Hinduism has grown by the incorporation of many tribal cults, until it has become a kind of federation of many tribal cult, and beliefs and practices...Which one can name as Hinduism. It is believed that Samlei Devi can be the savior or the destructor of the city and major she protects the residents of the city. She is considered to be the Jagannath of the Ganga kingdom in the coastal Orissa. (Mohapatra, 1990). Along with her some other deities such as Pteneswari, Raktambari, and Sureswari etc are also worshipped. They are considered all to be seven sisters.

- **Hinduisation of Tribal Religion**

Sachidanand (1964:96) adduces an elaborate account of how Hinduisation takes place among tribals. He shows how Hinduisation takes place among the Oraons. The Oraons have started performing Swami Pooja in Sawan (June-July) and offer a goat to the Devi or at the Devi mandap. The PAHAN (priest) leads the worship performed with incense, rice, beer, gur, ghee, vermilion and belapatra. Even a few Oraon youth learn Hindu mantra pathas. The people sing bhajans and celebrate different Hindu festivals. The marriage, birth and death rituals are also maoulded according to Hindus. Hindu Gods and Goddesses such as Ganesh, Lskshmi, Shiva and Saraswati are worshipped by tribal.

In recent terms again Hinduisation has developed a bhagat movement among the tribal where within five categories are marked such as – NEMHA BHAGAT (who are assigned the charge to retain the qualities of ceremonial purity and mahadeo), Hinduizied or Bachhidan Bhagats, Kabirpanthis Bhagat (Kabir followers who believe in *sat sahib sat kabir).* Tana Bhagat (mainly outcome of the bhakti cult), Vishnu Bhagat (who have joined Vaishnv cult).

- **Tribal, Christianity and Questions of Conversion**

As to the impact of Christianity, one can mark that it has been an important factor in the religious belief of the tribals. Christian missions belonging to various denomination have been working in tribal areas with the prime motive of conversion. Conversion involves a relatively radical change in the perspective. It refers to something more than simply joining a particular group or movement for which the term recruitment is often used. (Snow and Machalek, 1984; Robins, 1998)

Several controversies regarding conversions are experienced. The identity crisis emerges as some tribal accept the converted population and some reject them. The Graham Stain's murder case in 1998, Orissa is the burning example of the same.

Christianity has provided the first model of Westernised shape of church to tribal. Sahay (1963) suggests a set of five process taking place as the impact of Christianity on the tribal, i.e. Oscilation, Scrutinisation, Combination, Indigenisation, Retrovesion.

In relation to tribal being impacted by Hindu cults and church a specific model can be attached. In almost all religions, the religious organisations are the major carriers of the ideologies and conventional rules and regulations. So, Robertson (1970) derived a four-fold classification of religious organisation.

Self Conceived Basis of Legitimacy

	Particularistic Legitimate	Uniquely Legitimate
Exclusive	**Institutionalised**	**Sects**
Inclusive	**Denomination**	**Church**

Robertson's classification uses the two sects of distinctiveness to generate four categories, first, inclusive membership, that it is membership open to anyone, as compared to the exclusive membership where some test or qualification is essential to be eligible to be the member. Robertson calls the 'self conceived basis of legitimacy' which takes the form of either claim to sole possession of truth or where other groups are acknowledged also possess the essential truth. This classification essentially does not follow a linear development process and several complexities are attached to this process.

Impact of Buddhism and Islam on Tribal Religion

The Bhots of North West Himalaya and Bhutias, Lepchangs, Chakmas and Nagas of the North East Himalayan region are mainly Buddhist in consonance of the neighbouring Buddhist population. So far as the Islam population is concerned the Lakshadweep people are mainly Muslim. It is believed that originally the islanders were Hindu migrants from the mainland but were converted around 14th century A.D. (Dube, 1969:12), with the coming of the Muslim rulers. The Siddis of Gujarat and the Gujjars of the North Western Himalayan region are also Muslim. The Bhil, Dhankasi, and Kotis are some marked tribe who are largely influenced by Islam.

Conclusion

Thus, it is evident that other religious faiths like Hinduism, Christianity etc have had considerably influenced the tribal religion. Right from the nature of belief in Supernatural powers to the whole sacred complex of the tribal pantheon, has met with neighbours, the coming of missionaries in the tribal area, ritualisation or reform movement and soon have all had their impact. However, the engagement of tribal religion with Hindus always dominates other impacts. An optimistic initiation to overcome such tribal religious identity crisis and challenges is essential to safeguard the rights of the community.

References

Connolly, P.(ed.) 2007. *Approaches to the study of religion*, London and New York: Cassell publishers.

Ghurey, G.S., 1959. *The Scheduled Tribe,* Bombay: Popular Prakashan.

Gisbert, P., 1960. *Tribal India*, New Delhi: Manohar Publication.

Hamilton, Malcolm, 2007. *The Sociology of Religion: Critical Concepts In Sociology,* London and New York : Routledge, Tylor & Francis Group.

Hasnain, Nadeem, 1983. *Tribal India Today*, New Delhi: Harman Publication.

Hembrem,T., 1996. *The Santals: Anthropological Theological Reflections on Santali and Biblical Creations Traditions*, Calcutta: Punthi Pustak Publication.

Oraon, Karma, 2002. *Dimension of Religion, Magic and Festivals of Indian Tribe- The Munda,* New Delhi: Kanishka Publishers and Distributors.

Padel, Felix, 1995. The Sacrifice of Human Being: British Rule and the Kondhs of Orissa, New Delhi: Oxford University Press.

Pasayat, Chittrasen, 1997. "Tribal- Non-tribal Interaction in Orissa-A Study of Samleiswari Devi in Sambalpur", in Pfeffer, George and Behera. D.K (eds). *Contemporary Society: Tribal Studies,* Vol-II, New Delhi: Concept Publishing Company.

Radha, K. Manis. 1999. " The Tribes of India: Patterns and Problems of Identity", in Pfeffer, George and Behera. D.K (Eds.) *Contemporary Society: Tribal Studies,* Vol. IV, New Delhi: Concept Publishing Company.

Rai, B.K. and Vidyarthi, L.P., 1976. *The Tribal Culture of India,* New Delhi: Concept Publishing Company.

Singh, K.S., 1990. 'Assimilation Vs Integration in Tribal Society' (Article) *(JSTOR)*.

V.W. Turner, 1957. Schism and Continuity in an African Society, Manchester: Manchester University Press.

V.W. Turner,1967. *Revelation and divination in Nedembu Ritual*, Ithaci: Cornell University Press.

4

Inclusive Policy Approach on Disabled Persons: A Core Concept of Human Rights

—*Amritpal Kaur*

Abstract

The present paper emphasis the Persons with Disability Act, 1995 and National Policy for Persons with Disabilities (2006) is chosen for analysis. Though, the later is not a legislative document but it is the most recent relevant policy and therefore indicative of the Indian Government's stance on this issue. Policy forms the framework from which legislative change occurs and therefore Disability policy is the key to guiding government decision-making. The paper will focus on the human rights aspect as a core concept in the national policy on disabled persons.

***Key Words**:* Disability, India, policy, human rights.

Introduction

The status of vulnerable sections in the society is an important tool to determine the development. A truly compassionate society makes allowances for disabled, aged or sick in a non-intrusive, participative and sensitive manner, ensuring equal opportunities to all by providing a level playing field. According to 11th Plan (2007-2012), Persons with Disabilities could be as high as five to six per cent of India's total population. We need to make our society and systems inclusive for this substantial portion of our population, enabling them to lead a dignified, independent life while recognising them as valuable human resource to our country. All this is possible through an integrated approach, to include legislation, policies and concessions by the government, coupled with active participation by organisations, employers and in fact, every citizen. Moreover in developing countries only two per cent of persons with disabilities are able to meet the basic services and rehabilitation needs.

India has an important experience in making policy and proactive with respect to disabled persons from as early as 1872. In nineteenth Century Indian Lunacy Act, 1912 had specify provisions for mentally ill and retarded persons. In post-independence period Article 41 of the Indian Constitution specifically deals with the 'relief for disabled and unemployable persons'. However, it was in 1980's that the policy commitment to full participation of persons with disabilities in the Indian set up evolved. It has also been reflected in various key pieces of legislation such as Mental Health Act,1987, Rehabilitation Council of India Act,1992 (amended in 2000), the National Trust Act, 1999, the persons with Disabilities Act,1995 and National Policy on Disability, 2006. The major legislation among all these is the Persons with Disabilities Act,1995. The Act is based on the philosophy of promotion, protection, equalisation of opportunities, non-discrimination and affirmative action in favour of disabled persons. The idea is to build a bridge between the medical and social model of disability.

It is apparent that the entitlements or the commitments towards the persons with disability are divided in two groups. Firstly, the entitlement given in the form of legal rights and it has been reiterated or strengthened certain rights in the Act. Secondly, there are contingent entitlements whereby explicit proviso "within the economic capacity and development" has been added.

Though the Persons with Disabilities Act, 1995 is a comprehensive piece of legislation but there are a number of policy shortcomings in the design that are worth highlighting. The cross-cutting policy issues are discussed as follows:

I. The definition of the term 'disability' given in two (PWD Act 1995) under the Act is a kind of medical definition. This definition does not cover the wider group of disabled persons. The policy-makers have shown the reluctance to give an inclusive definition. The need is to develop policy whereby the definition of 'disability' is expanded to include multiple disability, autism, haemophilia, cerebral palsy, moderate speech impairment. The term 'mental illness' has also been vaguely defined (*ibid*). The proposed definition should be 'disorder of the mind which results in partial or complete disturbance in person's thinking, feeling or behaviour which results in recurrent or persistent inability to carry out the activities of daily living, self-care, education, employment and participation in social life. This approach is quite commonly used at the international level and could bc followed in India too.

II. Another policy issue with regard to the Persons with Disabilities Act, 1995 is related to the aspect of 'limits of economic capacity and development'. But the act has utterly failed to outline the levels of policies and interventions which are expected at different levels of economic development in India. It is important to highlight that this approach is used in certain important sections of the Act and the proviso has made the application of these sections of the Act quite uncertain. These important sections are identification of the Persons with Disabilities, prevention, treatment of disability and access rights of the persons with disability. Therefore, due to an absence of benchmark policy on such sensitive issues, the courts have become the main point of reference for the persons with disabilities to enforce their rights. However, the resources and the time needed to assess the courts is lengthy and it is tedious process too. Consequently, many persons with disability are excluded.

III. The enforcement policy of the Persons with Disabilities Act, 1995 is very weak. Chapter 12 of the Act deals with the appointment of the Chief Commissioners for the persons with disabilities. The Office of the Commissioner has weak powers. The major limitation is that the office of Chief Commissioner is to look into complaints with respect to the deprivation of the rights of persons with disabilities and to take up the matter with the appropriate authorities. No enforcement court or the administrative tribunal is given to the Chief Commissioner. It is a clear limitation.

IV. The overall policy approach has limited the roles of the actors such as NGO's or Panchayati Raj Institutions (PRI's) or civil society organisations. There is no explicit mention of PRI's though the act has been passed after 73rd Amendment Act, 1992.

V. The Sectoral Policy issues are:

Employment: The Act provides for three per cent reservation in public sector employment. The overall policy approach is that it is applicable to three disabilities only i.e. locomotors, hearing and visual with one per cent reservation for each. Therefore, full disability categories of the Act are not included in the reservation policy. It is a major lacuna which should be corrected.

Education: The policy is to provide education to 'Children with disabilities' in regular schools or setting up of special schools have been followed. The act provides a very limited guidance as to which approach is to be followed. Though subsequent policies have given more guidance but the rights of the parents to enroll their children is unclear.

Health: In health sector, the policy followed is quite ambiguous in the sense that it is difficult to interpret the terms of enforcement. The authorities are promoting pre-natal and post-natal care and create awareness of disability issues. Unfortunately, the combination of the economic capacity proviso and such general language has made these provisions simple statement of intent.

It is clear that there is diverse range of issues that persons with disabilities Act deal with. It is also not surprising that there are major

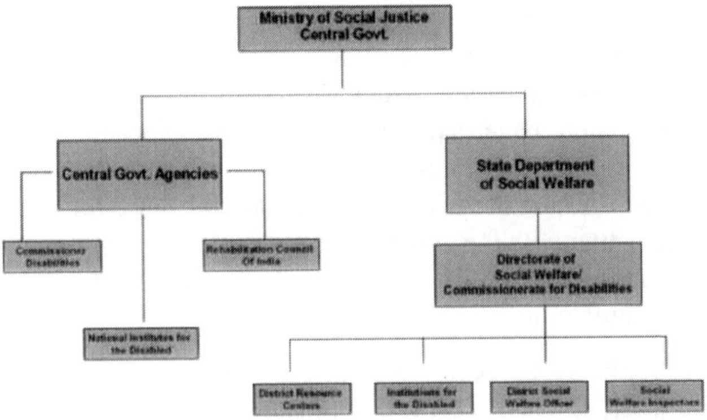

Fig. 3.1: Governmental Structure for Policy and Implementation of Programmes for the Disabled in India: Stylised Depiction.

challenges of institutional coordination in disability policy. These are between levels of the public sector (e.g. centre/state/districts and lower), within levels of the public sector (e.g. between social welfare, health, transport, education, and labour departments), and between the public and non-public sectors at all levels of the system. While this section focuses primarily on more formal institutions in disability policy and service delivery (both public and non-public), it is also important to stress the importance of informal institutions such as the families with disabled members. Undoubtedly, the family remains by far the most important institution in the lives of persons with disabilities in India (Harris, 1996).

VI. UNCRPD and Indian Policy on Disability:

India is a signatory of the UN Convention on the Rights of Persons with Disabilities. The Convention is a milestone in the priority accorded by UN members to disability, and the Government of India is undertaking consultations during 2007 to familiarise stakeholders on its implications for India. Three important obligations arise out of the Convention are (a) Implementation of provisions of the UNCRPD, (b) Harmonisation of Indian Laws with the UNCRPD and (c) Preparation of a Country Report by 2010. The Central ministries were directed to implement the provisions of the UNCRPD. It includes the focus on the women and children with disabilities. The Ministries were also requested to identify statutes and orders that require amendment in the light of the Convention and to initiate the process of amendment. All Chief Ministers of States and Administrators of UTs were similarly requested to refer to various obligations under the Convention that relate to the State Governments and to implement the same. State Governments/ UTs were also requested to furnish the status report for preparation of Country Report (*ibid*).

VII. Disability Policy: Recent Developments:

(a) National Policy for Persons with Disabilities (2006):

It is the most recent relevant policy and therefore indicative of the Indian Government's stance on this issue. No doubt policy forms the framework from which legislative change occurs and therefore Disability policy is the key to guide government decision-making (Aldersey and Turnbull, 2011).

The National Policy recognises that Persons with Disabilities (Hereinafter referred as PWD's) are valuable human resources for the country and seeks to create an environment that provides PWD's equal opportunities, protection of their rights and full participation in society. It is in consonance with the basic principles of equality, freedom, justice and dignity of all individuals that are enshrined in the Constitution of India and implicitly mandate an inclusive society for all, including persons with disabilities. The National Policy recognises the fact that a majority of persons with disabilities can lead a better quality of life if they have equal opportunities and effective access to rehabilitation measures.

The salient features of the National Policy are:

(i) Physical Rehabilitation, which includes early detection and intervention, counselling and medical interventions and provision of aids and appliances. It also includes the development of rehabilitation professionals.

(ii) Educational Rehabilitation which includes vocational training and

(iii) Economic Rehabilitation, for a dignified life in society.

It is to be noted that the Policy follows the structure of the PWD Act. Several observations can be made:

1. The policy represents progress in policy terms on some shortcomings of the PWD Act.
2. The Policy often repeats general commitments of the PWD Act, though remains more general on concrete strategies for implementing them.
3. There remains limited reference to the role of PWD themselves in policy development, implementation, monitoring and evaluation.
4. There remains no strategy for integrating disability concerns into the work of PRIs.
5. It is worth noting that the policy has mentioned "Capacity Building" 13 times and "Quality" was mentioned 10 times, "Accountability" was mentioned seven times, "Prevention"

and "Non-Discrimination" were mentioned six times each, "Family Resource" was mentioned five times "Protection from Harm" was mentioned four times while the terms "Entitlement" and "Access" were mentioned three times, "Contribution" and "Efficiency" were mentioned twice. The terms such as "Individualised Services", "Participation" and "Co-ordination of Services" were mentioned once only. (Infra note 14). Therefore, it is generally debated that the human rights of this group are not being fully realised.

(a) At the national level a wave towards inclusion of persons with disabilities in mainstream has been gaining roots. Ministry of Human Resources and Development (MHRD) report in 2005 released its policy statements which focus on the robust and concrete commitment to integrate children with Disabilities in regular schools.

(b) The states in our country are adopting disability policies. Though the number of states which have adopted such policy is quite low but an effort are made by the state governments shows a good sign. The states like Chhattisgarh, Karnataka, and Maharashtra have adopted the action plans for implementing the commitments to promote the rights of persons with disabilities. The draft of the Karnataka policy is the mirror reflection of the Persons with Disabilities Act, 1995 and the focus is on the implementation of the poverty alleviation programmes, education and health, exemptions on property tax for PWD. However, the draft state policy does not provide much more specific commitments or implementation guidance than the Act itself.

(c) Certain innovative programmes are also initiated by the states like Karnataka. The Karnataka Commissioner for Disabilities has introduced several progressive practices. These include:

   (i) *Regular Reviews:* The District Disability Management Reviews (DDMR's) are done. It involves regular reviews at state and district levels of all schemes which are targeted to Persons with Disabilities.

The process is intended to identify gaps/shortcomings in policy, programme coverage, and implementation. The reports are solicited quarterly from relevant departments in specialised format and the results publicised in the media. Collection of information is facilitated by a District Disability Welfare Officer. While reporting is timely, there remain concerns about the reliability of information from line agencies.

(ii) *Lok adalats for disability:* The periodic lok adalats (peoples' courts) are organised in districts for persons with disabilities so that they can air their grievances with respect to entitlements. These lok adalats are chaired by a senior official of the Commissioners' office and all district officials such as officials from social welfare departments, education, health, panchayati raj institutions and other departments are also expected to be present. This is very effective process as in many cases it leads to the immediate resolution of persons with disabilities issues, or in others accelerates judicial intervention.

(iii) *Voluntary organisations:* There are active partnerships with voluntary organisations to overcome its capacity constraints. Free legal aid is offered to persons with disabilities by alternative Law Forum in Bangalore through the Office. This not only includes issues with respect to Persons with Disabilities Act entitlements, but also the broader issues of access of justice are covered.

(iv) *Media:* The active use of media is taken in raising awareness of disability issues. It deals with wide coverage and publicity about violations of persons with disabilities rights. Not only the print media the regular phone-in programmes are also introduced to talk about the issues related to disability.

Suggestions

(a) The role of NGOs in service delivery and policy for persons with disabilities should be recognised. The programmes should be developed by Ministry of Social Justice and Empowerment (MSJE), central and state Commissioners' offices in collaboration with NGOs for awareness rising of officials, service providers, PRI representatives and communities on programmes for people with disabilities. A periodic monitoring of awareness, with particular focus on lagging states and remote regions, should be put in place to assess impact. States should also be strongly encouraged to develop their own disability policies.

(b) A more elaborated approach to education of children with disabilities is to be followed.

(c) A clearer acknowledgement of the role of media in awareness rising about disability issues has to be there. Similarly an acknowledgement of significant issues in collection of statistics on persons with disabilities should be improved.

(d) The State Governments must be urged to adopt "simple, transparent and client-friendly procedures." However, overall there is very limited sense in the Policy that even government of India's own assessments indicates serious implementation problems. A reiteration of the general commitments of the Persons with Disabilities Act will be insufficient to reinvigorate the disability sector.

(e) There is a complex institutional framework for operation of the disability sector in India. The nodal agency for disability is the Ministry of Social Justice and Empowerment (MSJE), whose overall mandate is to promote the interests of "disadvantaged and marginalised sections of society." This includes Scheduled Castes, Backward Classes, minorities, persons with disabilities, aged persons, street children, victims of drug abuse, and others. There are inherent challenges for any nodal ministry in such a multi-sectoral field as disability. To that extent, there is no "natural" nodal Ministry for disability issues as there may be in sectors such as education or telecommunications. There are areas where having MSJE as lead agency seems questionable and out of line with better international practice. The main example is special education. At present it is the mandate of MJSE, as are in-service training initiatives for teaching of children with special needs through RCI (which is administratively under MJSE). The consequence of this is that the vast majority of children with disabilities have their education under the mandate of MHRD while those in special schools are under another ministry. It is not good for any institution as it adversely affects the service delivery to the needy. Internationally the practice followed is that the education of all children is under educational authorities. It should be followed in India.

(f) The growing role of PRIs should also need to be tapped and it should be used to extend institutional reach to the village level. It will enhance the accountability at local level.

Conclusion

In India there is complex social structure, therefore all vulnerable sections of the society need to be covered in the policy documents so that their needs are addressed effectively. The national policy for persons with disabilities has covered 'youth and children with disabilities' but those 'suffering from chronic illness' and 'the aged' are ignored. It is true that with the passage of time 'the aged' suffers from physical and cognitive disabilities (Sudesh, 2008). Furthermore, there is scope for improvement in the policy framework for disability in India, particularly at state level where policy development has been largely piecemeal. The more fundamental issue is the extent to which the entitlements under the Act have been realised in the decade since its passage. The issue that is to be addressed is institutional mechanisms which the Act had put in place to enforce entitlements and increase accountability of providers, and how effective have they been in practice.

While further consultation is needed, some areas where the UNCRPD is likely to have implications for disability policy in India include a wider definition of "accessibility", going beyond the physical environment which is the focus of current access policies (e.g. access to information), greater focus on what "economic capacity of states" means in practical terms and expansion of the definition of disabilities to include some areas like developmental disorders which are not covered under the current Act.

The Government of India during 1998-2003 has spent just 1042 crores through its MSJE for welfare of the disabled persons. It amounts to 0.07 per cent of the total expenditure and 0.05 per cent expenditure by Government of India in 2000-2001, 2002-2003 respectively. It shows that Government of India places persons with disabilities at a lower scale in core programmes. MSJE does not have figures of other ministries which are spending on persons with disabilities so it fails to give an aggregate picture (Joydeep, 2015).

India has ratified the United Nation Convention on Persons with Disability in 2007. The Convention (ibid) obliges signatory States "to take into account the protection and promotion of the human rights of persons with disabilities in all policies and programmes." It is unfortunate to state that the India's current disability policy is of low quality with regard to encompassing the Human Rights of persons with disabilities. As mentioned above an introduction and comprehensive explicit inclusion of core concepts Human Rights and vulnerable sections are urgently required in India's National Policy for Persons with Disabilities (2006). An inclusion or integration of the persons with disabilities should mean that they are afforded the same dignity, respect and social inclusion as others and the equity gap is reduced. However, it is important to highlight that Indian government under the aegis of Ministry for Social Justice and Empowerment has taken a giant step by creating a Department of Disability Affairs in May 2012. Therefore, this is now responsible for addressing the needs of the disability community in India. It is hoped that it will help to shape the future services towards the persons with disabilities (Article, 14, UNCRPD). *It is true that "Too often we underestimate the power of a touch, a smile, a listening ear, an honest compliment, or the smallest act of caring, all of which have the potential to turn a life around."*

References

1. Aldersey, HM, Turnbull HR., 2011. "The United Republic of Tanzania's National Policy on Disability: A policy analysis" *Journal of Disability Policy Studies*, pp. 160-169.
2. Article 4 of UNCRPD.
3. Durocher, J, Defranco A., 2012. 'Disability and global development', *Disability and Health Journal,* pp. 132-135.
4. 2(i) In Indian context Physical Disability under Persons with Disability Act,1995 (hereinafter referred as PWD Act) is of different kinds: Blindness, Leprosy cured persons, Hearing Impairment, Locomotor Disability, Mental Illness and Mental Retardation, Autism, Cerebral Palsy, Learning Disabilities (Dyslexia), Writing Disabilities (Dysgraphia) etc.

5. Joydeep, 2015. Government Initiatives for Welfare of Physically Disabled in India, available at http://www.mapsofindia.com/my-india/government/welfare-of-physically-disabled-in-india-government-initiatives accessed on February 14, 2015
6. Jessica O'Dowd, 2015. *India's Disability Policy* available at https://global-health.tcd.ie/publications/publications/pdf/Indias_Disability_Policy_ODOWD.MANNAN.MCVEIGH.pdf accessed on February 14, 2015.
7. 2(q) of PWD ACT, 1995 'mental illness' means any mental disorder other than the mental retardation.
8. Harriss-White, 1996, For an insightful discussion of informal institutions in the field of disability.
9. Government Initiatives for Redressal of Disability in India, available at http://mospi.nic.in/Mospi_New/upload/disablity_india_statistical_data_11mar2011/Chapter%208%20-National%20redressal.pdf accessed on February 13, 2015.
10. Sudesh, V., 2008. "National and International Approaches to Disability", *Journal of the Indian Law Institute*,Vol. 50.

Further Readings

1. World Bank (2011).
2. Ministry of Social Justice and Empowerment (2006). National Policy for Persons with Disabilities. New Delhi, India.
3. United Nations Convention on the Rights of Persons with Disabilities (UNCRPD) (2007). UN, New York.
4. Ministry of Social Justice and Empowerment (2012). The Draft Rights of Persons with Disabilities Bill. New Delhi, India.

5

Political Marginalisation of Scheduled Castes in Elections to General Constituencies of Punjab Vidhan Sabha - A Case Study of 2007 and 2012 Elections

—*Dr Kamla*

The Brief Backdrop and Research Methodology

Seven hundred years after Guru Ravidas began preaching the oneness of God's creation, Scheduled Castes in Punjab and rest of India continue to be marginalised in socio-cultural and political arenas. They lie at the bottom of the Hindu caste hierarchy, of which Dr B.R. Ambedkar, wanted complete annihilation, to usher in an egalitarian society in India. His famous words in the book "Annihilation of Caste"[1] - *"Turn in any direction you like, caste is the monster that crosses your path. You cannot have political reform, you cannot have economic reform, unless you kill this monster"*- continue to rattle the conscience of moral crusaders. In a speech to the Constituent Assembly, he famously described democracy as 'top-dressing' on Indian soil. Customs, traditions, social practices and religious laws were all heavily loaded against the idea that all citizens should have equal rights. When Ambedkar said this, he had the practice of caste discrimination largely in mind.[2] The same phenomenon continue to stall political advancement of Scheduled Castes - also called *Dalits* - in so called liberalised democratic set-up. The rigid and socially maligned social hierarchies of Indian society meant that a commitment to equality and social justice was hardly a "natural" sentiment.[3]

In Punjab, they still constitute a low social, economic and political position. Because of poverty and illiteracy, their level of political awareness is low. Voting is the only political activity in which majority participates. Reservation in education, employment and political decision-making bodies (Panchayats and Legislatures) has not enhanced their political fortunes. What would have been the number of *Dalit* legislators in Punjab, had there been no constitutional provision for their reservations? In the light of contemporary political scenario, probable answers to this question, makes the political untouchability of former untouchables, palpably obnoxious for them.

Punjab has the highest concentration of Dalits (31.9 per cent) in the country.[4] The present study highlights the issue of political marginalisation of Scheduled Castes in Punjab *Vidhan Sabha* elections to general (unreserved) seats. It is a case study, based on general elections of 2007 and 2012 to Punjab *Vidhan Sabha.* The phenomenon under-study being rooted in the socio-cultural milieu combining dynamically with economic and political imperatives, inductive method of study has been used, with a degree of deductive reasoning. The data for the study is culled substantially from Statistical Reports on these general elections available on the websites of Election Commission of India. The study also referred newspaper articles/editorials, journal articles etc. for insights into psychological analysis.

II

Jatt Sikh community - the landed aristocracy of Punjab owing to their economic clout - serve as the hinterland for ruling elites. Schedule castes, making-up roughly one-third of state's population enjoy a very little political clout. The numerical preponderance of the *Jatts* in the Sikh religion and their hold over the landownership structure and politics of the state place them at the top of political ladder in the State.[5] Next to *Jatts* in the hierarchy are the urban trading castes, the high-caste Hindu elite-consisting of Khatris, Aroras and Baniyas, who control much of the urban trade and industry in the state and economically are quite well off. Punjabi Hindus do not generally identify with Akali politics and have served as the main support base of the Congress in the state. Hindu's support base is now getting divided mainly between Congress and BJP. Congress also draws strength from the caste divide with landowning Jats making up the upper crust of the Sikh community, who have little affiliation with *Dalits*, from both the Sikh and Hindu folds. In contrast the Scheduled Castes remain in a subordinated position to the *Jatts* and the trading castes.[6]

As is their wont, the Punjab political parties owing to land-owning background and traditional caste-bias, generally don't field SC candidates from constituencies other than the reserved ones for them. Coming into of Shiromani Akali Dal (SAD) and Bharatiya Janata Party (BJP) alliance since 2007, has aggravated the political marginalisation of Scheduled Castes (SCs) in Punjab. SCs are considered backwards in the social and cultural realms. Economically also, they can't match the clout of landed aristocracy of *Jatt-Sikh* community. The phenomenon of political marginalisation of SCs in Punjab is evident from the election data of "number of SC candidates given tickets" by the dominant political parties for contesting elections to 'general' seats to 2007 and 2012 State Vidhan Sabha Elections.

Total number of constituencies were 116 in 2007 and 117 in 2012 general elections [Table 4.1]. General (unreserved) seats were 87 and 83 respectively. Hence, there were 29 and 34 reserved constituencies in 2007 and 2012 respectively. No SC candidate contested election from as many as 23 general seats in 2007 and 16 in 2012.

Table 4.1: Number of Reserved and General Constituencies and number of General Constituencies from where no SC Candidate Contested Election

Election Year	*Reserved for SC Candidates*	*General seats*	*Total Number of Constituencies*	*Out of Column (4) Number of General seats from where no SC Candidate Contested*
1	2	3	4 = (2+3)	5
2007	29	87	116	23
2012	34	83	117	16

Source: Statistical Reports on 2012 and 2017 Punjab General Elections issued by Election Commission of India.

Dominant political parties in the state politics, generally desist from fielding SC candidates from general seats [Table 4.2]. Allocation of tickets to the SC candidates by them is restricted to the reserved constituencies only. In 2007 elections, there were 129 SC candidates in fray for the general seats. However, no SC candidate was given ticket for the general seats by SAD, BJP and INC. SC Candidates to general seats were fielded only by BSP (22), other parties (48) and independents (59).

Table 4.2: Party-wise Number of SC Candidates who Contested Election from General (Unreserved) Seats

Election Year	*Party wise Classification of SC Candidates who Contested Election from General (Unreserved) Seats*							*Number of SC Candidates who Contested election from General Seats*	
	SAD	*BJP*	*INC*	*BSP*	*IND*	*Others*	*Total*	*Won*	*Lost Security Deposit*
2007#	0	0	0	22	59	48	129	0	129
2012#	0	0	1	47	61	32	141	0	141

Source: Statistical Reports on 2007 and 2012 Punjab General Elections issued by Election Commission of India.

Abbreviations: SC - Scheduled Caste, SAD: Shiromani Akali Dal, BJP: Bharatiya Janata Party, INC: Indian National Congress, BSP: Bahujan Samaj Party, IND: Independents.

The Constituency/seat-wise break up of SC candidates who contested election from General seats in 2007 and 2012 Punjab Vidhan Sabha elections, is available in Appendix I and II, respectively, at the end of this paper.

Similarly, there were 141 SC candidates who contested election from 67 general seats in 2012 election. No SC candidate was put up by SAD-BJP alliance to general seats. Congress, however, made a lone deviation, by fielding Malkit Singh, an SC candidate from Jalalabad (W) seat against Sukhbir Singh Badal, presently Deputy Chief Minister of the State. All the remaining 140 SC candidates to general seats were from BSP (47), other parties (32) and independents (61). Success however eluded all the SC candidates from general seats in both the general elections. What further aggravated their insult was forfeiture of security deposit[$], of all of them. Further, SC legislators from reserved constituencies, if chosen as ministers, are generally assigned politically insignificant portfolios.

The political parties of the state do not tire in taking pride for welfare measures initiated by them for socio-economic and political advancement of *Dalits* in Punjab. However, not allotting ticket to any SC candidate, by the SAD-BJP alliance and INC, for contesting election to general seats in 2007 elections, exposes their hypocrisy. The same was the case in 2012 elections with solitary aberration by INC, giving ticket to an SC candidate from general seat of Jalalabad (W).

Table 4.3: Party-wise Number of SC Candidates who Contested Election from Reserved Seats

	Election Year -2007						*Election year - 2012*					
	SAD	*BJP*	*INC*	*BSP*	*IND*	*Others*	*SAD*	*BJP*	*INC*	*BSP*	*IND*	*Others*
Contested	25	4	29	29	90	60	29	5	34	34	97	88
Won	15	4	8	0	2	0	21	3	10	0	0	0

Source: Statistical Reports on 2012 and 2017 Punjab General Elections issued by Election Commission of India.

The behavioural pattern of dominant political parties, however, is contrastingly, different in respect of reserved seats [Table 4.3]. Here, the reason for allocating tickets to SC candidates lies in the 'sure' winnability prospects of one of the contesting SC candidates. For both the election years of 2007 and 2012, SAD-BJP combine contested all the reserved seats. INC also did the same. In 2007, all the reserved seats, except 2, were lapped-up by SAD-BJP alliance and INC. In 2012 general elections, SAD-BJP combine and INC accounted for all the successful candidates.

III

Reasons and Remedies

Ducks for BSP - a party supposedly of *Dalit* hinterland - in both the elections, is simply undigestible. The same however is attributable to a number of factors including absence of any strong Scheduled Caste leadership in the State of Punjab to organise *Dalits* as a potent political force. Entry of BSP in Punjab electoral arena, beginning with general elections of 1992, has led to the division of *Dalit* votes, hitherto pocketed by the Congress party. It did not yielded any political windfall for the BSP, but has considerably undermined the traditional mainstay of Congress in Punjab. There is however, no perceptible variance in voting pattern of *Jatt-Sikh* Community, which has little affinity with the *Dalit* folks. SAD-BJP electoral alliance since 2007 has further accentuated the political marginalisation of SCs in Punjab. Resultantly, support base of non-*Dalit* Hindu is now also getting divided, mainly between Congress and BJP. Division of votes of *Dalit* populace and non-*Dalit* Hindus in a multi-cornered contests, justifies the alienation of Congress and BSP and the rollicking success for the SAD-BJP combine since 2007.

Traditional hierarchies are too deeply entrenched to be reversed through one single measure. They need a concerted push backed by a strong will from different segments of society, including but not confined to politicians and politics.[7] But one doesn't has to be a rocket-scientist to suggest a remedy for the above diagnosis. The historic victory of Aam Aadmi Party - winning 67 out of 70 seats- in just held Delhi elections amply demonstrates that no political party can be considered a political under-dog for all the times to come. All the *Dalit* organisations should unite for the collective welfare of their community. The strategic seat-sharing alliance with the Congress will solve - once for all - the debilitating problem of cutting into each others vote-base, in multi-cornered contests, to their collective detriment. They only have to have a vision, road-map and commitment for an inclusive development of the state and its people, irrespective of caste, creed, religion or political affiliation, with however a softer corner for the hitherto botched-up populace on socio-economic, cultural and political matrices. Both the Bharatiya Janata Party and Rashtriya Swayam Sewak Sangh are now considering the possibility of actively mobilising *Dalits,* wthout losing the support base of the so-called upper castes. Ajay Gudabarthy, however, observes that "for Dalits, mobility by gaining acceptance looks far more tangible and achievable than the abstract idea of annihilating caste.[8]

Speaking at a function in Jalandhar in Punjab on the theme of "Life Teachings and Bani of Guru Ravidass" former Lok Sabha speaker and Congress leader Meira Kumar has given a call that the next Chief Minister of Punjab should be a dalit from Doaba. She said that Punjab had maximum population of *dalits* and *Doaba* was the area which had highest density of dalits.[9] She has provided a much needed food for thought and an action point, for all the concerned to lap it up. The imperative however is to match the call with a necessary vision, determination and wherewithals for a clean and value-based political governance model, to be placed before the electorate, for them to take a call on it.

Table -1: Punjab Assembly General Elections -2007

APPENDIX-I

Constituency Number	*Party Wise Classification of SC Candidates who Contested Election from General (Unreserved) Seats*							*Number SC Candidates from General Constituencies*	
	SAD	*INC*	*BJP*	*BSP*	*IND*	*Others*	*Total*	*Who Who*	*Won Forfeited Security Deposit*
2	0	0	0	1	0	0	1	0	1
3	0	0	0	2	0	0	2	0	2
4	0	0	0	0	1	1	2	0	2
5	0	0	0	0	0	1	1	0	1
13	0	0	0	1	0	0	1	0	1
17	0	0	0	0	0	2	2	0	2
18	0	0	0	0	1	0	1	0	1
21	0	0	0	1	2	1	4	0	4
23	0	0	0	1	1	0	2	0	2
25	0	0	0	1	0	2	3	0	3
26	0	0	0	1	0	2	3	0	3
27	0	0	0	0	1	0	1	0	1
28	0	0	0	0	2	1	3	0	3
29	0	0	0	0	0	2	2	0	2
30	0	0	0	1	0	1	2	0	2
31	0	0	0	0	1	0	1	0	1
34	0	0	0	0	0	2	2	0	2
35	0	0	0	0	0	1	1	0	1
36	0	0	0	1	2	0	3	0	3
38	0	0	0	1	2	3	6	0	6
40	0	0	0	1	0	1	2	0	2
41	0	0	0	0	2	1	3	0	3
42	0	0	0	0	0	1	1	0	1
44	0	0	0	1	2	1	4	0	4
45	0	0	0	1	1	0	2	0	2
51	0	0	0	1	0	0	1	0	1
52	0	0	0	0	0	1	1	0	1
54	0	0	0	1	0	0	1	0	1
56	0	0	0	0	0	1	1	0	1
57	0	0	0	1	0	1	2	0	2
59	0	0	0	0	1	0	1	0	1
60	0	0	0	0	2	1	3	0	3
68	0	0	0	1	0	1	2	0	2
69	0	0	0	0	1	1	2	0	2
73	0	0	0	0	1	0	1	0	1
75	0	0	0	0	3	0	3	0	3
76	0	0	0	0	1	0	1	0	1
77	0	0	0	0	1	0	1	0	1
79	0	0	0	0	1	0	1	0	1
80	0	0	0	0	3	1	4	0	4
81	0	0	0	0	1	0	1	0	1
83	0	0	0	0	0	1	1	0	1

(Contd...)

85	0	0	0	0	0	1	1	0	1
86	0	0	0	0	2	2	4	0	4
87	0	0	0	0	0	1	1	0	1
89	0	0	0	0	1	1	2	0	2
92	0	0	0	1	1	0	2	0	2
93	0	0	0	0	7	0	7	0	7
94	0	0	0	0	0	2	2	0	2
95	0	0	0	0	2	0	2	0	2
96	0	0	0	0	0	1	1	0	1
97	0	0	0	0	1	2	3	0	3
100	0	0	0	0	1	0	1	0	1
103	0	0	0	0	1	2	3	0	3
104	0	0	0	1	1	0	2	0	2
105	0	0	0	0	1	0	1	0	1
106	0	0	0	0	1	1	2	0	2
108	0	0	0	1	1	0	2	0	2
111	0	0	0	0	3	0	3	0	3
113	0	0	0	1	2	1	4	0	4
114	0	0	0	0	0	1	1	0	1
116	0	0	0	0	0	1	1	0	1
117	0	0	0	0	1	1	2	0	2
Total	**0**	**0**	**0**	**22**	**59**	**48**	**129**	**0**	**129**

Table -2: Punjab Assembly General Elections -2012

APPENDIX-II

Constituency Number	*Party-wise Classification of SC Candidates who Contested Election from General (Unreserved) Seats*							*Number SC Candidates from General Constituencies*	
	SAD	*INC*	*BJP*	*BSP*	*IND*	*Others*	*Total*	*Who Won*	*Who Forfeited Security Deposit*
1	0	0	0	1	0	0	1	0	1
4	0	0	0	1	0	0	1	0	1
7	0	0	0	1	0	0	1	0	1
9	0	0	0	1	0	0	1	0	1
12	0	0	0	1	0	0	1	0	1
13	0	0	0	1	0	0	1	0	1
15	0	0	0	1	1	0	2	0	2
18	0	0	0	1	2	1	4	0	4
21	0	0	0	1	0	1	2	0	2
22	0	0	0	1	2	2	5	0	5
23	0	0	0	1	1	0	2	0	2
24	0	0	0	1	0	1	2	0	2
26	0	0	0	0	0	2	2	0	2
27	0	0	0	1	0	0	1	0	1
28	0	0	0	1	4	2	7	0	7
31	0	0	0	0	1	2	3	0	3
32	0	0	0	1	1	1	3	0	3
35	0	0	0	0	2	1	3	0	3

(Contd...)

36	0	0	0	1	1	0	2	0	2
37	0	0	0	1	1	1	3	0	3
39	0	0	0	0	0	1	1	0	1
40	0	0	0	1	0	1	2	0	2
41	0	0	0	1	0	0	1	0	1
43	0	0	0	1	0	0	1	0	1
45	0	0	0	1	0	0	1	0	1
47	0	0	0	0	1	1	2	0	2
49	0	0	0	1	0	0	1	0	1
52	0	0	0	0	0	1	1	0	1
57	0	0	0	0	2	0	2	0	2
58	0	0	0	1	0	0	1	0	1
59	0	0	0	1	0	0	1	0	1
60	0	0	0	1	0	0	1	0	1
61	0	0	0	0	2	0	2	0	2
62	0	0	0	1	0	0	1	0	1
63	0	0	0	0	1	0	1	0	1
65	0	0	0	1	1	1	3	0	3
68	0	0	0	0	1	0	1	0	1
72	0	0	0	1	0	0	1	0	1
75	0	0	0	1	0	0	1	0	1
76	0	0	0	0	2	1	3	0	3
78	0	0	0	0	3	1	4	0	4
79	0	1	0	1	5	1	8	0	8
80	0	0	0	0	1	0	1	0	1
81	0	0	0	1	0	0	1	0	1
83	0	0	0	1	1	1	3	0	3
84	0	0	0	1	1	0	2	0	2
86	0	0	0	0	1	1	2	0	2
87	0	0	0	1	1	0	2	0	2
88	0	0	0	1	1	1	3	0	3
90	0	0	0	1	1	1	3	0	3
92	0	0	0	1	3	1	5	0	5
94	0	0	0	1	0	0	1	0	1
95	0	0	0	1	1	2	4	0	4
96	0	0	0	1	0	0	1	0	1
97	0	0	0	1	0	1	2	0	2
99	0	0	0	0	2	0	2	0	2
101	0	0	0	1	1	0	2	0	2
103	0	0	0	1	3	1	5	0	5
106	0	0	0	0	1	0	1	0	1
107	0	0	0	0	1	1	2	0	2
108	0	0	0	0	2	0	2	0	2
110	0	0	0	0	4	0	4	0	4
111	0	0	0	1	1	0	2	0	2
112	0	0	0	0	1	0	1	0	1
114	0	0	0	1	0	0	1	0	1
115	0	0	0	1	0	0	1	0	1
116	0	0	0	1	0	0	1	0	1
Total	**0**	**1**	**0**	**47**	**61**	**32**	**141**	**0**	**141**

Notes and References

1. Excerpts from speech prepared by Dr. B.R. Ambedkar for the 1936 Annual Conference of the Jat-Pat-Todak Mandal of Lahore but not delivered owing to the cancellation of the Conference by the Reception Committee on the ground that the views expressed in the Speech would be unbearable to the Conference.
2. Guha, Ramachandra, 2012. Parliament & Patriarchy. *The Hindu.* December 31.
3. Babu, D Shyam and Chandra Bhan Prasad. 2014. For a New Paradigm of Social Justice. Vishakhapatnam: *The Hindu.* September 1.
4. 2015. State Lagging in use of Funds for SC Schemes. Chandigarh: *The Tribune.* January 21.
5. Sharma, Neeru. Caste in Punjab: Political Marginalisation and Cultural Assertion of Scheduled Castes. *Journal of Political Science, 19(1).* pp. 27-29. [http://www.global.ucsb.edu/punjab/journal/v19_1/2- NeeruSharma19_1.pdf - Accessed on 30/11/2014]
6. *Ibid.* pp. 29-30.

$ As per Section 34 (1) (b) of the Representation of Peoples Act, 1951, a general candidate for contesting an Assembly election will have to make a security deposit of Rs 10,000. A candidate belonging to Scheduled Caste / Tribe will have to make a security deposit of Rs 5,000. A defeated candidate who fails to secure more than one-sixth of the valid votes polled in the constituency will lose his security deposit. [http://eci.nic.in/eci_main1/Contesting.aspx - accessed on 28/11/2014].

¥ These two successes belong to independent candidates - Charanjit Singh Channi from Chamkaur Sahib Constituency and Ajit Singh from Nihal Singh Wala Constituency.

7. Deshpande, Ashwini. 2014. Contours of Caste Disadvantage. Vishakhapatnam: *The Hindu.* September 25.
8. Gudavarthy, Ajay, 2014. A Rightward Shift in Dalit Politics. Vishakhapatnam: *The Hindu.* September 13.
9. 2015. Meira Kumar gives Call for Dalit Punjab CM. Chandigarh: *The Times of India.* January 5.

6

Ambedkar's Quest of a Mere Democratic India

—Dr Nirmal Singh

The encounter of democracy with caste is a historical process accommodating two sets of opposed values. There is a common understanding that caste is antagonistic to democracy. Indeed, the hierarchical universe of the caste system is theoretically at odds with the equalitarian requirements of substantive democracy. The political culture of Indian society is leading to more and more social contradictions. On one hand we aspire to become egalitarian society and, on the other, the caste culture negates this very aspiration. And what is more problematic we cannot become egalitarian without the help of this very caste culture, at least in economic sense.

Basic root of Ambedkar's philosophy was to establish a mere democratic India. Inequalities could not be the bases of this very system and in Indian context; he articulates a casteless society based on the principles of liberty, equality and fraternity. When Ambedkar tried to explore the hierarchical nature of Hindu Social orders, it did not mean that he was merely criticising the orders without any further planning. Ambedkar interrogated the caste ridden Hindu society on the criterion of democracy and observed that "Caste system is a grave impediment in the path of democracy. The roots of democracy lie not in the form of the government but in the social relationships and the terms of association between the people who form the society.

Community of purpose, desire of welfare, loyalty of public ends and mutuality of cooperation are essential hallmarks of the democratic society. A scheme of government does not exist in vacuum, it operates within the society. Its usefulness depends upon its relationships with the other sphere of society. Elections, parties and participation are, after all formal institutions of democracy. They cannot be effective in an undemocratic atmosphere. Political democracy means the principle of "one man one vote" which indicates political equality. But if oppression and injustice exists, the spirit of political democracy would be missing. Democratic government therefore, should be an expansion of a democratic society. Democratic society is characterised by absence of stratification of society into classes and the social habit on the part of individuals and groups which ready for the continuous readjustment of recognition of reciprocity of interests. Looking from this perspective, the purpose of democracy is not so much to put a curb on an autocratic king but to bring about the revolutionary changes in the social and economic life of the people without any bloodshed.

Ambedkar viewed democracy as an instrument of bringing about change peacefully. Democracy does not merely mean rule by the majority or government by the representatives of the people. This is a formalistic and limited notion of democracy. We would understand the meaning of democracy in a better fashion if we view it as a way of realising drastic changes in the social and economic spheres of society. Ambedkar's idea of democracy is much more than just a scheme of government. According to Ambedkar, Democracy is a way of life which requires everyone to respect the rights of every human being to be a person, a unique entity. Democracy is not an attempt at uniformity, which is impossible, but an integrated verity. He viewed that all men are not equal in their capacity but all men are equally necessary for society. We must begin by acknowledging the fact that there is a complete absence of two things in Indian society. One of these is equality. On the social plane, we have...a society based on principles of graded inequality which means elevation for some and degradation for others. On the economic plane, we have a society in which there are some who have immense wealth as against many who live in abject poverty.

Dr Ambedkar's View on Caste System

Caste is undoubtedly an all-India phenomenon in the sense of that they are hereditary, endogamous groups which form a hierarchy, and that each of these groups has a traditional association with one or two occupations. This is infect, a regression from Ambedkar's analysis of the place of labour in the caste system......Caste system is not merely division of labour; it is also a division of labourers......It is a hierarchy in which the divisions of labour are graded one above the other (Ambedkar, 1987: 263-64). For Dr Lohia, it is meaningless to talk of equality while maintaining separate castes. Castes have to be abolished. In 1935, at *Yevla* in Nasik district, Maharashtra, B.R. Ambedkar had declared his firm resolves to change his religion. He said that "To reform the Hindu society is neither our aim nor our field of action. Our aim is to gain freedom. We have nothing to do with anything else (Ambedkar, 1987)." The struggle for the emancipation of the depressed classes from the thralldom of untouchability and casteism has been in continuation for a pretty long time. However, the Dalit liberation movement got an impetus during the British period. With the dawn of democratic institution in India, the Dalit liberation movement steadily became more vocal, assertive and effective.

Dalit as a socio-political concept appears frequently in the contemporary discussion on Indian politics. It has become a form of academic violence which promotes casteist myths. Thus, Dalits become a static community. The term Dalit is referred to broken, ground downtrodden people who become subject to deliberate act of exploitation by those above them in a hierarchical social system (Manifesto of the Dalit Panthers, 1972). The term "Depressed classes" was mentioned in the Census report 1921, but since the enactment of the Government of India Act 1935, the Dalits are consistently referred to as "Scheduled Castes."

Mahatma Jyotirao Phule could properly realise the importance of education in improving the lot of the untouchables and backwards castes. He stated very categorically that, "For want of education intellect deteriorated. For want of intellect morality decayed. For want of morality progress stopped. For want of progress wealth vanished. For want of wealth the *Shudras* perished. All these sorrow sprang from illiteracy (Mahatma Phule, 1980: 189). The principle of graded inequality has been carried into the economic field. "From each according to his ability, to each according his need" is not the principle of the Hindu Social order. The principle of the Hindu Social order is: From each according to his need to each according to his nobility (The illustrations given above are merely drawn from imagination. They are facts of the history). For Dr Lohia, it is meaningless to talk of equality while maintaining separate castes. Castes have to be abolished. In 1935, at *Yevla* in Nasik district, Maharashtra, B.R. Ambedkar had declared his firm resolves to change his religion. He said that "To reform the Hindu society is neither our aim nor our field of action. Our aim is to gain freedom. We have nothing to do with anything else (Ambedkar, 1987)."

Phule strongly attacked the exploitation of peasants by the bureaucracy, Ambedkar and Periyar both supported and helped the organised movements of peasants against landlords. The denial of temple entry to Dalits by status quo and conservative caste Hindu is seen as a part of the social oppression that is still intertwined with class oppression as most of the Dalits are poor farm workers. Dalits have been denied entry into temples. Ambedkar's scathing comment on Hindu scripture culminated in a public burning of *Manusmriti* in 1927 and in 1935 Ambedkar announced his vow to leave Hinduism entirely and to convert to some other religion (Eleanor Zelliot, 2008: 193). Mahar satyagraha and *Kalaram* satyagraha were also an attempt to gain entry in the temples. The main figures of this larger anti-caste movement, Jyotirao Phule, B.R. Ambedkar, and E.V. Ramaswami 'Periyar' with many others throughout India attacked the system of exploitation at all levels, culturally, economically and politically. They asserted that Hinduism, had not been the religion and culture of the majority but rather it was an imposed religion. Phule tried to formulate a new theistic religion, Periyar promoted atheism, Ambedkar turned to Buddhism.

Through conversion movement, Dalits offer a new alternative religion, Buddhism, in negation of Hinduism. It started with Ambedkar's personal conversion announcement in 1935 which was followed by a *Mahar* conference in 1936 where Ambedkar declared, if you want to make the world in which you live, happy, change your religion; if you want independence, change your religion.

The conversion movement made an immense appeal to the Dalits, through its benefits are mostly limited to mental relax but other size impact is remarkable (B.R. Ambedkar, 1987: 192). If the Dalit question could be answered by religion, i.e., if the problem is somehow the bane of Hinduism alone, non-Hindu religion should have solved the problem a long time ago. What is the condition of Dalits, for example, in a state like Punjab where Sikhism, as egalitarian and non-Hindu religion has had to sway for three centuries? The charge is equally placed at the doorstep of Christianity (Shyam D. Babu and Chandra Bhan Prasad, 2009: 23).

Ambedkar asked that: Can a leopard change its spots? No, never. "Hinduism is like the leopard there can be no "Hindu" without a caste......untouchability is a part and parcel of Hinduism. If you become Muslims, you will get the political rights as Muslim; if you become Christian, you will get the political rights as Christians; if you become Sikhs, you will have your political safeguards as Sikhs. In short, our political rights will accompany us (B.R. Ambedkar, 1987). Through Sanskritisation movement, a section of untouchables who could improve their economic condition, either by abandoning or continuing their traditional occupations. A low caste was able, in a generation or two, to rise to a higher position in the hierarchy by adopting vegetarianism or teetotalism, and by sanskritising its rituals and pantheon (M.N. Srinivas, 1952: 32). They tried to justify their claims to a higher social status in caste hierarchy by inventing suitable mythologies. Ambedkar had famously declared that the untouchables had two enemies: Brahminism and capitalism. His first political party, the Independent Labour Party (ILP), was fashioned on the lines of the British Labour Party, which followed the Fabian line of peaceful transition to socialism but abhorred capitalism. Ambedkar's ILP was then the true leftist party of India, with the communities then going the Congress party. The ILP, on the other hand, demonstrated in practice how to embed caste and class in the struggle for social justice.

Ambedkar's Vision of Social Democracy

Ambedkar emphasises the need for bringing about an all-round democracy. Ambedkar's vision of social democracy emanates from his quest for a "just society" which is based on the idea of a casteless society. He not only provided a ruthless criticism of the existing social order but also came up with an alternative vision and alternative model of social order based on liberty, equality, fraternity and annihilation of caste. Dr Ambedkar says: "Democracy is not a form of government, but a form of social organisation.

After India's independence for dispensing social justice in the wake of emerging democracy in a hierarchically arranged society, Ambedkar discussed the operationalisation of principles of equality, liberty and fraternity, which were considered to be cardinal principles of any democracy. For social justice, he tries to find a creative combination of democracy and modernity. He looked at democracy as an initial condition or the sphere which could be used for converting opportunity into an asset. For him conversion could be achieved only through modernity. Ambedkar tends to treat democracy as an initial condition of social justice both as consciousness and also as a material possibility.

John Rawls developed the following principles of justice: (a) each person is to have an equal right to most extensive basic liberty compatible with similar liberty for others, (b) social and economic inequities are arbitrary unless they are reasonably expected to be to the advantage of the representative man in each income class, (c) inequalities are to attach to positions and offices equally open to all. Similarly, taking a leaf from Rawl's theory of social justice argues that, "the fundamental issue in distributive justice is equality; a more equal or at least a less unequal distribution of the benefits and of social co-operation." He opines that:

Rawls concept of social justice would mean giving every man his due. The basic aim of social justice is to remove the imbalances in the social, political and economic life of the people to create a just society. "In that sense distributive justice to go beyond equality in the purely formal sense: equality before the law, seeks to go beyond equality in the purely formal sense: equality before the law, the equal protection of the laws, or even formal equality of opportunity. Its central concern is, in the language of Rawl 'to address the bias of contingencies in the direction of equality'...Any attempt to promote distributive justice must begin with a consideration of the existing inequalities in society...it is essential to keep in sight both inequalities between individual and disparities. Disparities between groups have been historically go great significance in Indian society."

John Rawls idea of distributive justice opposed that "all social values are to be distributed equally unless an unequal distribution of any or all of these values is to everyone's advantage." Ambedkar's idea of social justice is tantamount of the concept of justice propounded by John Rawls, who includes in his theory of distributive justice an "element of the difference principles, in Ambedkar's case, it is the principle of special treatment. Both these principles of justice require a distribution of resources that will most effectively satisfy the needs of worst off (Gopal Guru, 2001). In terms of culture-specificity, the term social justice has a different meaning in Indian society. It means dispensing justice to those to whom it has been systematically denied in the past because of an established social structure. Ambedkar's Quest for social justice can be visualised in the philosophy, policy and ideals of the Constitution of India. On the basis of these, it can easily argue that Ambedkar has mentioned multiple principles for the establishment of an open and just social order in general and Indian society in particular. Ambedkar was of the opinion that social justice can be dispensed in a free social order in which an individual is end in itself. Similarly, the term of associated life between members of society must be regarded by consideration founded on liberty, equality and fraternity. In a way these principles of social justice are similar to the principles of social justice as mentioned in Rawl's theory.

To Ambedkar, "A democratic form of the government presupposes a democratic form of society. The formal framework of democracy is of no value and would indeed be a misfit if there was no social democracy. The political leaders never realised that democracy was not only a form of government; it was essentially a form of society. To Ambedkar, the aim of democracy is essentially the practical interests of society as a whole, and not of any class, group or community. Democracy as a social organisation is meant that it includes all members of society. For this purpose, Ambedkar had to fight against tyranny, injustice and false tradition in order to release the suffering people from boundage. He vigorously struggled against injustice, social slavery, inequality and poverty. To him, true socialism would not tolerate ill-treatment and oppression, because these are opposed to socialism. The present social orders are not suited to create a socialist spirit among the people.

State socialism is not based on bloody revolution as Marx argued. Ambedkar believed that bringing socialism is the duty and the responsibility of the state. State shall provide protection against economic exploitation and shall work towards making equalitarian society. Ambedkar said that "Caste is the monster that crosses your path, you cannot have political reforms, and you cannot have economic reforms, unless you kill this monster. Ambedkar said that political democracy cannot last unless there lies at the base of it social democracy. What does social democracy mean? It means a way of life, which recognises liberty, equality and fraternity as the principles of life. The Indian state needs to be reformed and reinvented are manifestly clear. The question is: do we have the state which can finally redeem the pledges made by the framers of the constitution which can make India, in Ambedkar term, a social democracy rather than a mere political democracy?

References

1. A.M. Shah. 2002. "The 'Dalit' Category and its Differentiation." *Economic and Political Weekly*, Vol. 37, No. 14, 6 April: 1317-1318.
2. Ambedkar, B.R. 1987. *Why Go For Conversion?* Banglore: Dalit Sahitya Akademy.
3. Ambedkar, Dr Babasaheb. 1990. *Yanche Bahishkruit Bharat ani Muknayak (Marathi) [translated to mean the Depressed India or Front runner].* Education Department. Government of Maharashtra.
4. Ambedkar, B.R. 1945. *What Congress and Gandhi have done to the Untouchables.* Bombay:Thacker & Co.
5. Anand, Mulk Raj and Eleanor Zelliot. 1992 (eds.). *An Anthology of Dalit Literature.* New Delhi: Gyan Prakashan.
6. Anand, Mulk Raj. 1990 (ed.). *Annihilation of Caste: Undelivered Speeches of Dr B.R. Ambedkar*. Delhi: Arnold Publishers.
7. B. R. Ambedkar. 1987. *Go For Conversion*, Banglore: Dalit Sahitya Acadamy.
8. B.R. Ambedkar. 1987. *"Why Go For Conversion*?" Banglore: Dalit Sahitya Akademy, p.192.
9. D.N. 1991. "Ambedkar and Separate Electorates Issues." *Economic and Political Weekly,* Vol. 26, No. 21, 25 May: 1328-1330.

10. Eleanor Zelliot. 2001. *From Untouchable to Dalit*, New Delhi: Manohar Publishers and Distributors.
11. Eleanor Zelliot. 2008. "Gandhi and Ambedkar: A Study in Leadership." In Ishita Banerjee (ed.), *Caste in History*. New Delhi: Oxford University Press, p. 193.
12. Emanual Nahar. 2007. Minority Politics in India. Chandigarh: Arun Publishing House Pvt. Ltd.
13. G.K. Karanth. 2004. "Replication or dissent? Culture and Institutions among Untouchable" Scheduled Castes in Karnataka." In Dipankar Gupta (ed.), *Caste in Question*. New Delhi: Sage Publication, p. 161.
14. Ganshyam Shah. 2001. *Dalit Identity and Politics*, New Delhi: Sage Publications.
15. Guru, Gopal and Geetha, V. 2000. "New Phase of Dalit-Bahujan Intellectual Activity." *Economic and Political Weekly,* XXXV, No. 3: 15-21 January.
16. Guru, Gopal. 2001. "The Language of Dalit Bahujan Political Discourse." In Ghanshyam Shah (ed.), *Dalit Identity and Politics*. New Delhi: Sage Publications.
17. Kalpana Kannabira. 2009. "Sociology of Caste and the Crooked Mirror: Recovering B.R. Ambedkar's Legacy." *Economic and Political Weekly,* XLIV, No. 4, 27 January, p. 37.
18. Lajpat Rai. 1909. Speeches and Writings, *Modern Review*, Vol.1, July.
19. Lata Murugkar, 1991. *Dalit Panther Movement in Maharashtra*. Bombay: Popular Prakashan, pp. 54-55.
20. Louis Dumont. 1999. *Homo Hierarchicus: The Caste System and its Implications*. New Delhi: Oxford University Press, pp. 66-67.
21. M.N. Srinivas, 1952. *Religion and Society among Coorgs of South India*. Delhi: Oxford University Press, p. 32.
22. M.N. Srinivas. 1972. *Social Change in Modern India*, Delhi: Orient Longman.
23. Mahatma Phule. 1980. *Samagra Vigmaya*. Bombay: Maharashtra Rajya Sahitya and Sanskriti Mandal, p. 189.
24. Nandu Ram, 1995. *Beyond Ambedkar*. Delhi: Har Anand Publications, p. 87.
25. Nirmal Singh. 2011. "Dr Ambedkar and the Renewing Scenario of Dalit Identity." In Dr S.S Randhawa and Sardool Singh (eds.), *Dr Ambedkar's Philosophy of Social Justice*. Chandigarh: Salaria Publication House.
26. Nirmal Singh. 2012. "Insight of Caste System in India: Its Reflection in 21th Century" International Research Analysis and Evaluation, International Indexed & Referred Research Journal, December: Vol. IV, Issue- 39.
27. Nirmal Singh. 2014. "BSP in Punjab: Analysing its Failure" *Economic and Political Weekly (EPW)*, November 29: Vol. XLIX, No. 48.

28. Rajni Kothari. 1994. "Rise of Dalits and the Renewed Debates on Caste." *Economic and Political Weekly*, Vol. 26, No. 26. 25 June: 1590.
29. Ronki Ram. 2001. "From Servitude to Assertion: Ambedkar's Subaltern Approach to Nationalism and Dalit Liberation." *Social Sciences Research Journal (Chandigarh).* Vol. 9, No. 2: pp. 146-170.
30. Ronki Ram. 2004. "Untouchability in India with a Difference: Ad-Dharm, Dalit Assertion and Caste Conflict in Punjab." *Asian Survey*, XLIX, No. 6, November-December: pp. 895-912.
31. Ronki Ram. 2009. "Regional Specificities and Caste Hierarchies in Punjab." *Indian Journal of Politics,* Vol. 43, No. 2: pp. 15-29.
32. Ronki Ram. 2009a. "Bhakti and Social Protest: Guru Ravidass and the Rise of the Dalit Consciousness in Punjab. *Indian Journal of Politics*. Vol. 43, No. 4: pp. 43-64.
33. Ronki. Ram. 2004. 'Limits of Untouchability, Dalit Assertion and Caste Violence in Punjab." In Harish K. Puri (ed.), *Dalit in Regional Context*, New Delhi: Rawat Publications.
34. Rudolph Lloyd I and Susanne Hoeber Rudolph. 1967. *The Modernity of Tradition*, Delhi: Orient Longman Limited.
35. S.R Bharati, 2002. "Dalit, a Term Asserting Unity." *Economic and Political Weekly,* XXXVII, No. 42, 19 October, pp. 4339-40.
36. Shyam D. Babu and Chandra Bhan Prasad, 2009. "Six Dalit Paradoxes", *Economic and Political Weekly*, XLIV, No. 23, 6 June, p. 23.
37. Surinder S Jodhka. 2003, "Caste Tension in Punjab", *Economic and Political Weekly,* Vol. 37, No. 28, July 12, pp. 2923-26.
38. Susan Bayly. 1999. *Caste, Society and Politics in India*. Cambridge: Cambridge University Press, p. 14.

7

Women with Disabilities: A Politics of Exclusion

—*Dr Kanchan Chandan*

Abstract

Women are a vulnerable and said to be the debilitated fraction of the society. In the complexity of Social Exclusion of Women these differences were debated for centuries, often in the form of complaints and accusations about what should be done and what not should be as part of social living. Many initiatives have taken to bring social inclusion in the society, still women are facing social exclusion in different walks of life, be it social, political, economic, social exclusion of women who are disabled or differently able is no exception in terms of exclusion of women in society. Women with disability are more marginalised and discriminated; attitude of the society is precarious towards them. This Paper tries to throw light on different prospective of social exclusion of disabled women in particular. This paper is an effort to illustrate plight of women who are not equal physically or psychologically with other section of the society, and are subjected to several kind of discrimination, and violence against them. There is an attempt to explore the means of social exclusion of this part of the society, and to analyze the issues and suggest the way forward. The dream of egalitarian society, a society in which men and women will no longer be differentiated in terms of status, power and prestige, abilities or disabilities. Women or disabled women in particular would not be subjected to experience inhumanity and violence by the society. Despite of gender equity enshrined in the Indian society; the past is evident of several types of discrimination in terms of gender inequality. It is my earnest optimism that working towards their issues will certainly give way to significant changes in these women's lives.

Keywords: Disabled Women, Disability, Social Exclusion, Gender Inequality, Violence, Discrimination.

"Being disabled should not mean being disqualified from having access to every aspect of life."

—***Emma Thompson***

Women are a vulnerable and said to be the debilitated fraction of the society. Women with disability are more marginalised and discriminated; attitude of the society is precarious towards them.

An estimated 10 per cent of the world's population experiences some form of disability or impairment (WHO Action Plan, 2006-2011). The term 'disability' has many different meaning. However, the term disability refers to loss of health, where health is conceptualised in terms of functioning capacity in a set of health domains such as mobility, cognition, hearing and vision (WHO, 2004). The number of people with disabilities is increasing due to population growth, ageing, emergence of chronic diseases and medical advances that preserve and prolong life, creating overwhelming demands for health and rehabilitation services (Srivastava and Khan, 2008). In South-East Asia, the prevalence of disability ranges from 1.5 – 21.3 per cent of the total population, depending on definition and severity of disability (Mont, 2007). Despite the increase in prevalence of disability worldwide, due to various reasons, not much attention has been paid to its evaluation, management and prevention (WHO, 2002).

The World Health Organisation (WHO, 1976) draws on a three-fold distinction between impairment, disability and handicap:

- Impairment is any loss or abnormality of psychological, physiological or anatomical structure or function.
- Disability is any restriction or lack (resulting from an impairment) of ability to perform an activity in the manner or within the range considered normal for a human being.
- Handicap is a disadvantage, for a given individual, resulting from impairment or a disability, which prevents the fulfillment of a role that is considered normal (depending on age, sex and social and cultural factors), for that individual.

Women have always been ignored and if they are disabled their degree of vulnerability increases manifold. There are various empowerment programmes running for women welfare but they also exclude issues of disabled women. Even the development programmes rarely address the needs of disabled women or include them in community development programmes. Disabled women are seen imperfect, incomplete, inferior, asexual, and non-productive and denied recognition as women and human beings.

The fact is women's movement is controlled by non-disabled women and disabled women lack the confidence and ability to raise their voice. In country like India, where sex selective abortions are rampant and girl child is not welcomed in the families till date, it is well understood the vulnerable condition of women with disabilities. Violence against women has a long history in Indian society, and when that woman is happened to be disabled then atrocities against them are multiplied. Women face widespread discrimination in India, and the rate of sexual violence against women and girls is appalling. If a woman has an intellectual or psychosocial disability, it makes her even more vulnerable to abuse. Women also face unique forms of neglect and abuse.

Review of Literature

Disability is a multifaceted and complex concept to define. Different conceptual models have been created to define disability (Altman, 2001).Women with disabilities are always neglected and subject to violence (Abramson *et.al*, 2000). There was a study by (Alexander *et.al*, 1998) about relationship between sexual and/or physical abuse, healthcare utilisation, and pain medication usage in female patients with fibromyalgia. Participants were 75 women with fibromyalgia. It was found that 57 per cent reported a history of sexual or physical abuse. Women with a disability continue to experience social oppression and domestic violence as a consequence of gender and disability dimensions. The study of Mays, J. M. (2006) explains the domestic violence and disability inadequately explain several features that lead women who have a disability to experience violent situations. May's article argues that material feminist interpretations and disability theory, with their emphasis on gender relations, disabilities and poverty, should be used as an alternative tool for exploring the nature and consequences of violence against women with a disability. Patel *et al.* (2009) using NSSO 2002 data, observed that locomotor disabilities are the most prevalent type of disabilities affecting of all ages in India. Mental disabilities are the highest in the working age population, whereas visual and hearing disabilities are the highest in the aged. Further, onset of locomotor and speech disabilities mainly occur at early ages, whereas onset of visual and hearing disabilities are highly concentrated at later ages. Onset of mental disabilities peaks at early ages and younger working age population. Severe disability is broadly concentrated at later ages (Patel *et al.,* 2009).

Disabled women are seen imperfect, incomplete, inferior, asexual, and non-productive and denial recognition as women and human beings. In a discussion of efforts to reduce global poverty, Yeo and Moore (2003) noted the marginalisation of people with disabilities. Meekosha (2002) revealed that there are three realms of social being - individual, society, and the state - interact in the making of the identities of disability. Morris (1991), a disabled feminist and activist, provides a feminist analysis to the study of the experiences of women with disabilities. Basing her arguments on the feminist principle that the personal is political, Morris eloquently challenges such issues as prejudice, abortion, and the notion that people with disabilities lead lives that are not worth living. Pride against Prejudice is a commentary on political activism and rights, and stresses the need to fight back against the prejudice, stereotypes, and oppression of an abelist culture. Women with disabilities in India face double discrimination due to prevalence of traditional gender roles and expectations, argue Thomas and Thomas (2002). Among older adults, there is empirical evidence that women are more likely to hide physical impairments if their spouse is still alive (older married women are less likely to report disabilities), and because of cultural differences, older women in northern India appear to be more disadvantaged as compared to their counterparts in the south (Sengupta and Agree, 2002). Furthermore, there is evidence that rural women with disabilities are most likely to be disregarded by survey enumerators (Jeffrey and Singhal, 2008).

There are differences of issues in the women disabilities in view with education, economic status, categorisation, culture and government policies of every state and country. Rao (1992) has developed manual improving communication skills in 300 mentally retarded children in terms of language disorder and articulation disorders, voice disorder, fluency disorder. Similarly, the World Bank reported in 2007 that in India, disability is associated with lower socio-economic status.

Social exclusion

Women with disabilities, especially from rural areas, are rarely part of family interactions and community activities. Most of the time they are subjected to social stigma and stereotyping within their own community, which leads them to feel devalue, lonely, and humiliated.

Even in case of employment opportunities for women with disabilities, they are the most excluded ones. While numerous projects exist which provide skills training for disabled women, but they are not good enough to meet the ultimate goal of providing a means of adequate income. Abuses within the family are quite common in Indian society. Women with disabilities are the easy prey for the exploitation within the family. People do not discuss these issues in public. Parents of mentally retarded daughters feel absolutely stranded, ignored and excluded from the social network. There is stress of who is going to care for their child who is disabled after parent's demise, no marriages or schooling for mentally challenged girls is available.

Abandoning girls with disability is another issue that needs strengthening. The measures required are to prevent abandoning by creating awareness and to improve their condition within the homes for them, which are often the epicenters of exploitation, humiliation and embarrassment. Adoption of children with disabilities is another issue, without which these children stay homeless.

Apart from economic independence, work is an essential means of enabling a person to develop a sense of identity and self-esteem. Thus, gainful employment is an important means of promoting the social integration of disabled women. From the perspective of the State, investing in the education and training of women with disabilities, and promoting opportunities for their employment, is sound economic and social policy. Gainfully employed women with disabilities contribute actively to the economy (Hidden Sisters, 1995).

Case Studies

1. A 'dumb and deaf' woman of 35 to 40 years of age, wife of a poor 'Rikshawala is the victim of rape by three persons at 10 P.M. in the Ram Nivas Bagh of Jaipur. The accused claims to be a student and young boy of 19 years of age. On the night of 9th May, 1981, Laxmi, a 'deaf and dumb' woman, wife of Arjun was coming back to her house after attending a marriage at Brahampuri at about 11.00 p.m. in the night. Ram Dhan Meena and one Sardar and one more person forcibly compelled her to get down from the Rickshaw and after taking her in some dark place, all the three accused forcibly committed sexual intercourse with her. The prosecutrix narrated the story to the husband in the night at about 1.00, and both of them went to the police station and produced the clothes having semen before the police and lodged the report. Laxmi was examined as she was deaf and dumb; she narrated the story with signs.

2. A teenaged deaf and dumb patient whose family complained that their daughter had been raped at the Bankura Sammilani Medical College Hospital by the hospital staff. The 18-year-old was admitted to the hospital on Monday on complaints of chest pain. Relatives of the girl said that the accused approached her on the pretext of a medical check-up. The mother of the 18-year old girl has complained to the hospital authorities that her daughter has been raped by a junior doctor.

3. Feb 2, 2014, in North Kolkata's Cossipore, a 16-year-old physically challenged girl who was allegedly lured, then abducted and locked in a house before being raped. The survivor was tied up in a bed and was in a half naked condition at the time of rescue. The accused Sk Ashfar Ali, a 26-year-old auto driver, was arrested. The accused knew the victim earlier and had lured her to follow him. However, he has denied the offence of rape and admitted that he had molested her.

4. August 15, 2013, in Mukund Vihar, Bhalswa Dairy area of northwest Delhi a 12-year old mentally challenged girl was allegedly raped by her neighbour aged 43 years, who has physical disabilities. When the victim was playing, the accused enticed her to follow him to the shop's godown. He then downed the shutter and raped the girl.

5. January 12, 2013, a physically handicapped married woman was allegedly raped at Padma, Hazaribagh, Jharkhand. The accused,

Ajit Kumar raped the woman near Padma power station in the evening hour when the victim was returning home after depositing her pension cheque in a bank.

6. One Jashiben, wife of Umedbhai Dahyabhai Solanki, lodged an FIR with Madhavpura Police Station, alleging that her niece Bhavna (not real name) was raped by Maheshbhai Ramjibhai Parmar in the midnight hours of 26-27th June, 2002. In the FIR the informant states that she was informed by the prosecutrix around 4.00 p.m., of 27.6.2002 about the incident saying that at about 12.00 p.m. in the midnight, the accused went to the cot, where the prosecutrix was sleeping, and gagged her mouth and raped her.

7. 15th November 2013, in Nagpur, a 40-year-old mentally unstable and physically challenged woman was allegedly raped in Dammanand Nagar locality in the city. The accused, identified as 35-year-old Ramsingh Gopisingh Mehto had been arrested under relevant sections of the IPC.

8. November 21, 2013, a five-year-old physically challenged girl was reported as a rape victim. She was raped by a 24-year-old in Beldara Seoni village in Raipur, Chhattisgarh, a village which is about 40 km away from the state capital. The accused, identified as Sanjay Verma, was arrested immediately after the incident. The girl, whose mother died during childbirth, was living with her grandparents. When her grandparents were away for work, the accused entered the house and sexually assaulted her. It was because of her shrieks that the neighbours' came to her rescue.

9. Jan 1, 2013, (Noida) : A case was registered in Dadri police station where the prosecutrix in her complaint has alleged that on December 29, 2012 when her mother had gone to Aligarh and she was alone at home, her father gave her some sedatives and she fell unconscious. Later, she was allegedly raped by her father. When her mother reached home, the minor girl narrated the incident to her mother.

10. October 31, 2013, a 16-year-old physically challenged girl was gangraped at Baduria in Bengal's North 24 Parganas district. The incident happened late when the victim was abducted by a group of men from a wedding she had gone to attend. They took her to a desolate spot and raped her.

11. A disabled woman was gang-raped allegedly by two persons after holding her husband captive. The incident took place when the woman had gone to a Dussehra fair in Sahabganj area following which she was gang-raped by two persons, who held her husband captive. The accused are friends of the victim's husband.

12. A man and his parents have been booked for allegedly raping a 28-year-old mentally challenged woman and confining her parents and brother. The brother of the rape victim, who was under depression, was also missing.

13. February 7, 2015, unidentified men raped and brutalised a 28-year-old mentally-challenged woman before killing her at Bahu Akbarpur in Haryana's Rohtak district. The woman's body was found without key organs on Wednesday along with sticks, stones and condoms stuffed into her private parts three days after she went missing.

14. A man was arrested on Friday for raping a 9-year-old mentally challenged girl in Chembur in Mumbai. The girl was raped in Rashtriya Chemical Fertilizers slum colony in suburban Chembur. The accused stays in the same neighbourhood as the girl and was arrested after the girl's family lodged a complaint.

Analysis

The above given case studies shows that how vulnerable are these women with disabilities. In most of the cases, the victims of the crime knew the accused person before either they are some friends, family or any other acquaintance. In some cases they were raped by their own relatives including the father. The cases also suggest that most victims were raped when they are alone and unprotected. Most of the minor and child victims were allured and enticed by the adult accused. Generally their voice are unheard or ignored. The law of state is also dumb and deaf in case of the women with disabilities. In many cases disabled women are unable to communicate the act of sexual assault they face and even if they communicate, the evidentiary value of their testamentary are not taken seriously either by the police or by the judicial system. As a result, even if the accused is convicted by the lower court, at the stage of appeal before Higher Court, the accused is acquitted. Women with disability is not only ignored at their homes, by their family members, but even State's policies play a big role in being discriminatory towards their well being, protection, security or giving them their due rights. Women with disabilities are the most marginalised people of our Indian society. They are deprived of all sorts of facilities such as political, social, economic, and health opportunities. The problems of women with disabilities become very complex with other factors such as social stigma and poverty. Women with disabilities have been largely neglected when it comes to research, state policies, the disability and women's movements, and rehabilitation programmes for the welfare of this population with disabilities.

Conclusion

Sexual violence against disabled women is a silent act in our country because in majority cases women are unsuccessful to comprehend that they are victims or are unable to narrate the act of violence. Even if it is communicated, the patriarchal society does not believe to their pleas. In majority of cases the perpetrators are hardly prosecuted. There is also fear that reporting the abuse could snaps bonds with the caretakers. Lack of information and awareness is found by the fact that peer group learning is very limited amongst disabled women as they are less likely to be sent to school. The social role or the absence of a role attributed to women with disabilities, in conjunction with the stereotypes that exist, contribute to their vulnerability and lead to violation of their rights. Hence, by way of legislating laws, state should not merely declare rights and entitlements but it should stipulate in detail the mechanisms by which rights can be protected. Women with disabilities must be afforded the same rights and opportunities as all other persons, irrespective of disability status and sex, with regard to employment. This is especially critical because employment impacts individuals on so many levels, both internally and externally. Women with disabilities have the potential to achieve high goals if given the opportunity. No longer should society ignore their presence and capabilities. Women with disabilities demand to be seen, recognised and valued for their abilities, and are increasingly demanding full participation and equality in the workplace.

References

Abramson, W. H., Emanuel, E. J., and Hayden, M. (Eds.). (2000 Fall). Feature issue on violence and women with developmental and other disabilities. IMPACT, 13(3). Minneapolis: Institute on Community Integration, University of Minnesota. Retrieved February 22, 2005.

Alexander, R. W., Bradley, L. A., Alarcon, G. S., Tirana-Alexander, M., Aaron, L. A., Alberts, K. R., Martin, M. Y., and Stewart, K. E. (1998). Sexual and physical abuse in women with fibromyalgia: Association with outpatient health utilisation and pain medication usage, Arthritis Care and Research, 11(2), pp. 102-115.

Altman, B M (2001): 'Disability Definitions, Models, Classification Schemes and Applications' in G L Albrecht, K D Seelman, M Bury (eds), Handbook of Disability Studies, Sage Publications.

Hidden Sisters, 1995c: Women and Girls with Disabilities in the Asian and Pacific Region (ST/ESCAP/1548), United Nations.

http://articles.timesofindia.indiatimes.com/2013-08-15/delhi/41412689_1_disabled-girl northwestdelhi-neighbour

http://timesofindia.indiatimes.com/city/gurgaon/Woman-raped-brutalised-and-murdered-in Rohtak/articleshow/46151730.cms

http://timesofindia.indiatimes.com/city/kolkata/Impaired-girl-raped-by-auto driver/articleshow/

http://www.abplive.in/crime/2014/10/07/article415524.ece/Disabled-woman-gang-raped-in-UP

http://www.deccanherald.com/content/302286/physically-challenged-girl-raped-father.html

http://www.firstpost.com/india/physicallydisabled - teenager-raped inkolkata229315.html.utm_source=ref article

http://www.hindustantimes.com/chandigarh/mentally-disabled-woman-raped-in-confinement/article1-1328002.aspx

http://www.ndtv.com/mumbai-news/man-arrested-for-raping-mentally-challenged-9-yr-old-girl-461085

http://www.thehindu.com/todays-paper/tpnational/physically challenged-girl gangraped/article5298723.ece

http://www.youthconnectmag.com/2013/11/21/5-year-old-physically-challenged-girl-raped/

http://zeenews.india.com/news/jharkhand/handicapped - woman - raped - accused -held_822543.html

http://zeenews.india.com/news/north-east/ constable - rapes - bru - woman -in - mizoram_881858.html

Jeffrey, Roger, and Nidhi Singal. 2008. "Measuring Disability in India," *Economic and Political Weekly 43* (12 and 13): pp. 22-24.

Maheshbhai v. *State,* http://www.indiankanoon.org/doc/493756/

Mays, J. M. (2006, March). Feminist disability theory: Domestic violence against women with a disability. Disability and Society, 21(2), pp. 147-158.

Meekosha, H., 2002. Virtual activists? Women and the making of identities of disability. E. Kittay, S. Silvers, and S. Wendell special issue: Feminism and disability ii. Hypatia, 17(3): pp. 67-88.

Mont, D. Measuring Disability Prevalence. Disability and Development Team. The World Bank Human Development Network Social Protection. 2007. Available at http://worldbank.org/DISABILITY/Resources/Data/20070606DMont.ppt

Morris, J. (1991). Pride against prejudice: Transforming attitudes to disability. Philadelphia: New Society Publishers.

Ramdhan Meena v. State of Rajasthan, 1981 WLN 520.

Rao, T.A.S., (1992), Manual of Developing Communication Skills in Mentally Retarded Persons, NIMH, Secundarabad.

Sengupta, Manisha, and Emily Agree. 2002. "Gender and Disability Among Older Adults in North and South India: Differences Associated with Coresidence and Marriage," *Journals of Cross-Cultural Gerontology* 17: pp. 313-336.

Srivastava, DK, Khan JA. Disability Needs Attention Now! *Indian Journal for the Practicing Doctor,* 2008; 5: pp. 3-4.

Thomas, Maya and M.J. Thomas. 2002. 'Status of Women with Disabilities in South Asia' Asia Pacific Disability - Rehabilitation Journal, Series 2, January 2002 downloaded from www.aifo.it/languages/english/apdrj/...

World Health Organisation. Disability and rehabilitation: WHO action plan 2006-2011. Geneva: World Health Organisation. Available at http://www.who.int/entity/disabilities/publications/dar_action_plan_2006to2011.pdf

World Health Organisation. Document A29/INFDOCI/1, Geneva, World Health Organisation, 1976.

World Health Organisation. Global Burden of Disease Report. Geneva: World Health Organisation, 2004. Available at http://www.who.int/healthinfo/global_burden_disease/GBD_report_2004update_part3.pdf.

World Health Organisation. International Classification Functioning, Disability and Health (ICF). Geneva: World Health Organisation, 2002.

8

Sex Preference and the Value of Sons and Daughters in India

—***Manjinder Kaur***

Abstract

In India, right from nineteenth Century onwards it has been repeatedly brought to light by social reformers, social researchers, national leaders, women's organisations and by International Agencies like the United Nations that for any Nation's or rather entire Globe's real progress and development it is absolutely imperative to improve women's situation and development. But what had not been adequately realised was that women's development acts and interacts with the development of the girl-child and that both are interrelated and interdependent. The present papers tries to focus on the issues related to such problems.

Keywords: *girl child, exploitation, mother, abuse, status.*

Introduction

The status of girl child is the key to achieving gender equality and the dignity of women in the future. The mould of the adult women is set in childhood. Girl children are a valuable asset of a nation; they are unit of reproduction and family and their welfare strengthens social and economic development. In most countries today, the girl child has a lower status and enjoys fewer of the rights, opportunities and benefits of childhood than the boy child who has first call on family and community resources. The situation of the girl child results commonly from prejudices rooted in culture and customs. Unfortunately, for the girl child, she is viewed in many cultures as a transient presence to be nurtured temporarily until she marries (UNICEF, 1991).

In India identification of a girl child as a special group and the need for devising specific group and the need for devising specific strategies to deal with its problem are relatively recent efforts. The very first problem faced in describing the situation of the girl child is the lack of gender-specific information about her. The data base is too inadequate that can offer socio-cultural and demographic insight about girl child.

Female-male ratio of the human population is one of the basic demographic characteristics, which is extremely vital for any meaningful demographic and gender-based analyses. The status of women and particularly the girl child is immediately judged by examining the sex ratio of a population. Indian Census has the tradition of bringing out disaggregated information by sex on various aspects of population. The first and foremost is the simple count of males and females. Changes in sex composition largely reflect the underlying socio-economic and cultural patterns of a society in different ways. Sex ratio defined here as the number of females per 1,000 males in the population, is an important social indicator to measure the extent of prevailing equity between males and females in a society at a given point of time. It is mainly the outcome of the interplay the sex differentials in mortality, sex selective migration, sex ratio at birth and at times the sex differential in population.

Table 7.1: Sex Ratio of Selected Countries

Sr. No.	*Country*	*Sex Ratio*	*Females Per 1000 males*
1	*2*	*3*	*4*
	World	986	984
1.	China	944	926
2.	India	933	940
3.	USA	10,29	1025
4.	Indonesia	1,004	988
5.	Brazil	1025	1042
6.	Pakistan	938	943
7.	Russian Fed	1140	1167
8.	Bangladesh	958	978
9.	Japan	1041	1055
10.	Nigeria	1016	987

Source: Census of India 2011, Provisional Population Totals, Paper-1 of 2011.

The composition of population by gender is not uniform and shows diverse patterns across different countries of the world. It has been estimated that around the year 2016, the world will have 984 females against 1000 males. As it is evident from Table 7.1, in USA, Russian Federation, Japan and Brazil females outnumber males, in the other six countries the balance is tilted towards the males. China, Indonesia, Nigeria and USA have shown a decline in the sex ratio in the present decade. The decline has been particularly sharp in Nigeria and Indonesia. The sex ratio in USA, Russian federation and Japan has always remained above unity despite minor variations.

According to the Census of India 2011, the sex ratio is 940 for the country as a whole. This is a welcome improvement from the 2001 census, which has recorded 933 females for every 1000 males. Table 7.2 presents the trend in sex ratio in India since 1901. The sex ratio in India had always remained unfavourable to females. Moreover, barring some hiccups, it has shown a long term declining trend. The sex ratio at the beginning of the twentieth century was 972, and thereafter showed continuous decline until 1941. In 1951, there was a marginal increase of one point, but thereafter it again dropped for two consecutive decades to reach 930 in 1971. In fact, between 1961-71, the country saw the sharpest decline of 11 points in the sex ratio. Thereafter, it has fluctuated marginally around 930 in successive censuses.

Table 7.2: Sex Ratio, India: 1901-2011 and Child Sex Ratio (0-6 years): 1961-2011

Census year	*Sex Ratio (Females per, 1000 Males)*	*Sex Ratio in age group (0-6)*
1901	972	-
1911	964	-
1921	955	-
1931	950	-
1941	945	-
1951	946	-
1961	941	976
1971	930	964
1981	934	962
1991	927	945
2001	933	927
2011	940	914

Source: Census of India 2011, Provisional Population Totals, Paper-1 of 2011.

It is clear that sex ratio in the age group 0-6 has declined at a much faster pace than the overall sex ratio of the country after 1981. The decreasing sex ratio in this child population perhaps has a cascading effect on population over a period of time leading to diminishing sex ratio in the country. One thing is clear that the imbalance in sex at this early age group is difficult to be removed and would remain to haunt the population for a long time to come. To say the least, demographically sex ratio of 914 of the population in the age group 0-6 does not appear to augur well for the future of the country.

The overall sex ratio of India is dependent on the sex ratio obtained in different states and union territories and their relative weight in terms of size of population. The sex ratio of the total population, sex ratio in the age group 0-6 and sex ratio of population aged seven and above for 2001 and 2011 for all the states and union territories. The diversity in sex ratio among the states and union territories is phenomenal. At the Census of India, 2011 the sex ratio among the major states ranged from 877 in Haryana to 1084 in Kerala. In 2001 also, Haryana among the northwest states of India with a sex ratio of 861 was at the bottom while Kerala in southern part of India was with 1058 females per 1000 males at the top. The changes in sex ratio of over time, therefore, are dependent on the changes in the ratio of the individual states and union territories and their relative share in population.

The child sex ratio (number of female children per 1000 male children in the age group of 0-6 years attempts to bring out the recent changes in our society in its attitudes and outlook towards the girl child. It is a broad indicator, which reveals the ground realities that exist in fabric of society. Moreover, the child sex ratio is a powerful index to examine the social response on female children. Present sex composition of child population determines the future vital events such as marriage rate, labour force, age structure, birth and deaths, migration, and replacement etc. Therefore, deficit in girl child population, leads to serious demographic imbalance and adverse social consequences. However, in recent decades, the drastic decline in child sex ratio is an issue of grave concern in India. Therefore, efforts are needed to solve the issue thereby create equal regard and affection for the girl child. Otherwise, the child population will become skewed leading to a host of several societal problems.

The decline in child sex ratio that came as a shock in the latest census figures shows 914 girls, and this is the lowest ever since Independence, slipping from 927 in 2001. The increasing trend has been seen in Punjab, Haryana, Himachal Pradesh, Gujarat, and Tamil Nadu, Mizoram, and the Andaman and Nicobar Islands, while in all, the remaining 27 states and Union Territories, the rate has shown a decline. It was the highest in Mizoram at 971, closely followed by Meghalaya (970), while at the rock bottom was Haryana with 800 and Punjab with 846. At the district level, Lahul and Spiti in Himachal Pradesh had the highest child sex ratio at 1,013, while in Twang district of Arunachal Pradesh, it was 1,005. It was shamefully low in Jhajjar and Mahendragarh of Haryana at 774 and 778 respectively.

The low sex ratio is generally viewed as an indication of existence of discrimination against female children, general neglect of girls, reflecting low status of women in the society. Understanding the trends, patterns and differentials for low child sex ratios is important as it helps to identify the areas, regions and social groups experiencing the decline and to take appropriate measures to improve the child sex ratio. However, identifying the factors for the low child sex ratio is a complex phenomenon than it appears. There are social, economic, biological and behavioural factors that skew the sex ratios and these factors sometimes affect the ratio directly and sometimes indirectly.

Family Size and Sex Preference

Age at marriage is known to influence the level of fertility. A few studies have found that age at marriage is directly related to the fertility-rate and average expected family size. It has been observed that high level of fertility is associated with early marriage and low fertility is associated with higher age at marriage (Skirbekk, 2008; Nayar, 2004). According to Bhadra (2000), the higher age at marriage shortens the reproductive span of women and also changes the fertility pattern towards fewer children.

In societies, where social and cultural values are in favour of a particular sex, sex of the child plays an important role in determining the size of the family. It has been observed that couples generally stop reproducing after the birth of a child of a desired sex or they keep on reproducing until they beget the child of the desired sex. Researchers like Arnold (1997) and Nayar (2006), have reported variation in the degree of son preference in India from one part of the country to another, like it is very strong in north and central India and somewhat weaker in the southern and western region of the country. Pande and Astone (2007) have documented that such a combination of high son preference with low or declining fertility can result in an increase of practices of female foeticide, infanticide, sex selective abortions, abandonment of daughters and skewed sex ratio.

Evils of technology and regressive social thought have had a disastrous impact in India in terms of a progressive imbalance in the sex ratio. Apparent preference for a son and neglect of the girl child has had a long history in our patriarchal society. The ratio of 972 females per 1,000 males (1991 census) had become 933 females per 1,000 males as per 2001 census. This has become marginally better (940 females per 1,000 males) as per the 2011 census. But the child sex ratio has dipped from 945 in 1991 to 927 in 2001 to 914 in 2011. Continued preference for the male child and relatively much lower status of the girl child is a reflection of this. Sociologists, economists and demographers have identified various practices such as female foeticide, female infanticide, and deliberate neglect of health and nutrition of the girl child, etc. that have contributed to the masculinisation of the sex ratio (Agnihotri, 1995).

Improvements in literacy, fertility rate and greater workforce participation of women have not significantly improved the lot of the girl child. 2001 census and 2011 census have revealed this discrepancy to be an almost pan-Indian phenomenon except for some of the southern and north-eastern states of the country. Places which are not so pronounced in patriarchal ideology and discrimination against girls and have never recorded any practice of female infanticide too are painting the same bleak picture of decreasing number of females in their population.

Kaur (2007) examines the socio-economic reasons for the steep decline in child sex ratios between 1991 to 2001 census. She has argued that continued preference of boys over girls in north and north-west India has to be seen in the light of changing inter-relationships between education, work, marriage and family status. Issues of stable future and old-age parental support lend credence to their choice of male children rather than female children. Also enhanced marriage and dowry expenditure for girls makes parents to plan their families without daughters. Basis for arousal of strong emotional feelings of 'son preference' and sexual mores that lead parents to kill unborn daughters has also been discussed by Patel (2007).

Numerous fertility surveys have repeatedly shown is that couples desiring large family want their large family composed of many sons, while those desiring small family size either have no sex preference or want two sons and a daughter (Bhat and Zavier, 2001). In other words, the desired number of sons is more elastic to changes in the desired family size than the desired number of daughters. Therefore, as fertility declines son preference falls rather than increases or remain unchanged.

Value of Children

In a patriarchal, male-dominated society like ours, the preference for a male child is inherent in the Indian psyche as he perpetuates the family name and line. Besides the mistaken notion that he brings salvation to the parents in the hereafter by carrying out proper rituals at their death, he is considered as a bread-winner and support in the old age. A girl on the other hand, usually leaves the family at marriage for her husband's home. In a sense she is considered merely a transitory member of a family and only indirectly participates in building its strength and prestige. Moreover, she is looked upon as a burden as she has to be married off possibly with a huge dowry. She is considered a liability and an economic drain on the resources of the family.

Although a daughter provides help in housework before marriage, she is considered to be an economic liability to her parents mainly because of the heavy dowry payment demanded by the grooms family (Kishor, 1995), as well as the high cost of the wedding, which is generally the responsibility of the bride's family to bear. Socially, the utility of having daughters is small compared with their cost. Although daughters are often considered to provide more emotional satisfaction to parents than are sons (Dharmalingam, 1996; and IIPS, 1994), they typically become a member of their husband's family after marriage and may have little continuing contact with their natal family. Parents also bear a large burden in arranging a suitable marriage for their daughters and protecting their chastity before marriage. At the wedding ceremony, in many cases the father of the bride has to assume a humiliatingly low posture in the presence of the groom and his family. According to Hindu tradition, however, there is one important reason for having a daughter: her parents can earn religious merit by selflessly giving her away in marriage (*kanyadaan).* Some parents also cite the need to have a daughter to cry at the time of their death (Dharmalingam, 1996).

In Indian society sons are given much more importance than daughters. Sons are considered to be assets for their parents whereas daughters are a burden (Mahadevan, 1979; 1989). In one of his studies, Mahadevan (1989) identified eleven reasons for valuing sons. They are:

- Economic support during old age;
- Better economic benefits of the family;
- Receiving dowry;
- Salvation of parents;
- Continuity of family tradition/lineage;
- Other family obligations;
- To inherit family property;
- Becoming on adult member and getting status;
- Company for parents and children;
- Physical force for power; and
- For physical protection of old parents;

Mortality

India's unfavourable sex ratio is primarily due to the higher female mortality rate as compared to that of males right up to the age of 35 (Women and Men, 1995). "It is noteworthy that every year about 15 million girls are born and despite being biologically stronger than boys, almost one quarter of them do not live to see their 15th birthday" (India Country Report, 1995). The greatest difference between male and female mortality rates is in the 0-4 age group. The mortality of the girls in this age group is about 15 times greater than that of any other five year age group.

Earlier when the technology was not available to know the sex of the foetus, the girl child used to be killed by putting a sand bag on her face or strangulating her or some poison used to be applied on the breasts of the mother. The irony was that neither mothers nor their family members used to express any kind of sorrow on the deaths of their baby daughters. Now the scenario has changed. With the help of new technologies one can easily detect the sex of the foetus. So the practice of female infanticide has been replaced by female foeticide.

Prior to 1971, abortion was illegal in India. As early as 1964, however, the Central Family Planning Board recommended legalisation of abortion. This was done in 1971, when the Medical Termination of Pregnancy (MTP) Act was enacted as a health measure to protect women. The MTP Act was revised in 1975.

The Medical Termination of Pregnancy Act requires that abortions take place in government — approved facilities. Largely because these facilities are in short supply, this requirement is not enforced. Moreover, the availability of approved MTP facilities varies considerably from state to state, with facilities concentrated in a few states that are more advanced on most indices of development. In the early 1990s, for example, Maharashtra had 23 per cent of total approved MTP facilities in the country but only nine per cent of the country's population, and Gujarat had ten per cent of MTP facilities but only five per cent of population. In contrast, Uttar Pradesh had only six per cent of MTP facilities but 17 per cent of population, and Bihar had only two per cent of MTP facilities but ten per cent of population. In the country as a whole, about five to six million abortions occur annually, and roughly 90 per cent of them take place in unapproved facilities (Khan, Barge, and Philip, 1996; Genatra, 2000; Arnold, Kishor, and Roy, 2002).

Female foeticide reinforces a girl's current subordinate position. "To pick a male is to declare that males are more valuable and female less so, which in turn perpetuates the preference" (Bennett, 1983).

The National Family Health Survey-3 data on under nutrition in children below five years had already flagged that 43 per cent of girls are under-nourished. Child marriage is a violation of child rights. According to NFHS-3 it was estimated that around 47 per cent of married women in the age group of 20-24 years were married before attaining the age of 18 years. In particular, child marriage has serious health repercussion on girls, such as frequent pregnancies, miscarriages and early motherhood.

Another important issue that has been broadly overlooked in the literature is the regional variation in socio-economic inequalities in India's infant and child mortality; India is a diverse country and the national averages are not representative of the different geographic regions. A recent study by Pathak and Singh (2011) reveals regional patterns in socio-economic inequalities in child malnutrition in India, so it is very important to examine the regional patterns in socio-economic inequalities in infant and child mortality. Such analysis may provide evidence to the Ministry of Health and Family Welfare (MoHFW), Ministry of Women and Child Development (MoWCD), Government of India and various state governments for formulating region-specific programmes and policies.

To ensure a male child, it was observed that people in all sizes visit holy sites such as 'deras' and 'maths', and seek the blessings of gurus/babas for a male child. There are many cases of couples across caste and class lines using 'herbal potions' to confirm a male child right at the time of first conception and later on abort the female foetus. It has been reported that in a large number of women who had taken such portions, the pregnancy culminated in miscarriages or stillbirth or in some cases children were born with defects. The desire for a son is so intense that despite congenital defects, nothing stops people from using these potions to have a male child (John *et al.,* 2008). Even if couples have availed of herbal potions/blessing of holy men, surety is guaranteed only by the 'machine'. Modern technology is an acceptable method to engineer size and composition. Abortion is also accepted as a mode of limiting family size, enabling spacing and regulating the sex composition of the family.

Conclusion

The low sex ratio is generally viewed as an indication of existence of discrimination against female children, general neglect of girls, reflecting low status of women in the society. Improvements in literacy, fertility rate and greater workforce participation of women have not significantly improved the lot of the girl child. Whatever may be the cause, the effect remains the same. The government always talks about equality between both the sexes in terms of health, nutrition, employment, education etc. but the study will attempt to study whether still patriarchal values are so culturally deep rooted in the minds of the people that they always give preference to male child and female child is still unwanted and has to be eliminated through abortions. The study will be sociologically significant to show attitudinal changes if any in the mindsets of the people. The study will analysc the existing social welfare schemes for the girl child and will like to suggest some policy changes, new schemes, etc. which can be formulated for upliftment in the status of girl child.

References

1. Agnihotri, Satish Balram, 1995. 'Missing Females: A Disaggregated Analysis', *Economic and Political Weekly*, 30(9 1): 2074-84.
2. Arnold, F., Rodolfo A. Bulatao; Chalio Buripakdi; Betty Jamie Chung; James T. Fawcett; Toshio Iritani; Sung JinLee; and Tsong-Shien Wu 1975. 'The Value of Children: A Cross National Study', Vol. 1, *Introduction and Comparative Analysis*. Honolulu: East-West Centre.
3. Arnold, F., Sunita Kishor, and T.K. Roy 2002. 'Sex-selective abortion in India', *Population and Development Review*, 28(4).
4. Arnold, Fred 1997. Gender preferences for children: Findings from the Demographic and Health Surveys, Paper prepared for the 23rd General Population Conference of the International Union for the Scientific Study of Population (IUSSP), 1997, Beijing, 11-17 October.
5. Bhatt, P.N. Mari and A.J. Francis Zavier, 2001. 'Fertility Decline and Gender Bias in Northern India', cited in P.N. Mari Bhat (2003) "On the Trial of 'Missing' Indian females"-II, *Economic and Political Weekly*, 37(52).
6. Bennett, N.G. (Ed.) 1983, *Sex Selection of Children*. New York: Academic Press.
7. Census of India 2011. Provisional Population Totals, India, Paper-1 of 2011. Delhi: Registrar General and Census Commissioner, India.

8. Committee on the Status of Women in India 1975. 'Towards Equality: Report of the Committee of the Status of Women in India,' cited in P.N. Mari Bhatt (2003) On the Trial of Missing Indian Females-II, *Economic and Political Weekly*, 37(52).
9. Dharmalingam, Arunachalam, 1996 'The social context of family size preferences and fertility behaviour in a South Indian village, cited in Rangamuthia Mutharayappa, Minja Kim Choe, Fred Arnold, and T.K. Roy (1997) 'Son Preference and Its Effect on Fertility in India', *National Family Health Survey Subject Reports*, No.3. Mumbai: International Institute for Population Sciences.
10. Genatra, Bela. 2000. 'Abortion research in India: What we know and what we need to know' cited in Radhika Ramasubbhan and Shireen J. Jeejeebhoy (eds.), *Women's reproductive health in India*. New Delhi: Rawat Publications.
11. India Country Report for the Fourth World Conference on Women 1995. cited in Vinaya Prabha V. Baligar (1999) *Mother and Girl Child*. Jaipur: Rawat Publications.
12. International Institute for Population Sciences (IIPS) 1995. *National Family Health Survey* (MCH and Family Planning), India 1992-93. Mumbai: TIPS. John, Mary E., Kaur, Ravinder, Palriwala, Rajni, Raju, Saraswati, and Sagar, Alpana (2008) *Planning families planning gender*. New Delhi: Action Aid/ IDRC.
13. John, Mary E., Kaur, Ravinder, Palriwala, Rajni, Raju, Saraswati, and Sagar, Alpana 2008. *Planning families planning gender*. New Delhi: Action Aid/ IDRC.
14. Kishor, Sunita 1995. 'Gender differentials in child mortality: A review of the evidence,' cited in Monica Das Gupta, Lincoln C. Chen, and T.N. Krishnan (eds.) *Women's health in India: Risk and vulnerability*, pp. 19-54, Bombay: Oxford University Press.
15. Khan, M.E., Sandhya Barge, and George Philip. 1996. 'Abortion in India: An Overview', *Social Change*, 26: 208-225.
16. Mahadevan, K. 1979. *Sociology of Fertility: Determinants of Fertility in South India*. New Delhi: Sterling Publishers Pvt. Ltd.
17. ______________ 1989 *Population Dynamics on Indian States: Fertility and Family Formation Variables*. Delhi: Mittal Publishers.
18. Nayar, Usha. 2006. *The unborn daughters of Delhi*. Delhi: The Women Press.
19. Pathak, P. K., and Singh, A. 2011. Trends in malnutrition among children in India: Growing inequalities across different economic groups. *Social Science and Medicine, 73*, 576–585.

20. Patel, Tulsi 2007. (eds.) *Sex-selective abortion in India: Gender, Society and new reproductive technologies*. New Delhi: SAGE.
21. UNICEF 1991. *The Girl Child an Investment in Future*. New York: UNICEF.
22. Women and Men in India 1995. Central Statistical Organisation, Department of Statistics, cited in Vinaya Prabha V. Baligar (1999) *Mother and Girl Child*. Jaipur: Rawat Publications. If there are images in this attachment, they will not be displayed. Download the original attachment.

9

Violation of Human Rights in Unorganised Sector: A Study of Excluded Group of Migrant Labour in Punjab

—*Dr Sucheta Singh*

Introduction

"Human Migration" denotes any movement by humans from one locality to another (migration), often over long distances or in large groups. Humans are known to have migrated extensively throughout history and prehistory. It has now become an essential characteristic feature of modern society as it consists of a variety of movements that can be described in aggregate as evolutionary and development fostering process operation in time and space to correct rural, urban, inter-urban and inter-regional imbalance. Migration is not just a process of people moving from one place to another but it also has certain impact on both the place of origin and destination (Chandna, 1986).

A person chooses to migrate, because of lack of opportunities at home, when he is able to earn sufficiently. According to early development economic migration has been considered as an effect of a distortion in development policy, which needs to be corrected. In modern times, movement of populations has become an essential component of economic development and has acquired special significance for agriculture and industrialisation (Chand, 2002).

An estimated 232 million people currently live outside their country of origin, many having moved for a variety of reasons in which the search for protection and the search for opportunity are inextricably entwined. Migration affects every region of the world, and many countries are now simultaneously countries of origin, destination and transit. Large numbers of migrants today move between developing countries, and around 40 per cent of the total global migrant population have moved to a neighbouring country within their region of origin (UNHR, 2014).

Migrants are often to be found working in jobs that are dirty, dangerous and degrading (the 3 Ds). While for some migration is a positive and empowering experience, far too many migrants have to endure human rights violations, discrimination, and exploitation.

Contributions of Migrants

Yet, migrants contribute to economic growth and human development in both home and host countries and enrich societies through cultural diversity, fostering understanding and respect among peoples, cultures and societies. Migration is also an important means for migrants and their families to improve life conditions and realise their human rights.

The United Nation convention on migrant workers 'Right is the most comprehensive international treaty in the field of migration and human rights. Adopted in 1990 and entered into force in 2003, it sets a standard in terms of access to human rights for migrants. However, it suffers from a marked indifference: only forty states have ratified it and no major immigration country has done so. This highlights how migrant remain forgotten in terms of access to rights. Even though their labour is essential in the world economy, the non-economic aspect of migration- and especially migrants' rights- remain a neglected dimension of globalisation (Cholewinski, 2013).

High Commissioner for Human Rights Navi Pillay has made promoting and protecting the human rights of all migrants a priority of the work of her office (OHCHR). "The protection of migrants is an urgent and growing human rights challenge. Governments have obligations to ensure that xenophobic violence, racism and related intolerance against migrants and their communities have no place in their societies."

Human rights violations against migrants, including denial of access to fundamental economic and social rights such as the right to education or the right to health, are often closely linked to discriminatory laws and practice, and to deep-seated attitudes of prejudice and xenophobia against migrants.

A Human Rights Approach to Migration

A human rights approach to migration places the migrant at the centre of migration policies and management, and pays particular attention to the situation of marginalised and disadvantaged groups of migrants. Such an approach will also ensure that migrants are included in relevant national action plans and strategies, such as plans on the provision of public housing or national strategies to combat racism and xenophobia.

Human rights mechanisms, such as the Special Rapporteur on the Human Rights of Migrants and the Committee on Migrant Workers, have been clear in stating that although countries have a sovereign right to determine conditions of entry and stay in their territories, they also have an obligation to respect, protect and fulfil the human rights of all individuals under their jurisdiction, regardless of their nationality or origin and regardless of their immigration status.

Similarly, Punjab has witnessed unprecedented changes in its economy, culture and social structure during the past half a century. The steep rise in agricultural economy, expansion of industrialisation/ urbanisation and corresponding infrastructure are some of the hallmarks on the development map of Punjab. The market has enveloped the entire life of the people into its own folds. In this process of transformation from subsistence agricultural economy to modern commercial agriculture, and its outward expansion towards secondary and tertiary sectors, migrant worker from other states of India has played a major role.

The earliest presence of migrant workers was recorded in the secondary and tertiary sectors involving primarily manual workers. Migrant workers of 1960s were first generation workers who were uprooted poor peasants/ agricultural labourers from rural hinterlands. They came bare handed and were in search of some urban niche to make their foothold on 'alien' lands. Thus, most of the work they were absorbed into was of the nature of harsh physical labour, such as, unskilled labour in manufacturing, construction, and rickshaw pulling. Since most of the early migrant workers in urban Punjab were first generation migrants, they maintained a live contact with their respective place of origin. They did not migrate with an intention of permanent settlement in Punjab. They came to seek immediate relief from hunger and unemployment within their respective place of origin. It was only in due course of time that their circulatory nature of migration ended up becoming a permanent feature as they did not find any let up in the 'push factors'. Eventually there emerged a new generation of migrants who were born and brought up in urban Punjab. The visible relief from the harsh working and living conditions, both at the place of origin and destination, acted as a major source of attraction for the potential migrants who kept on swelling the migration stream (Singh, 1980).

Some Glimpse of Ground Realities

In the Indian context, the caste system and the associated misdistribution of resources between and within castes affect migration differently between high and low castes. In an effort to cut down on the rent, five to six fellow workers are forced to live in a small room. During the course of study, it was also observed that migrants strictly followed the caste hierarchy wth upper caste Brahmins reluctant to stay in the *Vehras (a compound or building in local parlance)* populated by lower caste harijans and Ravidasias. So the notion of casteism, which they brought from their native land, was being practiced in Punjab also.

Having any kind of assets indicates the economic status of an individual. The migrants shifted to Punjab after facing various social and economical crises. Their main aim here was looking for a better livelihood. The maximum number of migrants lived in rented accommodation. The migrants who owned a house in at the place of destination revealed that they do not have any land and house at their place of origin but have build one here but their number is very less.

Contrary to the general perception, migrants here were not living in slums but in rented tenements called *Vehras*. In all the cities, which were taken for the study, migrants are living in such places built by the local people. The landlords were those who have converted their old village homes and a small part of their agricultural land, which have come within the municipal limits, into tenements housing the labourers.

In such places, there is hardly any space for washing their cloths with the result that some are forced to wash their clothes outside the tenements or in their rooms. It was also observed during the study that the migrants followed the caste hierarchy and that the upper castes were reluctant to stay in the *Vehras* populated by the lower castes.

Issues Pertaining to Human Right Violation

The tenements in which the migrants resided were very congested. On an average in each *Vehras* there were hardly two to three stinking toilets that are used by 100-150 persons. There is hardly any space for washing clothes with the result that some are forced to wash their clothes outside the rooms or in their rooms. It is very difficult for them to maintain hygiene as they do not have the enough space for other household activities.

Electricity is an important part of the urban life style. Today we are living in an era of modernisation and globalisation. But if we peep in at the life style of migrant workers who are living in the urban setting we found that they do not even have the basic facilities that are very essential for everyday survival. As we discussed earlier, the migrants here are living in dingy rooms without natural light and no ventilation. It was also found that in many places the workers do not have power connections.

Education plays a pivotal role in an individual's life. It also decides the limited avenues of employment open for a human being in his life. For migrant workers it is quite difficult to enroll their wards in schools in Punjab. Firstly, the poor economic condition of the workers does to permit them to educate their wards and secondly, their children are not comfortable with the local language.

The highest proportions of those not attending any schools were from the Scheduled Castes. Many parents whose children attended private schools said that they prefer to send their wards there because their children do not know Punjabi, though it is very expensive for them but they have no option. Those attending government schools were from the economically poor background and pay a very minimal fee.

This shows that government schools are still the only way the children of the poor families could ever hope to get an education. From the above discussion it is clear that the proportion of Scheduled Castes children going to government schools is quite large. It also a reflection on the high-end teaching shops that have failed to meet their social obligation of teaching kids from poor backgrounds.

The medium of instruction in the schools here is one of the major stumbling blocks in the education of the migrants' kids. Another is their inability to get birth certificates of their children from their native places forcing them to get their wards admitted to expensive private schools. Many parents also said that they left behind their children behind so that they could continue with their schooling, as education is quite expensive in Punjab. Owing to the long working hours and lack of nutritional diet and poor working conditions means that migrants fall prey to many chronic diseases.

Conclusion

It can be concluded that as a part of good governance government keeps on making policies or acts but no conscious action has been witnessed on ground to verify the fact that these policies have been effectively implemented or benefitted the mass or not. It can be safely said that after contributing their labour in the upliftment of the economy of Punjab. Migrants are quite far off from the benefits like social security, protection of the right to health, housing, education, water and access to sanitation. Beside this, they are kept isolated to the access to the right to identity, including birth registration.

References

Chand, K., 2002. *Migrant Labour and the Trade Union Movement in Punjab: A Case study of the Sugar Industry,* Chandigarh: Centre for Research in Rural and Industrial Development.

Chandna, R.C., 1986. *Geography of Population*, New Delhi: Kalyani Publishers.

Cholewinski, R., Paul de Guachteneire and Pecoud., A, 2013. *Migration and Human Rights: The United Nation Convention on Migrant Workers 'Rights'* Cambridge: Cambridge University Press.

Singh, M., 1991. *Labour Process in the Unorganised Industry*, Shimla: Indian Institute of Advanced Studies.

United Nation Human Right Convention a report, 2014.

10

Revisiting Delhi Gang Rape: Strategising Gender Empowerment at Linguistic Level

—*Nirat Pandey*

Abstract

Today the literature on the issues like social inclusion and exclusion is second to none in social sciences. These are the most discussed issues in academic in last two decades especially after the rise of 'Subaltern school'. This paper examines the news framing of Delhi Gang Rape by two highest selling English dailies that are Times of India and Hindustan Times. The framing theory of media studies and the method of qualitative content analysis have been employed for this research. The findings reveal various negative (misogynist and stereotypical) constructions by these papers through their lexical structure and with other linguistic nuances, while covering Delhi Gang Rape, which promote victim blaming and rape myths[1]. The paper argues that such negative coverage nurtures and reproduces patriarchal structure of society and makes existing hierarchies and marginalities more stringent.

Key Words: *Inclusion, Exclusion, hierarchy, gender stereotypes, media, Delhi Gang Rape, Content Analysis, Framing Theory*

Introduction

The media is all too powerful in twenty first century to let its capacity of mind colonisation go unchallenged. It is important to understand the underlying perceptions that guide media coverage, as these views are often internalised in society, reflect in public policy and entrenched in the legal system of society (Bonnes, 2010). It is not a trivial issue to skip that how an event or a phenomenon represented by media.

Rape is a taboo subject that is not frequently discussed. How we think about the rape is informed by different perspectives and projects of knowledge production (Dutton, 2010). It's portrayal is crucial because major part of the way the public understands sex crimes is through news account (Turkewitz, 2010). The media's coverage of rape cases influence beliefs about the nature of rape, offences and victims, in much the same way that the media's coverage of other social problems influence belief structures (Brooker, 2002).To understand how society views sexual assault, it is important to understand the media's discourse about sexual violence (Sampert, 2010). The fact that these presentations are presented to us as merely 'news' (some unbiased presentations of information) makes them even more effective at directing social thought and polity (Bissler and Conners, 2012, p. 3). There are number of studies that reveal that different depictions of rape impact mentality of masses differently (Franiuk, Seefelt, 2008 and Franiuk, 2008). The existing literature vividly revels that the structure of patriarchal power has worked against the interests of women in the way sexual crimes are reported in India and in other societies (Drache and Velegic, 2013).

Goal of the Paper

Prior to Delhi Rape case, occasionally, such as Shah Bano case or Sati Roop Kanwar tragedy had became central to mainstream media for some period and had bought women issues at the helm of discussion. But this time without any colour of caste or religion, Delhi rape case was discussed intensively by media. It is the most extensively covered rape case in recent Indian history (Drache and Velagic, 2013). Unprecedentedly, this rape provoked India to engage with the issue of gender justice. This paper is an attempt to understand the nature of Delhi Gang Rape's coverage by two English newspapers: *Times of India* and *Hindustan Times*.

Methodology

Theoretical Framework

Framing Theory

'Framing theory' is employed for the present research work. 'Framing theory' of social sciences is primarily associates with media studies. As noun, 'Frame' is the depiction of a "paradigm", if we put it in the Kuhn`s language, in which different narratives play their part. Frames are useful for comprehending shared understanding of situation (Boucher, 2008). So, one way to understand media coverage of sexual assault is through the "Framing Theory", which was first introduced by Erving Goffman in his book, *Frame Analysis: An essay on the organisation of experience* written in 1974. Framing theory is a broad theoretical approach that has been used in number of disciplines.

'Frame supplies contextual clues which provide order and meaning to problems, events and actions. Within mainstream media, frame guides the selection, presentation and evolution of information, by placing the stories into the familiar categories' (Dowler, 2006). Frame can reflect the views held in the wider society, and can originate from the outside of, and be reflected by, the media (Benjamin and Legrand, 2012). News frames suggest how readers should view events and issues. It gives us a 'preferred reading of facts' (Bishop, 2009). A frame activates certain schemes for readers, including perspectives that encourage reader to interpret an issue in a particular way. Frame not only explains us that how should we understand a particular event but also that what should be our reaction to it. As a verb 'Framing' is an attempt through which some narratives become more important than other. Framing is the form of wording choices, which includes a dimension of knowledge and dimension of emotion that give a certain interpretation of the social reality (Brown, 2001). It is the process of selecting information in order to define issues for readers. It gives range of possible explanations of heinous crimes, for example, abnormal perpetrators, an inevitable event in the dangerous city, poor security that compounded with poor choices and culturally violent masculinity (Worthington, 2011). If Rational choice theory focuses on the choices which people make, Framing theory focuses on the FRAME with-in which choices are presented, which beyond doubt impact the choices of people.

Framing literature has examined many social issues and crisis situations (Daniel, 2009). It reveals that how different media outlets because of their specific interests, ideologies and way of thinking lead them to explain some event in a particular way and sometimes same events in different ways. There is a large body of research that has focused on the way the media frame social issues, and because of depth and quantity of this area of research it is a good area to examine to see how media framing works. The present study sought to examine the framing of Delhi Gang Rape in two English newspapers.

Method

Data Collection

For this study, news items[2] from two newspapers from the period of 16th of December (When the girl was raped in Delhi) to 31st March are collected.

Newspapers are selected because they are the strong and prime source of information. Newspapers present news with authority (Turkewitz, 2010). They are one of the important sources of information through which people get exposure to various crimes. But it is also true that press is not the most important means of communication in a country like India, with its large illiterate population, yet, because of the prevailing power structure, which is dominated by those with access to education, the written word carries weight that is out of proportion to its outreach, therefore, its ability to influence the attitudes of both ordinary readers and policymakers cannot be underestimated (Joseph and Sharma, 2006). Although newspapers, films and television all focus on narrative story-telling, there are few important ways in which press acts differently as socialise than other types of media. One of them is that most mass media impart narratives that are fictional whereas newspaper reports are often seen as objective and true (Turkewitz, 2010).

The newspapers which I have selected are: *Times of India (TOI)* and *Hindustan Times (HT)*. Both of them are the mainstream English newspapers of India.[3] News Items from *TOI* and *HT* are available full text online, through the websites of each newspaper. This is really a legacy of India's colonisation experience, which made English the language of ruling class and the elite. However, the English language press continues to enjoy a position of prominence that is quite disproportionate to the size of its readership. Even after the several decades of independence English is still the language of governing class and policy-makers (Joseph and Sharma, 2006). From national politicians to influential business class, from bureaucracy to top army officials, from academicians to scientists, from players to Indian film stars, we can notice the robust hold of English language. So the contributors and the recipients of ideas of the English press are those who are at the helm of the driving force of this country. So how an event presented to the forerunner of this county is not a trivial issue to skip. Moreover, the incident which I have studied that is Delhi Rape and eventual public outburst which it attracted is more or less an urban phenomenon. The prime consideration in the selection of daily newspapers for study was their readership which is according to the latest readership survey highest. In combination, their readership consist of nearby 1.35 crore people. Moreover, it is generally believed that actual readership is much higher as newspaper is read my more individuals than who purchase them (Benjami and Legrand, 2011).

The collected data is not only confines to the incident to rape itself. It's subsequent events like protests, legislative reaction etc. is also in the ambit of this research. Rise of such events in the context of rape incident were unprecedented in Indian history.

In the present analysis, I choose not to comment either on the political and ideological or on the editorial polity of selected newspapers. The findings of this paper are comment only on the type of coverage of these two streams of media of the incident of Delhi Gang Rape.

Total number of news items is studied as follows.

Newspapers/Websites	***Number of News Items***
Times of India (TOI)	1046
Hindustan Times (HT)	556
Total	**1602**

Data Interpretation

To operationalise the above mentioned conceptual framework, the method of Content analysis is used. It is very popular in the field of communication. As its name suggest, it is the analysis of the content of communication. The method of content analysis has travelled a long journey. It's earliest application is known as its usage by church in Seventeenth century when church conducted a systematic examination content of early newspapers. Most immediate ancestors to modern content analysis, however, are the studies that sought to evaluate the content of mass media in early twentieth century.

The content analysis is a research tool focused on the actual content and the intern features of media texts. As a research technique, it can make replicable and valid inferences from the data (Kripendorff, 2004). A content analysis is a detailed and systematic examination of the contents of a particular body of material for the purpose of identifying patterns, themes or biases (Dowler, 2006). It's capacity to deal with large amount of as well as unstructured data, ability to provide empirical evidence for specific messages, its objectivity, systematic approach, requirement of no special equipment expect text are its favourable points as method. 'This (content analysis) is a social-scientific method of describing and analysing the "content" of a range of media texts, either in qualitative and quantitative terms.

Employing content analysis, this research sought to systematically and critically explore the presentation of Delhi Gang Rape in the selected English Dailies.

Data Analysis

There have been as wide range of types of textual criticism of media culture, ranging from quantitative content analysis that dissects the number of, say, episodes of violence in a text, to qualitative study that examines images of women, blacks, or other groups, or that applied various critical theories to unpack the meanings of a texts or to explicate how text function to produce meaning. For the present research I only used qualitative content analysis. Technically such content analysis is known as *Discourse analysis.* It allowed me to capture the style of the argument of a particular news story. Discourse analysis tends to focus on how particular phenomena is presented (Krippendorff, 2004). Obviously, the meaning of words, phrases, or terminology is subjective in nature, that's why qualitative analysis is used.

Qualitative Analysis

This section has deeply analysed the nuances of language and narration used by these two newspapers in the framing of Delhi Gang Rape. I find four dominant framing after my analysis as follows:

Framing of victim

Times of India

The victim is framed as highly responsible, hardworking, intelligent, brave and courageous girl. *TOI* writes 'Her family was banking on the victim of financial assistance as her two young brothers are still studying {....} Parents spent all money on her education and were hoping she would financially support the family.[4] Her father, the man of modest means, was counting on her help to educate his children.[5] She took tuition to pay for her school and college education.[6] In her exams, her score were 'excellent'.[7] She was mentor to her younger brothers, a pillar of support to her father and life of the family.[8]

Some opinion pieces also reproduce this framing. Jitender Verma writes 'The girl we must remember was only shaping up to provide for her brother`s education and had earnestly worked for a life that would have taken not only her but her family from a remote part of UP forward in life.[9] Sharanya, S. Hegdge writes 'A girl had to lose her life, a family and India a bright daughter to a heinous crime.''[10] "The bubbly girls who was the pride and joy of the family could not live to fulfill her found dreams" writes Durgesh Nandan and Vishv Mohan.[11] Her bravery was mainly frames during the reporting on her medical condition. In one report it states "Brave girl like her doesn't need anybody`s sympathy."[12] 'Despite the serious injuries and two major surgeries, she was hanging on tenaciously and even attempting to breathe on her own.[13] She has overcome many obstacles, be it poverty or in her studies and she will keep fighting.[14] Similar idea is expressed in opinion pieces. One piece says "She wasn`t a victim, but a paragon of a soldier who fought until the day her breath stops'.[15] Rupa Sen

Gupta writes “Nirbhaya’s refusal of victimhood in her darkest hours teaches what we always knew: that human dignity is inalienable and human spirit indomitable.”[16]

Hindustan Times

Like *TOI, HT* also portrays victim in a heroic, responsible and hardworking frame. One of its reports says ‘her struggle started with her family poverty and ended in the hospital fighting against brutal injuries. Born into family from Ballia, the young woman, family friends said, was hard working and desired to forge ahead in life ahead.[17] Other one narrates “She was the entertainer of the household, the perennially smiling one who had her brothers in splits with her jokes at the dinner table. It’s editorial states “She was the brilliant student who gave tuitions for younger kids when she was 14 to help her lower middle class parents to run their home.”[18] National commission for women claimed her as ‘martyr’.[19]

But *HT’s* framing goes beyond this picture of victim’s heroism. There is one another type of framing in *HT’s* reporting on victim. That is of: Victim Blaming. At various levels *HT* has used such type of narratives which leads to victim blaming. As in one report it writes:

> ‘*It was when he asked Ram Singh, the prime accused, who has questioned his friend`s morality by her decision to travel in his company and was reeking of alcohol, to mind his own business that all hell broke out in the white luxury bus.* ’[20]

This narration vividly points that if victim’s friend did not initiate any quarrel with Ram Singh then everything might have go fine. The other report says “not realising that it was not a regular bus on route, on route 23 year old and his friend boarded it.[21] Singh (prime accused) claims that they had done nothing to lure the couple on to the bus instead of offering to go to Noida and claiming that theirs was a chartered bus.[22] These narrations clearly give sense that because of the fact that victims did not choose right bus to travel, that unfortunate incident was inevitable.

Framing of Accused

Times of India

TOI frames accused as an insane and abnormal beings. In one opinion piece it states that 'the men who victimised Nirbhaya were monstrous products of this society'.[23] Alisha Sharma in other opinion piece writes "They (accused) may look like normal people but have a diabolic mindset."[24] Explaining the character of prime accused (Ram Singh) it writes, ' Ram Singh, 33, prime accused, is a volatile man, known among friends as mental'.[25] Commenting on their behaviour after rape it says 'They are remorseless human beings. They have no regrets. Most of them returned to work, 2 spent rest of night watching music channels on television.'[26] *TOI's* narration of rape incident clearly focuses on the fallen nature of accused. In a news report it says:

"When she resisted and bite his (talking about one of the accused) hand, he got very angry. Alcohol and victim's defiance, made him go berserk. He picked up the rod and hit the two (victims) everywhere."[27]

TOI frames juvenile accused, also, as an insane criminal creature. It's one of the report says 'He said to be the most brutal of six who alleged gang raped Nirbhaya.' She later died of her injuries. At the time of incident, he was 17 and half years old, a juvenile in the eyes of "law."[28] Other one says 'The boy everyone calls juvenile beat her with iron road. He inserted it into her body till it went all the way up and yanked it out, and with it, her intestine. As she shouted for him to stop, he screamed at her 'Sali mar' (Die Bitch). Yet the law calls him juvenile.'[29] Such narration clearly shows that *TOI*'s framing of accused is sensationalistic with ghastly and gory details, which are absolutely avoidable.

Other two issues through which *TOI* frames criminality of accused were of death penalty and juvenility. On the issue of Juvenility *TOI* firmly supports the amendment in Indian Penal Code so that one of the Juvenile accused of Delhi Gang rape got punishment equivalent to others accused. *TOI* argues that changing societal circumstances demands firmly to change Juvenile act accordingly. 'The sixth accused - alleged to be the most brutal a lot- has been left out of the charge sheet."[30] But problem is not only with this specific rape case. It's other report says "The NCRB figures show that various states have highest number of juvenile crimes in the country. Among all crimes rape tops the chart followed by murder."[31] It is important to amend law, so that any juvenile, convicted in any heinous crime, would not let the off hook without facing proper punishment. "It is the systemic failure by all stake holders in implementing the Juvenile Act, 2006, (amendment) has ensured that juveniles get away with heinous crimes'[32] More over "in other countries juveniles tried as adults for heinous crimes."[33] Giving logical and intellectual support to such demands Jug Sauriya writes in an opinion pieces that "A child labour- whatever her chronological age might be- is force to accept the responsibility of earning the life of livelihood for herself and her family. She cannot claim social and legal privilege of being a 'juvenile'. By same token juveniles who commit acts of criminal violence must be made to accept the responsibility for their actions and be made to pay the price for them."[34]

TOI dominantly favours death penalty for rapists. It criticises President of India on commuting the death sentence of various convicts. Himanshi Dhawan in one of the opinion pieces claims that 'There have been at least four cases in the recent past where rapists awarded death penalty manage to escape noose after President commuted their sentence to life imprisonment.'[35] Similar idea is propounded in other opinion piece by Alisha Sharma in "Give death to rapists" December 22, 2012. Other opinion piece says "Although I firmly believe that no punishment can or will let Nirbaya's soul be contented. But oh dear Lord!!!! we demand from you let the Nirbhaya`s soul incarnate, may her soul be adhered to hang man, who will hang their culprits till death.[36] On similar lines other piece writes "There has been a long debate on banning capital punishment in India, but I believe this is the only option to deal with culprits of such heinous crimes."[37]

Other tactic *TOI* adopts too justify its pro-death penalty stance is by giving too much space to violent ideas of angry protesters who support brutal punishment for rapists. Giving space to an idea of one of the protesters it writes 'I think we need to study laws of Arab countries. Laws are so stringent there that no one would dare to even tease a girl: one protester said'.[38] Other reports expresses 'one said: India should bring in the law similar to what gulf countries have.

The offenders should be given painful punishment before they are hanged to death: other claimed'[39] 'If need be, women will come out in the streets to castrate rapists, then don't tell us to be patient: one said.[40] For these people (rapists) even the death penalty seems too mild a punishment for the ghastly crime: another one claimed.[41] They should be made to suffer before they are hanged to death.[42] 'Can there be a crime more heinous than this. An innocent girl is battling for life because of the brutality of the monsters. All rape accuses should be hanged till death'.[43] "Most of the girls *TOI* spoke to were furious so much so that they were almost unanimous in their demand for Arab country like delivery system which allows shooting the offender in full public view."[44]

Hindustan Times

Like *TOI*, *HT* has also frames accused as insane devils and declared them as 'Gang of Beasts.'[45] It was 'Most unheard and worse than animal behavior' "today has been a disturbing day."[46] Explaining their habits it states 'They had very bad habits. Every evening you could find them in an inebriated state.[47] Ram Singh, prime accused, is said to be a quarrelsome, alcoholic and bully.[48] He (Ram Singh, the prime accused) was known to everyone as 'mental'.[49] 'The apparent streak of violence that seemingly characterised him elicited two strict instructions from him neighbours both for women and children staying in locality. One was not to look him in the face or react whenever he passed lewd remarks and other to stay clear of him and his house after dark'.[50]

Various opinion pieces reproduce similar frame. One of them says "An alcoholic and having a severely violent sadistic streak was what motivated him (Ram Singh) to participate in the bestial physical and sexual assault on victim."[51] Commenting on Ram Sing's character other opinion piece says 'A quarrelsome, evidently frustrated bully by day and a volatile brute enslaved by a fetish for drunken sexual gratification and innate misogyny that night'.[52]

Juvenile accused is also frames in the similar lines. Like *TOI,* this paper also considers juvenile accused as most brutal and favours highest available punishment for him. One report says 'Even after victim had passed out after the ordeal, the juvenile, who had still retain some energy, kept brutalising her in a ways which cannot be discussed.[53] Other report narrates 'he extracted her (victim's) intestine with his bare hands and suggested she be thrown of moving vehicle devoid of her clothes.[54] But juvenile justice board declared that minor accused deserve a chance at reformation instead punishment.[55]

HT publishes various reports to justify its blaming on juvenile accused. For example, one of the reports gives the data regarding the dramatic increment in the number of juvenile criminals in past few years.[56] Other report says "Unofficial Delhi police estimates put the numbers of juvenile delinquents apprehended for sexual assault, including unnatural sex, at half the total number of minors for nabbed their alleged involvement in heinous crimes.[57] Similar ideas continue in the opinion pieces as well. Criticising Indian Juvenile Justice Act one opinion piece says, "Indian Juvenile justice act does not take into account the level of mental and physical maturity of juvenile offenders nor does it take into account the nature and severity of crime."[58] Other piece claims "Call it an irony of the legal justice system" or what that.[59] Other opinion piece claims 'the gravity of an offence should be determined the punishment and whether the person should be tried as an adult in case of heinous offences'.[60] In other one opinion piece George Thomas argues 'the rational behind providing such a safeguard for juveniles lies in the assumption that they can't distinguish between right and wrong and are prone to act harshly. In theory, such rational is sound. However, such formula will not ensure justice for the victims. The heinous nature of crime committed by juvenile in Delhi buttresses this argument.[61] But one opinion piece by Srishti Jha claims that it is a complex problem with any straight answer. She argues ' what experts agree on though is that it is a vicious cycle with no straight solutions and answers'.[62]

HT, like *TOI,* dominantly supports death penalty for accused. It adopts various linguistic tactics to convey their readers that demand of death penalty is justified. It claims "Hang them!! Demands India."[63] *HT* prints victim's medical condition in very 'inflated narratives' repeatedly, which left readers with the sense that culprits deserve nothing than death for example: " There was remorseless brute behind the rape."[64] Even "Doctors say never seen such brutality"[65], " She is in 'Very Bad Shape' in the hospital."[66] "She is getting infusion of morphine to reduce the pain but the pain is so excruciating that despite morphine dose she is conscious."[67] "The girl is in critical condition and faces the prospects of never being able to eat a meal in her life if she survives."[68] It believes that deterrence will be the real tribute to Nirbhaya.[69]

Similar ideas reproduce in the opinion pieces and editorials as well. One of the opinion pieces says "criminal justice system should hand over the most deterrent of punishment to the 6 perpetrators."[70] Other opinion piece states "they (culprits) should be dealt with so severely, that for generations to come they can't imagine lifting a figure on women. Nothing worse than solid aridity confinement, flogging or castration needs to be considered.[71] Its editorial says "we need time bound investigation, fast rack court harsher punishments and protection of witnesses." Other opinion piece by Arghya Sen Gupta argues "There is much that is wrong with the India's retention and enforcement of the death penalty. However, abolishing the death penalty itself does not follow as a consequence. Doing so in this ground would be the grave error."[72] Its one of the editorials states "Taking an easy way out is hardly a deterrent. It is not just the case of having the right laws in place. It is only the certainty and severity of penalty can deter criminals and prevent cases of rape like the recent one in Delhi"[73] One of the opinion pieces says "Every time when there is a gruesome tragedy, mostly man made, which could have been prevented by good governance there is invariably a knee jerk reaction of the government that be to enact more stringent laws for punishing the culprits, without the necessary focus on the means to prevent similar incidents in future."[74]

On the issue of Juvenility, *HT* favours stringent punishment for juveniles in case of heinous crimes. Commenting on the culpability of the juvenile accused it reports that 'it was this juvenile who encouraged the couple to take the bus.'[75] But instead of this incident specifically, it claims that the juvenile delinquency as a phenomenon on dramatic rise from past few years. It report says "Rape by minors five fold since 2000".[76] *HT* criticises those who support juveniles in such cases. For example, while reporting Chief Justice of India's wife views on juvenility it writes "Finding no shortcoming in the present juvenile justice act, she (Wife of Chief Justice of India) said, 'The boy is entitle to just and fair trial under a separate law if he is under 18 years of age and he has right to be provided with legal aid to defend himself'.[77]

Framing of Fear

Times of India

TOI presents rape in a manner that it perpetuates a rape myth that 'Rape is bad than death'. Such myth nourishes patriarchal nature of society. All regressive concepts like of women`s body as the site of respect and dignity enters in because of such perceptions. Commenting on after rape psychology it states "the trauma is chronic. It changes the personality of victim and makes it turbulent. It may result in the victim not being able to have or maintain normal relationships. Many victims suffer from post-traumatic stress disorder"[78]. Other report says "Rape victim not only forced to live with an impaired self esteem for life but also faces social stigma'.[79] That`s why it claimed 'Rape is a bigger crime than murder from women point of view.'[80]

Out of the fact that victim of Delhi incident raped in a moving bus, relationship of women and transport has discussed intensively. Commenting on the gender insensitivity of transport system, it states 'Commuting in the public transport is a daily distress for the women.'[81] 'They are harassed on almost all bus routes in the city'.[82] According to a survey '9 out of 10 women using public transport face eve teasing on regular basis'.[83] Putting this situation in more sensationalistic manner it states "Getting home safer at night is an achievement."[84] That's why "they should be alert on road, act to protect themselves."[85] Such narration clearly instills fear in the mind of reader.

TOI perpetuates fear through its sensationalist coverage. It starts from narrating on the medical condition of victim. It's one report says "We are giving her medicines to treat the infection. There were serious injuries in her intestine. If the infection is not contracted then we might have to operate. But at present she is not in the condition to undergone second surgery: said doctor."[86] "An intestine transplant is the last resort for patients with irreversible intestine failure. The only surgical option with Nirbhaya is an isolated intestinal transplant."[87] At her hospital, battling for life Victim claims 'Maa mujhe bacha lo mai jeena chate hun' (save me mother, I want to live).[88] She expressed it through muffled speech and hand gestures that she wants to take fight back to men who raped her.[89] In narrating rape incident it writes 'For 40 minutes, 6 men violated her body inside a bus in the most brutal way. It was savagely beyond words {....} their final outrage was to throw her out of the moving bus'.[90] Reporting somewhere else it states 'A 23 year old physiotherapy student was left battling of her life after being brutally beaten up and raped by 7 drunken men in a private bus.'[91] She was brutalised and condemned to the slow and painful death.[92]

The streaks of sensationalism continue in opinion pieces also. Aravind S. writes "what the rapist has done to Delhi girl is intolerable."[93] Other one states 'her sodomized, gangrenous intestines have been removed surgically and yet her heart feebly beats on'.[94] Other one states "we can never feel the pain that she did in last few days; we never fully understand what her family have been through in last few days, unless we and our own are victims of same horrendous crime.[95] Other piece claims 'Every time there is a rape, we the city residents cower in the fear because our daughters, sisters and wives go out to work along with the very same routes slaked by depraved men who think nothing of violating, maiming and torturing women."[96] "Be it the congested shared auto where men just look for chance to touch and brush their bodies or the over-crowd buses where people pass lewd comments or do all sort of shameful deeds, commuting in public transport is a daily distress for women."[97] Vastla Shrangi and Aaditi Isaac in their opinion piece argue "Fear has become the part of their lives. No matter what measure are taken, no place is completely safe."[98] One writes " Nirbhaya is the story of the millions of Indian Women, open to insult, subject to ambush, vulnerable to attack, destined for demonisation."[99] "For the first time I am unpatriotic. I am not sure if I want to be Indian any more. I am pained, ashamed and disgraced at being Indian" Wendell Roderick writes.[100] Riyan Ramanath claims "Little pleasure like going to movies or hanging out at shopping malls is marred by the nuisance created by mischief mongers and eve teasers for girls. Women are force to be on their guard at all times even at such publically crowded places."[101] Apoorva Anubhuti says "we fail to realise that we do not even access basic freedoms on the daily basis. This not just about taking buses, but ability to walk freely at the place of my choice, without being stared at."[102] *TOI* captures the reaction from political class in the aftermath of gang rape vividly. It reports 'The brutal assault on Nirbhaya seems to have jolted the political class into recognising the urgent need to tighten anti-rape law.[103] Parliament voiced shock and anguish over barbaric rape. In that environment of emotional hysteria many MP's demanded capital punishment for accused of such heinous crime.[104] Government took so many knee jerk reactions. For example, 'Government proposed to have the case heard by fast track court' *TOI* discusses the weakness in Indian Policing regime. It starts from the pathetic, biased and insensitive approach of Indian police in rape cases.[105] The police take their own time to register cases of rape and molestation. Other report says 'Men in Khaki often fail to collect evidence properly enfeebling the prosecution case in the court. This police ineptness leads to low conviction rate[106] Reporting Delhi Police words it states "we are aware of the fact that figures belie the actual situation because many cases of rape are not reported. Fear of social stigma and retaliation by perpetrators and long legal procedures stop victims filing police complaints.[107] The indifference of police resulted in girls getting harassed even after making formal complaints with cops.[108] This turning of blind eye by Police to the lawlessness unfurled by men in public transport vehicle.[109] So, *TOI* feels gender insensitive police is inept for sexual assault cases.[110]

Hindustan Times

HT constructs fear by depicting Indian society as a complete lawless society where there is no policing at all. In an opinion piece Brinda Karat arguers "It is tragic but true that had the police and the government performed their duties, the 23-year-old student who was gang raped on December 16 could have been safe. Guidelines such as prohibiting tinted windows in vehicles and action against those who do not comply, which were formulated by the home ministry and the police after discussions with women's organisations, have not been implemented. The callousness is exemplified by the fact that the young woman had to go through the torture of recording her statement twice by those who should have put her interests above their inflated egos."[111] One of the report writes "The 28-year-old friend of the physiotherapist who died in a Singapore hospital after being brutally raped in a moving bus on December 16 said they had seen the worst faces of humanity and the police on that fateful evening. "They wanted to run us over, to kill us," the girl's friend told Zee News on Friday. "Three PCR vans reached us, saw us — just like so many people who were there. But the police kept fighting about jurisdiction and no one stepped forward to help us.[112] Other report says "He (victim's friend) also claimed that the police took them to a government hospital when it had the option of going to a private one that was nearby, and that he had lain on a stretcher for four whole days after the event with a broken leg.[113] Similar ideas float in the opinion pieces as well. It does not require a social philosopher to make the observation that police in India lack the trust of the citizens or that the majority of citizens consider the force a necessary evil.[114] Shivani Singh writes "An average Delhi cop is insensitive to the crime against women.'[115] Indrajit Hazra writes in an Opinion pieces that 'The police takes sexual violence as seriously as drivers across India take zebra crossings.'[116] In one of the opinion pieces Sitaram Yechury, writes 'Universally in every state in India and for the country as a whole, the ratio of policemen to population is one of the lowest in the world.[117] Lamenting over the investigating procedure in one of the opinion pieces Shilpa Jain argues "Investigation in criminal cases is left to the lowest rung of the police officers."[118] While narrating the story of conservative attitude of police one of editorial says 'The war on feudal and patriarchal mindsets will be long and hard one was clear again last week even when nation was debating gender sensitivity when Punjab police rape victim: How did they touch your chest? Did they first open the shirt or jeans?[119]

HT also has highly sensationalistic overtones. One of the news reports says "It appears to be that a rod was inserted into her and it was pulled out with so much force that the act brought out her intestine along. She was brutalised so badly that she had only 5 per cent of her intestine left inside her when was brought to the hospital.[120] Other claims "It is suspected that rusty iron road used to assault victim caused infection.[121] "She was in the pool of blood but conscious. There was blood over the face. I cannot even imagine the agonising pain, she must be in."[122] The pain was so excruciating that despite morphine dose she is conscious.[123] This can be done only to someone who is dead. How can someone assault a person in the matter they did when there is still life left in the person?[124] Sensationalism continues in editorials and opinion pieces. Its editorial says "It (Delhi Gang Rape) was an attack so vicious that even doctors, usually used to such cases, were shocked to their core.''[125] Other editorial writes "on Saturday her smile froze into the sad permanence in the memories of those who knew her, and her brilliance flickered for a final time."[126] Other editorial states "A young women who was on the threshhold of a promising life journey is no more today." "Even doctors said we never seen victim of such assault subjected to such brutality.''[127] One opinion piece states "Rape" or "Gang Rape" with its description of a venal pack mindset, does not come anywhere close to describing the hell that descended on 23 years old women on the evening of December 16.[128] Shivani Singh writes in an opinion piece '23 years old suffered unimaginable on December 16.''[129] Other says "we speak not just of blander word 'rape', but an iron road that was forced into her body, wrenching out her intestine.[130] Galltaman Bhaskaran writes 'At the recent rape in Delhi a teenager used an iron rod to rip out her intestines. How horrifying can things get? How did she become such a monster? I shudder to think of the horror he perpetrated'. Amrita Penumudi says "While 23 years old rape victim fights for her life in Delhi, the rest of the country is shocked at the kind of brutality she is subjected to'.[131] Telling about her own experience, one woman writes in an opinion piece that 'I don't wears high heels so that I can run.'[132] Other lady writes 'The brutal gang rape of 23 years old girl has so disturbed me that every night sleep eludes me and my thoughts revolve around what the girl must have gone through'. Other lady narrates her friend's experience in very sensationalistic manner. She writes "A few weeks earlier, she was in the bus and felt about a dozen hands crawling all over her. They points to her legs, breasts, back and buttocks. No spot on her body was spared. She jumped off the bus. She was in the tears.''[133] Namita Bhandare in her opinion piece writes "A terrible thing happened to that girl who was trying to get back home after a movie.''[134] 'The gory nature of the crime makes it difficult to explain to children'.[135]

Framing of a city

Times of India

Other noticeable framing by this paper is of framing Delhi as a 'rogue city'. *TOI* frames Delhi as a 'rogue city'- place where exploitation is inevitable. Crimes like rapes cannot be averted because of inherent criminal nature of the city. As our Capital has had a long history of such crimes.[136] It is among worst place to live in India.[137] Putting it in more sensationalistic manner it states ``to think that India is ruled from Delhi is a matter of fear and shame now."[138] There is every reason for girls to feel vulnerable while moving out on their own.[139] Fear has become the part of their lives.[140] They are maltreated everywhere.[141] Other report writes 'After Nirbhya`s barbaric rape in December last year, thousands of determined Delhiites had taken to streets demanding a safer city. Barely four months later, Delhi is probably unsafe than it has been in long while. According to police statistics most kind of crimes have risen sharply in the city since the January 1.[142] Women felt unsafe whenever they stepped out and whatever transport they took.[143] If a girl walk on an empty road, there is every possibility of a car pulls up near her and people in the car start teasing her or at times forcibly pulling her in the vehicle.[144] Citing the incident to show the vulnerability in the city it stated 'They (Victims of Delhi Gang Rape) were picked up around 9:10 pm, a time when many Delhiites are still out in the city.'[145]

Hindustan Times

Like *TOI, HT* also portrays Delhi as 'Rogue city' where women are vulnerable round the clock. It report says "over 90 per cent of accused in Delhi are first time of offenders, showing scare regard for law in the national capital where the crime graph has been rising steadily." Other one says 'the capital continues to witness sharp rise in rapes and molestation even after the incident of December 16 rape.'[146] 'Till march three, 247 cases of rape were registered in comparison to 110 last year- an increase in 124 per cent.'[147] Many other reports also give such sensationalistic facts like: 'More Shame: 5 rapes 2 days, 12'.[148] The year that ended with most brutal cases of sexual assault reported in the capital also recorded the highest numbers of rape, attempts to murders, rioting and robbery in the entire decade, according to Delhi police annual report.[149]

Deductions

The above stated qualitative content analysis revels four dominant framings of selected newspapers.

Framing of victim

Regarding victim two types of frames are prominent. First frame portrays her as responsible and hardworking women. Other frame portrays her as brave and courageous girls. Both type of framing are problematic because of their exclusionary nature.

The former framing is problematic because it teaches us to sympathise only with a victim who is 'ideal' according to patriarchal standards. If any victim does not fit into the traditional stereotypical definition of 'victim', unlike Delhi Gang Rape victim, she will have to face blaming from media which will restore responsibility of rape on her than on accused. For example, existing literature clearly reveals that those who were rape in bar or in an intoxicated condition faced what is called 'victim Blaming' from media. So, media perpetuates gender stereotypes while covering rape reports through the framework of, what Helen Benedict (1992) called as, Virgin and vamp. She is framed as hardworking as well as an intelligent girl who had pursued her study even in difficult financial times. Collectively, papers leave no stone unturned in framing this victim as an 'ideal victim'. Hence, her death was a 'national loss'. Such framing reproduces the cultural boundaries of, as stated above, ideal and non-ideal rape victim. The non-ideal rape victims (for example, those who were not intelligent, hard working, those who were from lower caste, from lower class, those who consumed alcohol before they got raped etc, those who were raped in the places like bar, discotheque, those who were wearing sexually revealing clothes, those who were raped at late night parties, those who were at night outs, those who choose to do outing at late night with friends) do not get concentration, support and sympathy neither from media nor from public. Such victims are termed as 'bad girls' and are 'themselves responsible for their rape' (Benjamin, 2012). Their voices get marginalised in the process. If such cases get noticed then victim has to face the blame of rape on herself rather than sympathy. For the framing of such victims most painful rape myths that is 'women ask to be rape' is used. 'Women ask to be rape' is an umbrella under which more specific ideas such as she was walking by herself at night, she was asking to raped in that outfits, she enjoy rape etc. can be categorised (Allison and Wrightsman, 1993). Why men subject women to blame for being attacked is unclear but their actions create a culture of impunity that allows rape to continue (Bates, 2012).

The latter framing is problematic for some other reasons. The bravery of the girl is framed on two instances. One, when newspapers narrate the incident of rape. Out of the fact the victim gave tuff fight to her rapists, papers praise her courageous attempt of retaliation. Such framing is problematic because every type of rape victim does retaliate strongly against her rapists. The assumption of strong retaliation based on a rape myth that rape occurs between strangers (Benjamin, 2012). But in various rape cases like date rape, marital rape, drug facilitated rape etc, generally either the retaliation is low or sometimes completely non-existent. The victims of such type of rape do not come under the ambit of 'ideal victim'- as defined by patriarchal society. The media does not take interest in the coverage of such rapes and if it does, it perpetuates victim blaming rather than an unbiased reporting.

Second instance when victim's bravery is framed while reporting her medical condition from hospital. According to papers, as I revealed in upper section, he fought a courageous fight against her pain and injuries. This perpetuation of medical heroism of victim by these papers support the long standing criticism against media's coverage of rape that is 'where women are savagely beaten, when women are assaulted unconscious, these incidents get more coverage (Capua, 2013). As it also states by Darche and Velagic (2013) that violence against women is the permanent fixture in the Indian language press, with most brutal cases garnering the greatest attention? There is a famous quip of the newspapers industry 'if it bleeds, it leads'. Media shows no interest in the rapes where there are less or no injuries. But in reality, majority of acquaintance rapes, as stated above, are such kind of rapes in which very less violence is involved. The literature shows that marital rape does not always involve physical violence (Langhinrichse and Monsoon, 1998). Media as well as society treats such cases lightly out of a dominant rape myth that is 'the perpetrator usually uses a weapon and leaves the victim physically injured (Benjamin, 2012).

Framing of Accused

Both *TOI* and *HT* have framed accused (including juvenile accused) as insane and abnormal people and hence dominantly support capital punishment for such culprits. In *TOI* and *HT* 'a variety of sources were quoted suggesting that attack was a manifestation of abnormal behaviour on the part of assailant (Worthington, 2013). The rapists are projected as crazy psychopaths (Russel, 1984). The rapists are portrayed as subhuman, looking stranger, violent, mentally deranged, impulsive, with no access to consensual sex.

Papers used number of linguistic tactics to frame insanity of accused. One of them is through the narration of rape incident. Ghastly and gory details of the incident are expounded.

Such projection of rapist is problematic because of mainly three reasons. Firstly, such projections make readers to understand perpetrators as 'other' than a genuine part of the society which force them to believe that any act of gender discrimination, for example, rape is a rare phenomenon and hence refrain them from getting sense of deeply entrenched patriarchal nature of society. Secondly, by calming accused as an uncontrolled person, victim shares the responsibility of attack by making poor choices, a familiar victim blaming discourse that often emerges in news account of gender violence (Benedict, 1992). By encouraging victim blaming, the articles potentially supported the myth that the rape is the victim`s responsibility and some way women deserved the attack (Tosh and Philips, 2009). Thirdly, such insane perpetuators are framed as people who have uncontrolled sexual desire. Such portrayal leads to the dissemination of a rape myth that is 'rape is purely an expression of a sexual desire' (Benjamin, 2012) and not of 'violence'.

Both papers strongly demand death penalty for all accused. Not only these papers themselves support death penalty but also give substantial space to the violent ideas of protests of death penalty from the marches. Rather than educating people against such short-term angry retaliations, papers themselves were indulged in such kind of immature knee-jerk reactions.

Framing of Fear

These two newspapers cover Delhi rape in highly sensational manner. Such sensational coverage by these dailies was their paramount tool through which they disseminate fear. Unnecessary usage of 'heightened' and 'inflated' narratives evoke fear in society. Their coverage of rape incident and of medical condition of victim explicitly perpetuates a rape myth that is 'rape is bad than death'. While discussing flaws in Indian institutions like police, judiciary, legislative, these papers, portrayed the situation of complete lawlessness in Indian society. Such depiction, beyond any doubt, has created intensive fear in the psyche of readers. 'The fear of crime arguably has important implications in the lives of women (Brennon, 2004).' "Describing rape in this way, as it is done by these two newspapers, potentially increases fear in female readers as rape is constructed as life threatening experience that they are unable to protect themselves from" (Tosh, Philips, 2009). Such fear of crime leads social control of women (Pollock, 2009) and reproduces patriarchy.

Framing of city

Both of these papers frame Delhi as a 'rouge city'. A town where violence and lawlessness might be expected (Worthington, 2011). Such projection gives sense to readers that a particular place is very dangerous to reside and portrayed gender discrimination as a geographically specific phenomenon rather than deep imbibing societal value.

Conclusion

The foregoing framing analysis suggests that coverage of Delhi Gang rape by these two papers give way to sensationalism, victim blaming, less thought- knee jerk reactions and mainly to various types of rape myths. The development of the concept of rape myth started with the pioneering work of Brownmiller (1975) and Burt (1980) and since then has been extensively used in research on sexual violence. The existing literature clearly reveals that it is not only in the case of Delhi Gang Rape, we are living in a world in which female victims are blamed, stigmatised, re-victimised and showered with abuse (Bates, 2012). All rape myths sprouted out of a grand narrative of patriarchal society that is of 'purity'. This grand narrative teaches us to treat a virgin, feminine, fearful, less exposed, less talkative, non-argumentative and woman who is not in any romantic relationship, who never prefer to go out in night, who has less friend of opposite gender, who is hardworking, intelligent, responsible as a 'pure' woman and as an 'ideal victim' if get rape. This research clearly reveals that the coverage of Delhi Gang rape by two selected newspapers also disseminates similar type of gender stereotypes and orthodoxies. Such stereotypes not only reproduce but also make existing gender hierarchies more stringent and strong. There are number of studies that reval that different depictions of rape impact mentality of masses differently (Franiuk, Seefelt, 2008; and Franiuk, 2008).

At broader level it would not be wrong to claim that both paper cover Delhi Rape through episodic reporting than thematic reporting. Whole focus of these papers is on incident and characters involved rather than understanding general patriarchal and masculine nature of society. 'Developing a back story through interviews with family, friends (neighbours, teachers, doctors) the press highlights the personal lives of victims and accused (Drache and Velogic, 2013). Such personalisation of a particular rape incident does not allow readers to understand gender discrimination at the broader framework of society.

As media is one of the most important tool, not only to communicate but also to educate, we must develop a mechanism to monitor media's narratives in short as well as in long-term so that it can be misused for disseminating gender biased stereotypes and orthodoxies.

References

1. Allison, J A and Wrightsm, LS. (993. Rape, the misunderstood crime. Thousand Oaks: Sage.
2. Bates, Laura. 2012. A Crime upon a crime: Rape, victim blaming and stigma. (Blog article). Retrieved from http://www.womenundersiegeproject.org/blog/entry/a-crime-upon-a-crime-rape-victim-blaming-and-stigma.
3. Benedict, Helen. 1992. *How press covers sex crimes. Virgin and Vamp.* New York: Oxford University Press.
4. Benedict, Helen. 1993. The privacy rights of rape victims in the media and the laws, *Fordham Law Review*, 61(5), 1141-1145.
5. Benjannin, Lisa and Legland, Cathleen. 2012. Sound and Fury: Newspaper coverage of marital rape debate in New Providence. *International Journal of Bahamian Studies,* 18 (4), 16-35.
6. Bissler, Denise and Joan, Conners (eds). 2012. *The harms of crime media. Essays on the perpetuation of racism, sexism and class stereotypes.* North Cardina: Macfarland and Co Inc.

7. Bonnes, Stephen. 2010. *Gender and Racial stereotyping in rape coverage: An analysis of rape coverage in Grocotto's mail* (Master Dissertation). Retrieved from file:///C:/Users/hp/Downloads/BONNES-MA-TR10-05%20(2).pdf

8. Bonnes, Stephanie. 2011. Gender and Racial stereotyping in rape coverage: An analysis of rape coverage in a South African newspaper, Grocotto's mail. *Feminist Media Studies,* 13(2), 208-227.

9. Brooker, Joanne and Susan, Mac Donald. 2002. Media attributes of blame and sympathy in 10 rape cases, *The Justice Professional,* 15(1), 3-18.

10. Brownmiller, Sussane, 1975. *Against our will: Men, Women and rape,* New York: Simon & Schuster.

11. Burt, MR. 1980. Cultural Myths and support of rape. *Journal of personality and social psychology*, 38(2), 217-230.

12. Cupa, Joe. 2013, April 30. Better Coverage of rape is needed. *Voice of America News,* Retrievedfrom http://www.voanews.com/content/rape-media-30apr13/1651676.html

13. Daniel, Emory. 2009. A game that cannot be won: Media framing of the Duke Lacrosse rape scandal. (Master's Thesis)

    Retrieved from http://scholar.lib.vt.edu/theses/available/etd-05152009-105054/unrestricted/EmoryStephenDanielthesisETD.

14. Dowler, Kenneth. 2006. Sex, lies and video tapes: The presentation of sex crime in local television news. *The Journal of Criminal Justice*, 34(4), 383-392.

15. Drache, Daniel and Velogic, Jennifer. 2013, June. *A report on sexual violence journalism in four leading English language publication before and after Delhi Bus rape.* Paper presented at the ICA pre-conference workshop on South Asian Communication Scholarship, London, UK.

16. Dutton, Jessica 2010. Thinking through the politics of shame as a contemporary form of colonial discourse: Analysing media representations of the baby T shepang rape case (Master Thesis), Retrieved from https://open.uct.ac.za/bitstream/handle/11427/10341/thesis_hum_2011_dutton_j.pdf?sequence=1.

17. Franiuk, Renae, *et al.* 2008. Prevalence and effects of rape myths in print journalism. The Kobe Bryant case, *Violence against women,* 14(3), 287-309.

18. Franiuk, Renae, *et al.* 2008. Prevalence of rape myths in headlines and their effects on attitudes towards rape, *Sex Roles,* 58(9), 790-801.

19. Joseph, Ammu and Sharma, Kalpana. 2006. *Whose news? The media and the women's issues,* New Delhi: Sage Publications.

20. Krippendorff, Klaus. 2012. *Content Analysis: An introduction to its methodology*. New York: Sage Publications.

21. Langhinrich and Monson. 1998. Marital rape: Is the crime taken seriously without co-occuring physical violence, *Journal of family violence,* 13(4), 433-44.
22. Somport, Shannon. 2010. Let me tell you a story: English Canadian newspapers and sexual assault myths, *Canadian Journal of Women and Law,* 22(2), 301-328.
23. Tosh, Jenna and Phillips, Jeremy. 2009. *How 'THE SUN' newspaper portray rape?, Qualitative Methods in Psychology,* 7(8), 5-9.
24. Turkewitz, Rebecca. 2010. All the news that is fit to print: A content analysis of newspaper's portrayal of rape and sexual assault (Doctoral Dissertation). Retrieved from http://wesscholar.wesleyan.edu/cgi/viewcontent.cgi?article=1544&context=etd_hon_theses.
25. Worthington, Nancy. 2011. *Gender Discourse and Ubuntu media philosophy, Journalism Studies,* 12(5), 608-623.
26. Worthington, Nancy. 2013. Explaining Gang Rape in 'Rough Town': Diverse voices in gender violence news online. *Communication, Culture and critique,* 7(4), 103-120.

Notes

1. Rape Myth refers to the false beliefs and stereotypes regarding forced and attempted sexual intercourse and the victims and perpetrators of such act (Burt, 1998).
2. The term 'News Item' which has used frequently in whole dissertation used in a very comprehensive manner. It denotes to news articles, news reports, opinion pieces, columns, editorials etc.
3. According to latest Indian readership survey these two English dailies are at top in regarding their readership.
4. Chitlangia, Risha, (2012, December 20). Save Me I Want To Live, Delhi Rape Victim Tells Kin, *TOI.*
5. TNN (2012, December 28). Delhi Gang Rape: Attack didn't kill victim's spirit, *TOI.*
6. Ghosh, Dwaipayan, (2012, December 30). Delhi Gang Rape Victim Worked Hard to Realize Her Ambitions. *TOI.*
7. Kunwar, SD. (2013, January 24). Nirbhaya Scores 73 Percent in Last Exam of Her Life. *TOI.*
8. Pandit, Ambika. (2012, December 30). All Nirbhaya Wanted Was A Government Job, *TOI.*
9. TNN. (2012, December 30). 'Salute The Brave heart', *TOI.*
10. Hegde, Sharanya. (2012, December 30). No Man Should Dare It Again, *TOI.*
11. Jha, Durgesh. (2012, December 31). Don't Let Nirbhaya's Fire Die, *TOI.*

12. PTI. (2012, December 22). "Gang Rape Victim Showing Composure, Health Is Better: Doctors", *TOI.*
13. TNN. (2012, December 21). "Gang Rape Victim's Will To Leaves Doctors Amazed", *TOI.*
14. TNN. (2012, December 25). Victim's Father Appeals For Calm, *TOI.*
15. Singh, Akhilesh (2012, December 29). Nirbhaya the revolutionary, *TOI*
16. Sengupta, Rupa. (2012, December 30). Nirbhaya's Story. *TOI.*
17. IANS. (2012, December 29). Gang Rape Victim Took Tuitions To Pay For Her Education, *HT.*
18. HT, (2012, December 30). She Lit A Flame, *HT.*
19. HT. "(2012, December 29).Gang rape victim is martyr for the cause of women's security", *HT.*
20. Anand, Jatin. (2012, December 30). Rapist Ferried School kids, *HT.*
21. HT correspondent. (2012, December, 19). Out On The Joy Ride, Gang Robbed A Man Before Brutalizing Women. *HT*
22. Anand, Jatin. (2012, December 20). Delhi Gang Rape: Victims Were Not Selected, Says Accused Ram Singh, *HT.*
23. Staff Reporter. (2012, December 30). Nirbhaya's Story, *TOI.*
24. Sharma Alisha. (2012, December 22). Give Death To Rapists, *TOI.*
25. Shekhar, Raj. (2012, December 19). Delhi Gang Rape Case: Main Accused Went Berserk After Victim Bite Him, *TOI*
26. Ghosh, Dwaipayan. (2012, Dcember "Accused Have Tea, Watched TV after Rape", *TOI,* December 23, 2012.
27. Raj, Shekhar. (2012, December 19). Delhi Gang Rape Case: Main Accused Go Berserk After Victim Bite Him, *TOI.*
28. Singh, Smriti. (2013, January 5). With Older Juveniles Getting Away, Juvenile Justice Act Needs To Be Amended, *TOI.*
29. Mathur, Swati. (2013, January 13). Juvenile Deserves Death Sentence: Nirbhaya's Mother, *TOI.*
30. Singh, Smriti. (2013, January 4). Delhi Gang Rape Case: Juvenile may go free in months, *TOI.*
31. Aggrawal, Priyangi. (2013, January 8). "Juvenile offenders' major crimes. *TOI.*
32. Veyas, Hetal. (2013, January 1). Minors get away with major crimes, *TOI.*
33. Singh, Smriti. (2013, January 30).In other countries juveniles tried as adults for heinous crimes, *TOI.*
34. Suraiya, Jag. (2013, January 22). Age old question, *TOI.*
35. Dhawan, Himanshi. (2012, December 20). President Pardon saved rapists the nooses, *TOI.*

36. Singh, Akhilesh. (2012, December 29). Nirbhaya the revolutionary, *TOI.*
37. TNN. (2012, December 30). There is no fear of law, *TOI.*
38. TNN. (2012, December 21). Chorus of death penalty gins pitch, *TOI.*
39. Chaudary, Sayantanee, (2012, December 24). Rape rage refuses to die down, *TOI.*
40. Vyas, Sharad. (2012, December 21). Maharashtra supports death penalty of gang rape convicts, *TOI.*
41. Sharma, Alisha. (2012, December 22). Give death to rapists, *TOI.*
42. TNN. (2012, December 22). Delhi united in anger and grief, *TOI.*
43. PTI. (2012, December 23). Delhi Gang Rape: Students seek justice for victim, *TOI.*
44. Tiwary, Deeptiman. (2012, December 29). Why talk about Delhi when Patna is too unsafe, *TOI.*
45. Anand, Jatin. (2012, December 30). Delhi Gang Rape: Rapists Tried to Run Over Couple, *HT.*
46. Bollywood Hungama. (2012, December 29). Today has been a disturbing day: Amitabh Bachhan, *HT.*
47. PTI (2012, December 24). Hang them over, we will serve justice, say neighbours, *HT.*
48. PTI. (2013, March 12). Odds against Him, Rape Accused Needed Counseling: Psychiatrists, *HT.*
49. Anand, Jatin. (2012, December 22). 3 days Later, Two Rapists Still At Large, *HT.*
50. Anand, Jatin. (2012, December 22). Remorseless Brute Behind the Rape, *HT.*
51. Anand, Jatin. (2012, December 23). Emotional vacuum aids crime, *HT.*
52. Anand, Jatin. (2012, December 21). Remorseless Brute Behind the Rape, *HT.*
53. Gupta, Anant. (2012, December 22). Minor Among Two Held For Sunday Gang Rape, *HT.*
54. PTI (2013, January 3). Delhi Rape: Juvenile Raped Her Twice and Ripped off Her Intestine", *HT.*
55. PTI. (2013, January 29). Delhi Gang Rape: Juvenile May Get Away With Least Penalty, *HT.*
56. Anand, Jatin. (2012, December 22). Number of Juvenile Delinquents on Rise, *HT.*
57. Anand, Jatin. (2012, December 24). Emotion vacuum aids crimes, *HT.*
58. Kishore, RR. (2013, March 14). Remove The Legal Shield, *HT.*
59. HT Correspondent. (2012, December 30). Most Brutal among the rapists, won't even have to go to jail, *HT.*

60. HT. (2013, January 7). When the young aren't innocent, *HT*.
61. Thomas, George. (2013, January 14). This is an age of unreason, *HT*.
62. Jha, Srishti. (2013, February 17). Inside the juvenile mind, *HT*.
63. HT Correspondent. (2012, December 19). Hang them!! Demands India, *HT*.
64. Anand, Jatin. (2012, December 21). There was remorseless brute behind the rape, *HT*.
65. TNN. (2012, December 18). Even "Doctors say never seen such brutality", *HT*.
66. TNN. (2012, December 18). She is in 'Very Bad Shape' in the hospital, *HT*.
67. HT Correspondent. (2012, December 24). Victim is critical, putting up spirited fight, *HT*.
68. TNN. (2012, December 24). Delhi Gang Rape victim critical, writes on the piece of paper: mother I want to live, *HT*.
69. TNN. (2012, December 30). It believes that deterrence will be the real tribute to Nirbhaya, *HT*.
70. Girimaji, Pushpa (2012, December 23).Transport department, cops liable for negligence in Delhi Gang Rape, *HT*.
71. Singh, Jairaj. (2012, December 18). Delhi please stop raping your women, *HT*.
72. Sengupta, Arghya. (2013, March 4). It is not just the question of life and death, *HT*.
73. Editorials. (2012, December 19). A nightmare on the street, *HT*.
74. Verma, JS. (2012, December 20). Focus on means to prevent similar incidents in future, *HT*.
75. TNN. (2012, December 23). Delhi Gang Rape: Juvenile could be let off lightly, *HT*.
76. TNN. (2013, January 7). 'Rape by minors five fold since 2000', *HT*
77. Mukherjee, Upasana. (2013, January 7). Don't try juvenile in adult courts: CJI's wife, *HT*.
78. TNN. (2012, December 24). Sexual assault victim spared death but not society's barbs, *TOI*.
79. TNN. (2012, December 31).Castrate rapists: said BJP ministers, *TOI*.
80. Pradhan, Ashok. (2012, December 29). Majority wants death in new rape laws, *TOI*.
81. Sinha, Alisha. (2012, December 20). Commuting in Masculine space, *TOI*.
82. TNN. (2012, January 2). 'They are harassed on almost all bus routes in the city', *TOI*.

83. TNN. (2012, December 22). "Horrors of social stigma haunts women, encourages eve teasers", *TOI.*
84. John, Ekatha. (2013, January 2). Mapping areas where crime against women are high, *TOI.*
85. Devidayal, Namita. (2012, December 20). They should be alert on road, act to protect themselves: Expert, *TOI.*
86. TNN. (2012, December 19). Victim battles for life, Sonia Gandhi turns up, *TOI.*
87. Isalkar, Umesh. (2012, December 21). Once Nirbhaya stabilizes, intestinal transplant is the only surgical option, *TOI.*
88. Chitlangia, Risha. (2012, December 20). Save me, I want to live, *TOI.*
89. Ghosh, Dwaipayan. (2012, December 23). I won't vanish without a fight, they will have to pay, Delhi Gang Rape victim says, *TOI.*
90. TNN. (2012, December 29). Delhi Gang Rape: Attack didn't kill victim's Fighting Spirit, *TOI.*
91. (2012, December 18).Delhi Gang Rape Case, *TOI.*
92. Pandit, Ambika. (2012, December 31). All Nirbhaya wanted was a government job, *TOI.*
93. S Arvind. (2012, December 24). Don't dictate us on the dress, *TOI.*
94. (2012, December 25). Her Story. Our Story, *TOI.*
95. Ravinder, Sharmila. (2012, December 29). The death of India's Daughter, *TOI.*
96. Times View. (2012, December 19). Enough talks, let's make women safe, *TOI.*
97. PTI. (2012, December 19). Zero Tolerance, *TOI.*
98. Shrangi, Vatsala. (2012, December 19). Do girl students feel safe in Delhi, *TOI.*
99. Sengupta, Rupa. (2012, December 30).'Nirbhaya's story', *TOI.*
100. Rodricks, Wendell. (2012, December 31). Today something changed in me, *TOI.*
101. V. Riyan. (2012, December 23). Eve teasers spoil girl's fun, *TOI.*
102. PTI (2013, January 17). Delhi Mentality, *TOI.*
103. Singh, Mahendra. (2012, December 30). Political class consensus on tightening rape laws, *TOI.*
104. TNN. (2012, December 19). Outrage MP demanded death for rapists, *TOI.*
105. TNN. (2012, December 18). Activists woe low conviction rate, long trail, *TOI.*
106. Deshpande, Swati. (2012, December 24). Low conviction rate spurring sexual assault cases in India: Legal experts, *TOI.*

107. Kannan, Sindhu. (2012, December 19). All rape cases aren't reported, police admit, TOI.

108. Prashar, Saurab. (2012, December 26). Harassed victims push cops out of inaction, *TOI*.

109. Reddy, Srinivas. (2012, December 26). Women fear taking public transport, *TOI*.

110. TNN. (2012, December 29). Activists seek trained staff to tackle sexual assault, *TOI*.

111. Brinda, Karat. (2012, December 26). A constant threat, *HT*.

112. HT correspondent. (2013, January 5). Cops didn't help: Delhi Gang rape victim's friend, *HT*.

113. HT Correspondent. (2013, January 8). Angry over gang rape forces probe into police responses, *HT*.

114. (2012, January 12). Not with you, not for you, *HT*.

115. Singh, Sivani. (2012, December 24). Let‘s make our anger count and demand lasting reform, *HT*.

116. Hazra, Inderjit. (2012, December 30). Terrify the scum, *HT*.

117. (2013, January 7). Two sides of the same coin. *HT*.

118. Jain, Shilpi. (2012, December 21). Ensure responsible officers handle investigation, *HT*.

119. Editorial. (2012, December 30). Don't let her life go to waste, *HT*.

120. Kaul, Rhythma. (2012, December 20). Delhi gang rape victim critical, writes on piece of paper Maa I want to live, *HT*.

121. Bhalla, Jaya. (2012, December 27). Delhi Gang Rape: Infection spreads, victim very critical, *HT*.

122. PTI. (2012, December 20). Victim 'fighting for life', arrest made, *HT*.

123. HT Correspodent. (2012, December 20). Victim is critical, putting up spirited fight, *HT*.

124. HT Correspodent. (2013, January 5). Burn them alive, she said, *HT*.

125. Editorial. (2012, December 19). A nightmare on the streets, *HT*.

126. Editorial. (2012, December 30). She lit a flame, *HT*.

127. Raju, S. (2012, December 18). Main accused arrested, *HT*.

128. Hazra, Indrajit. (2012, December 30). Terrifying the scum, *HT*.

129. Singh, Shivani. (2013, January 7). 'Every resistance helps to built the culture of Zero tolerance, *HT*.

130. Halarnkar, Samar. (2013, January 3). Dark and silent night, *HT*.

131. Mycity. (2012, December 23). Time to teach respect, *HT*.

132. Variyar, Mugdha. (2012, December 20). I don't wears high heels so that I can run, *HT*.

133. (2012, December 18). Delhi stop raping your women, *HT*.
134. Bhandare, Namita. (2012, December 22).A tipping point of change, *HT*.
135. HT Correspondent. (2012, December 23). A wounded nation seeks answers, *HT*.
136. Singh, Smirti. (2012, December 18). Ghastly rapes Delhi's undoing for long, *TOI*.
137. Supriya, Sharma. (2012, December 18). Delhi tops rape tally among metro states, *TOI*.
138. TNN. (2012, December 19). Delhi should take leaf out of NE, *TOI*.
139. Gyanesh, Aaditi. (2012, December 20). Women resort to training, safety devices, *TOI*.
140. Shirangi, Vastala. (2012, December 24). Do girl students fell safe in Delhi?, *TOI*.
141. Nezami, Seezan. (2013, January 12). Women feel unsafe everywhere in the world, *TOI*.
142. Ghosh, Dwaipayan. (2013, March 26). Delhi reels under surge in crime since 1, *TOI*.
143. Sodhi, Parerna. (2012, December 18). Unsafe in any hour in big, bad city, *TOI*.
144. Keslaya, Kelly. (2012, December 16). Students, parents in the state shaken by Delhi Gang Rape, *TOI*.
145. Chuhan, Neeraj. (2012, December 18). Delhi Rape case: Victim battles for life, 3 accused held, *TOI*.
146. TNN. (2013, January 9). 3 rapes in 2 days in Delhi, *HT*.
147. Haider, Faizan. (2013, March 5). Delhi is still not safe for women, *HT*.
148. TNN. (2013, March 9). More Shame: 5 rapes 2 days, 12, *HT*.
149. Special Coorespondent. (2013, January 19). Crime up in Delhi, Rapes at 10 years high, *HT*.

11

Between "Exclusion" And "Unfavourable Inclusion": Realising the Right to Food for Dalits

—*Tejinder Pal Singh*

Abstract

In India, Dalits – officially known as Scheduled Castes – constitute one-sixth of the population. The traditional caste-based ascribed roles manifests in few alternate livelihood opportunities for dalits, a situation perpetuated by the abstract commitments of inclusive policies and programmes as well as the poor implementation of laws prohibiting caste discrimination. This paper makes an attempt to analyse various meanings and dimensions of "social exclusion" given by Amartya Sen, and also explores the inextricable linkage between the condition of food security, the Right to Food in India, as well as the 'hidden apartheid' (in terms of prevalence of hunger and malnutrition) to realise an equitable, inclusive and sustainable path to development.

Keywords: *social-exclusion, dalit, traditional-Hindu-social-order, food-security, right-to-food.*

Introduction – Conceptualising the Social Exclusion

The term "social exclusion" is of relatively recent origin. There is a large number of growing literatures on this subject. The idea of social exclusion has conceptual connections with well-established notions of deprivation, discrimination, poverty, powerlessness, oppression, inequality, injustice as well as insecurity. Therefore, the term 'social exclusion' has become influential in the intellectual corridors debating about inclusive policy.

Buvinic (2005) summarise the meaning of social exclusion as "the inability of an individual to participate in the basic political, economic, and social functioning of the society", and goes on to add that social exclusion is "the denial of equal access to opportunities imposed by certain groups of society upon others." The concept of social exclusion has four distinguishable features—*firstly*, it involves the denial of equal rights to persons belonging to a particular group due to their shared identity; *secondly*, social exclusion entails the denial of equal rights to the group as a whole, that is members of the group face exclusion due to ascribed rather than achieved features, beyond individual agency or responsibility; *thirdly*, exclusion is embedded in social relations, and it is through social inter-relation that the groups are wholly or partially excluded from full participation in the society in which they live (Sen, 2000), and *finally*, social exclusion involves the denial of right and entitlement, it impoverishes the excluded groups and induce a high level of poverty among them.

The manifest as well as latent consequences of exclusion, thus, depends crucially on the functioning of social and economic institutions through a network of social relations, and the degree to which they are exclusionary and discriminatory in their outcomes. Social exclusion is '*social*' because it is social in the sense which encompasses all the aspects of life such as civil, economic and political, and it is systematic and structured – there is a definite pattern to social exclusion in a society. Thus, exclusion is reflected in the inability of individuals from the discriminated groups to interact freely and productively with others, which also inhibits their full and meaningful participation in the civil (including the freedom of speech and expression, rule of law, right to justice etc.), political (that is, the right and means to participate in the exercise of political power), and socio-economic (that is, the right to property, freedom of occupational choice, education etc.) life.

For further clarification, we need to make a clear distinction between the exclusion of a 'group' from the exclusion of an 'individual'. Social exclusion essentially refers to the processes through which a 'group as a whole' is wholly or partially excluded, on the basis of the group identities of its members, from full participation in the social, economic and political life of the community. Theoretically speaking, in the case of 'group exclusion', all persons belonging to a particular social/cultural group are excluded because of their cultural (group) identity, and not due to their individual attributes. The social and cultural identities, such as caste, ethnicity, religion, gender etc., become reference points for exclusion and discrimination and cause the exclusion of all persons sharing that particular group identity. On the other hand, the exclusion of an 'individual' is fundamentally different from the exclusion of a 'group'. Individuals (both from the excluded and non-excluded groups) often get excluded from access to economic and social opportunities for various reasons specific to them rather due to their group identity. For instance, individuals may face exclusion in access to education due to the lack of minimum qualification and merit, or their inability to meet the high cost of education. Similarly, an individual may be excluded from employment due to the lack of requisite educational qualifications. Also, an individual may be excluded from access to input and consumer markets due to lack of income and purchasing power or inability to receive credit due to lack of security.

Amartya Sen (2000) draws attention to the various meanings and dimensions of the concept of social exclusion. For him, the "*unfavourable exclusion*" is a situation wherein some people are being kept out (at least left out), the "*unfavourable inclusion*" (or, *selective inclusion*) is a situation where in some people are being included (maybe even being forced to be included)—in deeply unfavourable terms. Thus, with unequal treatment, it may carry the same adverse effects as the former. For casual analysis and policy response, Sen has also differentiated between active and passive exclusion. "*Active exclusion*" means fostering of exclusion through deliberate policy interventions by the government or by any other wilful agents (to exclude some people from some opportunity) while "*Passive exclusion*" works through the social processes in which there are no deliberate attempts to exclude, but nevertheless, may result in exclusion from a set of circumstances.

Right to Food and Constitutional Mandate in India

Food is the first and foremost basic necessity of life. The Universal Declaration of Human Rights (1948) recognised the right to food as a core element of an adequate level of living. Food security as a concept emerged at the United Nations Food and Agriculture Organisation (FAO) World Food Conference in 1974. The 1996 World Food Summit (WFS) declared, "Food security at the individual, household, regional, national and global levels exists when all people, at all times, have physical and economic access to sufficient, safe and nutritious food to meet their dietary needs and food preferences for an active and healthy life" (FAO, 1996). In 2009, the World Summit on Food Security stated that the four pillars of food security are availability, access, utilisation, and stability.

Food security is a pre-condition for realising the Right to Food. The International Covenant on Economic, Social and Cultural Rights (ICESCR) recognises the "right to an adequate standard of living, including adequate food", as well as the "fundamental right to be free from hunger." The "right to adequate food" is a much higher standard, including not only absence of malnutrition, but to the full range of qualities associated with food, including safety, variety and dignity, in short all those elements needed to enable an active and healthy life. Inspired by this definition, the Special Rapporteur on the Right to Food in 2002 defined it as "The right to have regular, permanent and unrestricted access, either directly or by means of financial purchases, to quantitatively and qualitatively adequate and sufficient food corresponding to the cultural traditions of the people to which the consumer belongs, and which ensure a physical and mental, individual and collective, fulfilling and dignified life free of fear." The former Special Rapporteur on the Right to Food, Jean Ziegler, defined three dimensions to the right to food:

- *Availability* refers to the possibilities either for feeding oneself directly from productive land or other natural resources, or for well functioning distribution, processing and market systems that can move food from the site of production to where it is needed in accordance with demand.
- *Accessibility* implies that economic and physical access to food is to be guaranteed. On the one hand, economic access means that food should be affordable for an adequate diet without compromising other basic needs. On the other hand,

physically vulnerable, such as sick, children, disabled or elderly should also have access to food.

- *Adequacy* implies that the food must satisfy the dietary needs of every individual, taking into account age, living conditions, health, occupation, sex, culture and religion, for example. The food must be safe and adequate protective measures by both public and private means must be taken to prevent contamination of foodstuffs through adulteration and/or through bad environmental hygiene or inappropriate handling at different stages throughout the food chain; care must also be taken to identify and avoid or destroy naturally occurring toxins.

Furthermore, any discrimination in access to food, as well as to means and entitlements for its procurement, on the grounds of race, colour, sex, language, age, religion, political or other opinion, national or social origin, property, birth or other status constitutes a violation of the right to food.

The Constitutional mandate of India is based on the notion of a Welfare State. India's Constitution upholds the obligation of the State to be proactive in ensuring food security, especially for the most vulnerable and marginalised sections. Article 21 of the constitution guarantees the fundamental right to life. The duties of the State in the context of the right to food are understood in relation to the Directive Principles of State Policy. Article 39(a) directs the State to ensure through policy that all citizens have the right to adequate means of livelihood, and Article 47 makes explicit the duty of the States to raise the level of nutrition and standard of living of the people. Also, the Constitution of India prohibits any forms of discrimination based on caste.

Further, India has ratified several international human rights treaties including the International Covenant on Economic, Social and Cultural Rights (ICESCR), the Convention on the Elimination of Racial Discrimination (CERD), the Convention on the Elimination of Discrimination against Women (CEDAW), and the Convention on the Rights of the Child (CRC). India has binding obligations under international framework as well as constitutional democratic ethos with respect to justice, liberty, equality and non-discrimination in ensuring food security for the most vulnerable and marginalised sections.

In response to the growing Right to Food movement in the recent years, the Supreme Court following the Constitution stipulated that the Central Government, when introducing new food-related schemes should include specific provisions for the prevention of caste-based discrimination and exclusion in the implementation of social welfare and food-related programmes. Despite the presence of the above provisions, public interest litigation (PIL) questioned the efforts of the national government to ensure the food security of its most vulnerable populations. The litigation generated widespread support and inculcation of democratic ethos across civil society, the media, judiciary and administrative circles and subsequently resulted in a series of measures that paved the way for existing schemes to be converted into legal entitlements or guarantees of food security. The Supreme Court of India also established an independent monitoring mechanism to track the progress of food, livelihood and social security programmes being implemented across the country. In 2001, the Court recognises the right to food, thereby, transforming policy choices into enforceable rights. Ultimately, this culminated into a larger public Right to Food Campaign.

In 2005, India enacted National Rural Employment Guarantee Act, later renamed as the Mahatma Gandhi National Rural Employment Guarantee Act (MGNREGA), aims to ensure livelihood security in rural areas by providing at least 100 days of wage employment in a financial year to every household whose adult members volunteer to do unskilled manual work. The recently enacted the National Food Security Act (NFSA), 2013 guarantees subsidised food to 50 per cent of the urban population and 75 per cent of the rural population, i.e., approximately two-thirds of India's 1.2 billion people. The beneficiaries are entitled to 5 kilograms per person per month of cereals at the following prices: Rice at Rs 3 per kg, Wheat at Rs 2 per kg, and Coarse grains (millet) at Rs 1 per kg. Also known as the Right to Food Act, it converts into legal entitlements for existing food security programmes of the Government of India such as the Midday Meal scheme, Integrated Child Development Services (ICDS) Scheme and the Public Distribution System (PDS).

Regarding India, the Special Rapporteur has commented that "India provides one of the best examples in the world in terms of the justifiability of the right to food. The Constitution of India prohibits discrimination and recognises all human rights. The right to life is recognised as a directly justifiable fundamental right (Article 21), while the right to food is defined as a directive principle of State policy (Article 47). As it has interpreted these provisions, the Supreme Court of India has found that the government has a constitutional obligation to take steps to fight hunger and extreme poverty and to ensure a life with dignity for all individuals."

Within the context of this paper, the term malnutrition specifically refers to the phenomenon of under nutrition, rather than over nutrition. Under nutrition, is one of India's most serious and persistent problems, and outcomes are even worse for tribal communities. Under nutrition refers to the outcome of inadequate intake of food (calories) or essential micronutrients that the body needs to grow, resist infection and disease, learn, perform physical work, and complete other essential bodily functions.

- There is more than enough food in the world to feed everyone, but the number of people affected by hunger and malnutrition is still 'unacceptably high' (FAO, 2014), with disproportionate impacts on vulnerable and marginalised sections.
- India transformed from being a food deficient to food surplus nation. Earlier we faced the problem of scarcity, but now there is problem of plenty where the millions of tonnes of wheat rot because warehouses are overflowing and huge quantities of wheat and rice are stored in open spaces risking decay. The Supreme Court, in 2010, urged the government to distribute grain free to the hungry rather than let it go to waste in warehouses and open fields, but that hasn't happened.
- The High Level Committee (HLC) on re-structuring of Food Corporation of India (FCI), submitted its report in January 2015, highlighted the leakages in the Public Distribution System (PDS) range from 40 to 50 per cent, and in some states go as high as 60 to 70 per cent.
- UNDP survey (2008) of 16 districts in the seven poor states of India showed that for 7.5 per cent of respondents access to

food is highly inadequate, and for another 29 per cent of the households it is somewhat inadequate.

- According to UNICEF, malnutrition is more common in India than in Sub-Saharan Africa and one in every three malnourished children in the world lives in India.
- Malnutrition in children is not affected by food intake alone; it is also influenced by access to health services, quality of care for the child and pregnant mother as well as good hygiene practices. Girls are more at risk of malnutrition than boys because of their lower social status.
- The anthropometric indicators of nutritional status for children in India are among the worst in the world. According to the National Family Health Survey (NFHS), the proportion of underweight children remained virtually unchanged between 1998-99 and 2005-06 (from 47 to 46 per cent for the age group of 0-3 years).
- As per the new provisional data from the 'Rapid Survey on Children' conducted by the Union Ministry of Women and Child Development and UNICEF shows that the proportion of underweight children in India might have declined from 45.1 per cent in 2005-6 to a historic low of 30.1 per cent in 2013-14. Even so, India still has the highest number of underweight children under five in the world and 70 per cent of children are anaemic.
- The 2014 Global Hunger Index (GHI) ranked India at 55th out of 76 countries, before Bangladesh and Pakistan, but still trails behind neighbouring Nepal (rank 44) and Sri Lanka (rank 39). While no longer in the "alarming" category, India's hunger status is still classified as "serious."

These are appalling figures highlights that India is among the most "undernourished" countries in the world. Further, paradoxically, India is a surplus producer of grain and yet thousands starve; Indian produced grain is often exported or sold in the open market, however the poor cannot afford to buy grain at market rates; with increasing droughts/ drought-like conditions in India and rising prices of grain, levels of hunger and food insecurity are set to increase.

The implications of malnutrition are dire both from the perspective of intense human suffering for the individual as well as the cumulative implications for society. The condition is known to perpetuate poverty and have a significant impact on human development, from birth into adulthood. The economic costs of malnutrition are staggering for both individuals and societies: individuals earn 10 per cent less over a lifetime and the world economy loses two to three per cent of its Gross Domestic Product (GDP) due to malnutrition annually.

Caste-based Violation of Right to Food

The insight from the preceding discussion on the concept of social exclusion is relevant for understanding the social structure of Indian society, which is characterised by a unique social institution called "Caste." The members of a caste group shares obligations and privileges which are fixed by ascribed criteria (birth), sanctioned and supported by social customs and religion. In other words, in Indian society, exclusion revolves around societal institutions that discriminate, deprive, oppress and even isolate (ostracize) some groups on the basis of ascribed group identities. The caste designation of a community in rural India, still, has a significant impact on the ability of members of that community to access and control critical productive resources like land, water, credit, livestock, agricultural inputs, training and extension services, technology, market information and access.

The nature of exclusion associated with the institution of caste particularly needs to be understood while analysing the situation of food security and realising the Right to Food. Being relegated to the bottom of the caste hierarchy, dalits lack access to and control over livelihood opportunities and productive resources, thereby violating their Right to Food. The causes of hunger and under nutrition are often not a scarcity of food but an inability to access available food in a caste stratified society.

In Indian society, historically, the Traditional Hindu Social Order (THSO) regulated the civil, social and economic life through certain socio-religious customary rules and norms, based on the occupational division of labour in which the rights and privileges of each social (caste) group are pre-determined or ascribed by birth and made hereditary. Therefore, the entitlement to rights is, however, unequal and hierarchal (graded). This stratified social order, with the fundamental characteristics of rigid social structure, implies the "forced exclusion" of one caste from the civil, socio-cultural, economic and political rights of the other castes. Extreme caste-based exclusion manifests in the form of 'untouchability', thus reflects in the inability of individuals from the lower castes to interact freely and productively with others, and also inhibit their meaningful participation in the socio-cultural, economic and political life of a community.

The Dalits are recognised as the "untouchables" (formally known as the "Scheduled Castes"), the fifth group below the four varna in the THSO. Being relegated to the bottom of the caste hierarchy and considered as 'a varna', they have limited livelihoods viewed as deplorable or deemed too menial by higher caste groups, such as removing human waste (known as 'manual scavenging'), dragging away and skinning animal carcasses etc. Their caste designation also renders them socially "polluted" or "untouchable" and is used to justify exclusionary and discriminatory practices, for instance, a segmental division of labour, restrictions of feeding and social intercourse, civil and religious disabilities, restrictions on occupational choice and marital relations. Majority of them are poor, exploited, illiterate, landless and work as farm labourers. Although the term "untouchability" has been abolished in law, yet dalit are known to suffer severe caste-imposed discrimination that affects every aspect of life (IHEU, 2010; Minority Rights Group International, 2010).

The 2011 Census recorded nearly 20.14 crore people belonging to various Scheduled Castes in the country. As per the 2001 Census, the number was 16.66 crore. The dalit population showed a decadal growth of 20.8 per cent, whereas India's population grew 17.7 per cent during the same period. Though there is an increase in the population of Dalits in the country, many States with a considerable number of Dalits don't have any legislation to protect the interests of the community. Many Dalit families lack access to productive and livelihood resources such as land or any other property. In case whatever access they had, in reality they lack control over these assets. Many Dalits are landless and efforts to empower them by giving free land have not been successful in many states with deeply entrenched feudal mode of production.

In addition, the "paradoxical" situation is such that while the Constitution of India and other special laws guarantee equal status for all citizens and outlaws untouchability practices, various forms of discrimination and exclusion still persist. Even under the Scheduled Castes and Scheduled Tribes Prevention of Atrocities Act, 1989, the Muslim and Christian dalits are not included as Scheduled Castes and thus are not eligible for the same protections as Hindu dalits. Though democratic political and human rights movements have shaken some traditional caste barriers, but caste continues to be used to justify exclusionary, discriminatory, violence, cruel, and inhuman treatment, especially in rural areas where caste-designation still dictates rigid roles and entitlements.

Under the impact of the global human rights movements, the constitutional democratic ethos and the neo-liberal economic policies, the caste system as an institution has also undergone some change from its original form, for instance, from "exclusion" to "unfavoured inclusion." Yet there are social and economic costs associated with change, which discourage the structural transformation of the unjust caste system. Also, the principles of free-market laissez-fairism, based on high economic growth rates, have failed to 'trickle down' and improve the food security situation of rural India, especially for this disadvantaged community.

Food security mainly relates with the production, distribution and pricing of food grains and thus brings agriculture, Public Distribution System (PDS) and the subsidy structure into focus. The reform measures that predominantly affect them are reduction in fiscal deficit, reduction in subsidies, capitalist mode of production through green revolution to increase the productivity, centralised model of corporate farming, high input cost, land acquisition for non-food crops like horticulture, export orientation and costlier agricultural credit due to unregulated informal credit institutions. Further, the international market for agri-products being an oligopoly of few giant companies, which control over the majority of market networks, may impair the food security of the local population.

Even in government schemes, designed specifically for the welfare of the traditionally discriminated communities, the members of such communities, often, find themselves excluded, both from participation and partnership in the implementation of such schemes, as well as, from the tangible and intangible benefits of the schemes. This is notably the case in Right to Food-related government programmes such as the Mid-day Meal Scheme (MMS) and the Targeted Public Distribution System (PDS) (Indian Institute of Dalit Studies, 2006). There are manifest as well as latent forms of caste prejudices that operate in the functioning of these programmes and the entrenched ways in which discrimination pervades the right to food. There are low levels of physical and economic access the Dalits had to these food security programmes; the degree to which they participated in their administration; and the nature of community-level access to each programme. The State seems to be committed in passing laws and adopting policies, but has done too little to address widespread failure to implement these measures. The Public Distribution System (PDS) has been to a large extent dismantled over the post-1991 period. This process accelerated with the introduction of the Targeted PDS in 1997, which divided consumers into so-called Below Poverty Line (BPL) and Above Poverty Line (APL) households. Prices for the latter were raised to virtually the level of market prices, effectively driving them out of the PDS. By various methods, including the use of the fraudulent official poverty line, the majority of the poor were simply excluded from the BPL category; being the poorest sections, the Dalits and Adivasis were particularly affected. By 2004-05, less than 40 per cent of dalit households in rural areas had either a BPL card or an Antyodaya card (a scheme for the 'poorest of the poor'). Among landless households (which describes the majority of rural dalit households), 51 per cent did not have a ration card at all, and another 24.5 per cent had an APL card (NSS Report no. 510). More so, the economic compulsions and sanctions imposed by the markets, in the globalised era, are demanding fiscal consolidation through rationalisation of subsidies (actually meant for weaker sections) and reduction in public expenditure on the social sector.

The causes of hunger and malnutrition are often not a scarcity of food but an inability to access available food in a caste stratified society. Caste-based discrimination and exclusion has inextricable linkage with the prevalence of hunger, undernutrition and poverty among the Dalits, thereby violating their Right to Food and freedom from hunger and poverty. This "hidden apartheid" creates obstacles in realising an equitable, inclusive and sustainable path to development. There is a growing body of evidence to suggest that despite controlled socio-economic factors, Dalit communities are at a distinct disadvantage in relation to food and nutrition security and well being owing to the prevalence of discriminatory practices. According to NFHS-III (2005-06) data, 54 per cent SC/ST kids are stunted as against 41 per cent among upper castes. Among OBCs, 49 per cent kids are stunted. Sure enough, malnutrition among Dalits is also caused by the caste order. Further, 48 per cent of SC children (below the age of five) in India are underweight as against the national average of 42.5 per cent, and 54 per cent of SC children are affected by stunted growth as opposed to the national average of 48 per cent. Severe malnourishment among Dalit children is 18.5 per cent. Nearly one-third of all Dalit children are severely stunted (27.6 per cent) and nearly 10 per cent are severely wasted as per government data. Anaemia among Dalit children is recorded at 72 per cent against the national average of 69.5 per cent. Nearly half of all Dalit children (47.3 per cent) are either moderately or severely anaemic. Data on micronutrient intake among Dalit children below the age of five also shows a less than average intake. The prevalence of malnourishment and anaemia among Dalit women is consistently higher than the national average, with 58.3 per cent of Dalit women suffering from anaemia and 18.5 per cent reported as moderately or severely underweight. The corresponding national figures are 55.3 per cent (anaemia) and 15.8 per cent (moderately or severely underweight). The recently published HUNGAMA study (2011) too estimates that 50.6 per cent of the SC population was malnourished as opposed to 36.3 per cent of the 'general' population. Likewise, SC children are 1.4 times more likely to be malnourished than children from other social groups.

Further, Poverty in India has been 'feminised' as well as 'dalitised'. Economically, most of them are still the poorest of poor. The situation of Dalit women, who have less access to ownership of land, households and livestock, is significantly worse than that of Dalit men. When the effects of caste and gender discrimination are combined, Dalit women end up at the bottom of the socio-economic scale. Poverty is a sum total of all the deprivations. In India, governmental definition of poverty is based on the sole criterion of minimum food requirement for survival. Thus, the poverty line is decided by the income sufficient to buy food equivalent of 2400 calories in rural and 2100 calories in urban areas. The database for poverty estimates is provided by the quinquennial surveys of NSSO. In 2009-10, in rural areas, Scheduled Tribes exhibit the highest level of poverty (47.4 per cent), followed by SCs (42.3 per cent), and OBC (31.9 per cent), against 33.8 per cent for all classes. In 2009-10, in urban areas, SCs have HCR of 34.1 per cent followed by STs (30.4 per cent) and OBC (24.3 per cent) against 20.9 per cent for all classes.

In rural areas, more than 57 per cent of SCs do not have any land under cultivation compared to 42.8 per cent in the general population; 21 per cent cultivate less than one acre (0.4 hectares); and another 13 per cent cultivate between one acre and two and a half acres (one hectare). The proportion of households cultivating larger holdings of size 4.01 hectares and above was the highest among other category of households (about five per cent), followed by OBCs (about 3 per cent). Between the ST and SC categories of households, the proportion of households operating such large holdings was a little higher among the households belonging to the STs (two per cent) than among those belonging to the SCs (one per cent). Ninety one per cent of the SC households in the rural areas are either landless or operate what are termed 'sub-marginal' or 'marginal' holdings (NSS Report no. 516). Although the statistics indicate that Dalits have made a significant progress on almost all parameters during the six post-independence decades, the relative distance between them and non-dalits seems to have remained the same or increased.

The actual social condition of rural Dalits, however, is hardly conveyed by such statistics. Although about 70 per cent of India's population continues to depend on agriculture as its primary source of livelihood. In 2005-06, marginal and small farmers accounted for 83 per cent of the operational holdings and 41 per cent of the operated area in India. The lack of adequate land often overlaps with social disadvantages, especially caste related. Some 32.3 per cent of marginal and small farmers belong to the SC and the ST categories, compared with 22.7 per cent of medium and large farmers. The incidence of landlessness is relatively higher (12.8 per cent) among ST households, followed by SC households (11.3 per cent) as compared with 10 per cent of all landless households in India. This is important as they are likely to face discrimination and exclusion in the delivery of public services such as credit; critical inputs such as water, power, seeds and fertilizers/manure; neglected by extension services and crop research; limited market access etc. Added to this is the rapid increase in land acquisition for non-agricultural use, and the continuing shift of land from subsistence to commercial farming, despite legal restrictions, resulting in the development-induced displacement, lack of adequate compensation, resettlement and rehabilitation, loss of livelihood opportunities and violation of the right to live life with dignity.

Bonded by the chains of caste and gender, the Dalit women are considered as "excluded among excluded", as they are placed at the very bottom of caste, class and gender hierarchies. They suffer multiple forms of exclusion and discrimination – as Dalits, as poor, and as women. Dalit women are considered to be intrinsically impure and 'untouchable', which sanctions gender-based violence. The vast majority of them are impoverished; they lack access to basic resources; they are subjugated by patriarchal structures, both in the general community (public) and within their own family (private); and violence and inhuman treatment serve as a social mechanism to maintain their subordinate position in society. Dalit women and children are likely to be the most poorly nourished sub-groups in India. Social status of Dalit women within the household also has the potential to bear upon nutritional status of their children. This affects the holistic development of their children and also hinders the socio-economic development of the society and the nation. In India, Dalit women are often met with violence when attempting to assert their rights in terms of access to drinking water, housing, the public distribution system (PDS), education or open spaces for open defecation. A careful look at the economic situation of Dalit women reveals that their work force structure is such that they rarely own any land. A large majority of them are agricultural labourers. The rate of unemployment among them is also quite high. About 90 per cent of women working in unorganised sector are mainly from lower castes. Thus, there are several welfare and inclusive programmes, policies, legislations and budget provisions like Special Component Plan for the benefit of marginalised sections, however, the Right to Food of Dalit women is so far neglected area in the mainstream policy and legal discourse, despite of the fact that dalit women are the worst affected victims of this caste ridden, patriarchal society across the Indian sub-continent.

Further, Dalit women face additional limitations, since in families with land, they typically own none and what they might own is seldom in their control. On the one hand, they are major contributors to agricultural production, and increasingly agriculture is being feminised with male outmigration; and on the other hand, they have little access to and control over the basic means of production. Women workers who are counted as "cultivators" in national statistics tend to be largely unpaid workers on family farms. Various field studies on the ownership of land under cultivation revealed that most of the land under cultivation by Dalit women has no legal title and thereby they are in constant threat of eviction by the State (on common lands) or leased in land from the dominant caste groups. The lands 'leased in' by Dalit women are very less productive as they do not get any support from the government or private agencies for investment. It is also a fact that, most of the legal land holdings of Dalits are dry land in nature and lack any support for their irrigation needs, agricultural inputs compared to the wetland owned and cultivated by other caste groups with all support from the government services. A Field Study in Andhra Pradesh, which has achieved largest amount of assigned land for landless Dalits particularly Dalit Women reveals the following:

- Assignment of land is on paper only and the physical possession has not been endowed with;
- The poor have been evicted out of their assigned lands;
- Some women are in cultivation of government lands but their title and possession is not regularised. So they couldn't claim any government credit support for improving land condition. Land is under possession, but cultivation has not been done due to the threat and encroachment of dominant caste men;
- The poor do not have sufficient technical or financial resources to cultivate the land and may, in fact, lease out their land and work as wage labourers on it;
- In many villages, where there is land in the name of Dalits have been mortgaged or sold to dominant caste for very meagre amount etc.

In is well known that in Indian society rural women are extensively involved in agricultural activities. The mode of female participation in agricultural production varies with the landowning status of farm households. In the globalised world, the impact of World Trade Organisation (WTO) rules and policies of trade liberalisation in the agriculture sector on women is distinctive. Being a primary seed keeper and processor, the WTO impacts her expertise and productive functions throughout the food chain. The Trade Related Intellectual Property Rights (TRIPS) agreement impacts women's knowledge of and control over seed and community resources. The Agreement on Agriculture (AoA) impacts women's livelihood security. Further, as globalisation shifts agriculture to capital as well as chemical intensive systems, women bear disproportionate costs of both displacement and health hazards. When WTO destroys rural livelihoods, it is women who lose the most, as they carry the heavier work burden in food production, and because of gender discrimination get lower returns for their work.

Suggestions

How to overcome social exclusion has been the subject of a central concern for inclusive policy-makers. The development planning in India has focused on formulation of policies and programmes aimed at bringing the marginalised, deprived and poor sections of society into the mainstream. Indian society is characterised by multiple forms of exclusion associated with group identities like caste, ethnicity, gender etc. Therefore, any inclusive policy to overcome discrimination, deprivation, oppression and violence, must understand the various dimensions of exclusion in a stratified society like India.

The development experience of the last six decades and the capitalist mode of production, particularly the post-1990s, make some groups believe that the benefits of social and economic development have not been shared fairly by these excluded groups, or grabbed by the privileged within these groups. It is in this background that various new groups have begun to demand for the group specific policies to ensure an equitable, inclusive and sustainable path to development.

Given the general exclusionary character of Traditional Hindu Social Order (THSO), the core governing principle of the caste system is not inequality alone, but "graded inequality", which implies hierarchical-unequal entitlement of rights to various castes. With the entitlement to rights being hierarchically unequal, every caste (except the higher castes) suffers from a degree of denial and exclusion. But all suffering castes do not suffer equally. The castes located at the bottom of the caste hierarchy, such as the Dalits, suffered the most in the terms of violation of the Right to Food. By implication, inclusive food security policies will necessarily be different for different caste groups depending on the nature of discrimination and exclusion faced by them and their socio-cultural, economic and political situations. Further, the group-specific problems need to be addressed in the formulation of food-related programmes and other social welfare initiatives.

Also, special programmes are needed to improve the access to and control over income earning assets and skills and educational levels and consequently enhance the livelihood opportunities, particularly of Dalit women. In addition, the loopholes in the legal mechanisms have to be understood and the laws should be strictly implemented with effective redressal mechanism and strong political commitment.

There is imperative need to make the "invisible" visible in the national statistics and social research. Improving the ability to gather data disaggregated by caste, gender and other features associated with exclusion is essentially the foremost step for governments towards promoting inclusion. Such information is necessary for designing better programmes and for more effective targeting and programme evaluation (Buvinic, 2005). Recently, the government has commenced the Socio-Economic and Caste Census (SECC) 2011 through a comprehensive door to door enumeration across the country, yet it is still incomplete.

Conclusion

Since our society, economy, and polity are characterised by exclusion of various dimensions and magnitudes, it is imperative to develop a comprehensive inclusive policy to ensure the fair representation and meaningful participation of the hitherto excluded sections in the food security system. Thus, World Bank writes "Social inclusion aims to empower poor and marginalised people to take advantage of growing various global opportunities. It ensures that people have a say in decisions which affect their lives and that they enjoy equal access to markets, services and political, social and physical spaces." In this context, thus, food security system can be defined as where all people at all times have physical and economic access to adequate amounts of nutritious, safe, and culturally appropriate foods, which are produced in an environmentally sustainable and socially just manner, and that people are able to make informed decisions about their food choices.

References

1. Buvinic, Mayra. 2005. "Social Exclusion in Latin America", in Mayara Buvinic, *et al.* (eds.), *Social Inclusion and Economic Development in Latin America*, Inter-American Development Bank, Distributed by New York: John Hopkins University Press.
2. FAO 2009. *Declaration of the World Food Summit on Food Security.* Rome: Food and Agriculture Organisation of the United Nations. Retrieved 1 March 2015.
3. Haan, Arjan. 1997. "Poverty and Social Exclusion—A Comparison of Debates on Deprivation", *Working Paper No. 2*, Poverty Research Unit, Sussex University, Brighton, United Kingdom.
4. Sen, Amartya. 2000. "Social Exclusion—Concept, Application, and Scrutiny", *Working Paper*, Asian Development Bank, Manila, Philippines.
5. Special Rapporteur on the Right to Food 2008: para. 17; quoted in Special Rapporteur on the Right to Food 2012a.
6. Special Rapporteur on the Right to Food 2008: para. 67.
7. Study on "Establishing Links between Empowerment of Dalit Women and their Secure Land Rights", ActionAid India- April 2013.
8. Thorat, Sukhadeo, 2013. *Caste, Social Exclusion, and Poverty*, Gautam Printers, New Delhi, pp. 6-7.
9. Thorat, Sukhadeo and Kumar, Narender, 2008a. *B.R. Ambedkar: Perspectives on Social Exclusion and Inclusive Policies*, Oxford University Press, New Delhi.
10. United Nations Conference on Trade and Development. 1995. *UNCTAD Statistical Pocket Book*, p. 69.
11. http://www.unicef.org/india/children_2356.htm.
12. http://www.thehindu.com/news/national/malnourishment-declined-sharply-among-children-in-india-says-unicef/article6497025.ece.
13. http://www.ifpri.org/sites/default/files/publications/ghi14.pdf. p. 12.; International Food Policy Research Institute (IFPRI) (2014), *2014 Global Hunger Index*, Washington, DC: IFPRI.

14. http://timesofindia.indiatimes.com/india/Half-of-Indias-dalit-population-lives-in-4-states/articleshow/19827757.cms
15. http://fciweb.nic.in/app/webroot/upload/News/Report%20of%20the%20High%20Level%20Committee%20on%20Reorienting%20the%20Role%20and%20Restructuring%20of%20FCI_English_1.pdf.
16. http://www.dailypioneer.com/columnists/gupshup/caste-responsible-for-malnutrition.html
17. http://nutritionfordignity.org/malnutrition-among-dalits.html#tabs-b
18. http://planningcommission.nic.in/news/press_pov1903.pdf.
19. http://indianeconomy.columbia.edu/sites/default/files/working_papers/working_paper_2013-02-final.pdf.
20. http://indiacode.nic.in/acts-in-pdf/202013.pdf.
21. http://planningcommission.gov.in/aboutus/committee/wrkgrp12/agri/wg_Final_Report_sent.pdf.

12

Crime against Dalit Women

—*Parminder Kaur*

Abstract

Dalits are the most vulnerable section of Indian society. But Dalit women are in a worse position than Dalits in general in terms of sex ratio, wages, employment, occupation, assets, health, social mobility. Sexual exploitation of scheduled castes women is also high. The impunity enjoyed by both dominant caste community and the state officiates continues largely due to the insensitiveness and the continuous failure of the continuous failure of criminal justice administrative system. The higher degree of deprivation among Dalit women is reflected in other indicators of well being-under nutrition and health. Caste, class and gender discrimination prevents Dalit women from enjoying their basic human rights, particularly to dignity, equality and development. At last paper is concluded with some of the suggestive measures to curb the issue.

Keywords: *Dalit, women, deprivation, dignity, equality, development.*

Introduction

Sociologically defined social security means that government, which is the symbol and representative of society is responsible for fixing a minimum standard of living for all its citizens [G.H.D Cole]. Social security is an instrument for social transformation and progress and must be preserved, supported and developed such as. Furthermore, far from being an obstacle to economic progress, as is all too often said, social security organised on a firm and sound basis will promote such progress, since men and women benefit from increased security and are free from anxiety for tomorrow, they will naturally become more productive social security manifests the nature desire of communities for protection from life's problems from uncertainty from disease and deprivation...(its) the protection which social provides for its members through a series of public measures against the economic and social distress that otherwise would be caused by the stoppage or substantial reduction of earnings resulting from sickness, maternity, employment, injury, unemployment, invalidity, old age and health the provision of medical care and the provision of subsidies for families with children. [ILO,1998].

Social Security and Indian Women: Women be it from a higher caste or lower, from a rich class or poor, educated or uneducated, in home or outside home is not safe anywhere. In this patriarchal social set-up she has to rely on the pity of their opposite sex. She is harassed, tortured, threatened or are ill-treated. Centuries of maltreatment and oppression resulted in the total loss of their identity and individuality. Today, the greatest numbers of crimes are committed against them and these starts with its mere existence in the womb of her mother. Female foeticide, infanticide, dowry deaths, rape, molestation, acid attacks, sexual harassment etc. are some of the most common forms of violence against women persisting in all parts of the state. Women consist half of the human population, have been treated as weaker sex in all societies of the world. Women represent the most vulnerable section of the society in spite of their celebrated and priviledged position as referred to by the ancient Indian scriptures. Women are treated as unequal by society for genetic sin of her discriminated sex. The Government of India from time to time has moved legislations that concern social security of women. Although all its acts are gender sensitive, however, never dimensions have been provides to make women. The Hindu Marriage Act, 1956 reasons out the division of property in a Hindu joint family structure and the right of a women maternity leave for working women in various sectors during and after childbirth. In case of separation, the women are given the equal right to leads to a high degree of emotional security. We therefore, understand that various laws have been enacted by the governing bodies to provide inbuilt support system for providing social security to women. Also recently, the Supreme Court of India has given landmark judgment protecting women against Sexual Harassment in workplace.

Insecure Indian Dalit Women

Dalit women are the most vulnerable and face untouchability, discrimination and violence much more than their counterparts. The position of Dalit women in the society is reflected by the nature and number of atrocities committed on her. Being a Dalit women, abuse is used to remind her of her caste and keep her oppressed. On an average, about 1000 cases of sexual exploitation of Dalit women are reported annually and in the year 2001 alone, 1316 cases of rape was reported (NCRB, 2001). Not only their performance with regard to human development indicators are much lower compared to their counterpart from rest of the women, also the instances of atrocities are far higher than non-dalit women. Every 18 minutes a crime is committed against a Dalit. Every day three Dalit women at least are raped. Every day two dalits at least are murdered, 11 dalits are beaten or two dalit houses are burnt in India.

National crime statistics indicate an average of over 1,000 rape crimes against dalit women are reported annually, the highest of any social group.

The fundamental and core feature of India's social structure is its caste system. Even after sixty years of Independence, caste and the entrenched caste hierarchy still remain the symbol and essence of Indian society, differentiating it from other societies. This hierarchy, which accords some the privilege and the power to dominate over other castes, has been present in Indian history since time immemorial. The discrimination and deprivation arising out of the caste system and untouchability have affected them far more adversely than any other group in Indian society (Thorat, 2006). The dominant Brahminical cultural code accords the so-called lower castes a highly inferior position in society and has drained them of dignity and self. The lower castes or Dalit as they prefer to the upper castes who have forced them to remain within the confines of their lowly birth-based menial occupations [Narayan, 2006]. Gender-based discrimination is rooted in all aspects of social, economic and political existence. Women's subordination in all round- economic, social, religious, cultural, political and ideological, each of which reinforce to other one (Acharya, 2003). Scheduled castes women have continued to toil in the lowest rung of the social order in the Indian society. They have been relegated to lower status compared to men within scheduled castes groups themselves are placed at the lowest level in the society. The scheduled castes women therefore constitute the most distressed and poverty stricken section of the Hindu society. The scheduled castes women were perceived to be the essence of epitome of ignorance, illiteracy, poverty and pollution not long ago (Kalpana, 200l).

Eighty million Dalit women in India encounter the cumulative impact of discrimination in their day-to-day lives. This is a widespread phenomenon found in India, Pakistan, Bangladesh where caste-based discrimination subjects millions of Dalit women to inhumane living conditions and systematic human rights violations [www.idsn.org]. In India the Dalit constitute about 16.20 per cent of India's population in 2001 with less than half being women, which means that 80 million Dalit women face multiple forms of discrimination in this country alone. They are denied of their dignity, livelihood and social security and everything that is humane and just women continued to suffer discrimination based on "work and descent", which lead to social exclusion, physical separation, degrading of occupation like manual scavenging, violent appropriation and sexual control by men of the dominant caste, evident in systematic rape of Dalit women and perpetuation of forced prostitution in the name of religion through the Devadasi system. Crime against women have roots in the male dominated socio-economic, legal and political order. Assaults on women are often visibly associated with their social status, their communal, ethnic and caste identities (Mukherjee, Rustogi, Krishnaji, 2001). The state and non-state actors act with impunity, violating domestic and international human rights law. Violence against Dalit women reinforces caste norms wherein they are seen as available for all forms of violence, especially sexual violence. Dubey (2003) explored the relationship between caste and gender, it examined the way caste affects on women's lives and explores the role of maintaining it. He focused on the rules regarding the performance of caste-based labour and ultimately the gendered regulation of sexuality. According to India's National Commission for Women, "In the commission of offences against [Dalit] women the [dominant caste] offender try to establish their authority and humilate the community system subjecting their women to indecent and inhuman treatment." [NCW, 1996].

Forms and Frequency of Violence against Dalit Women

There are nine major forms of violence against Dalit women, six being violence in the general community- physical assault, verbal abuse, sexual exploitation, forced prostitution, kidnapping and abduction, and three being violence in the family- female feticide and infanticide, child sexual abuse and, domestic violence and rape in descending order.

The more frequent forms of violence that are perpetrated against the majority of Dalit women are verbal abuse, physical assault, sexual harassment and assault, domestic violence and rape in descending order. Rajawat (2005) has elaborated that there is a huge difference in the status of Dalit and non-dalit women. Dalit women are more vulnerable to exploitation. They are suffering from social, economic, political and sexual exploitation at the hands of high caste men as well as by their own caste men.

Child sexual abuse in terms of particular early child marriages and sexual relations with minor Dalit girls below the age of 16 years is also prominent.

Dalit women are also especially vulnerable to violence by private actors who commit violent offenses with impunity. As the majority of landless labourers, Dalit women came into greater contact with landlords and enforcement agencies than upper-caste women, rendering them more susceptible to abuse. Dalit Women also comprise the majority of victims of gang rapes in India. Human Rights watch reported that on April 5, 2003, for example, four upper-caste men abducted a fourteen year-old Dalit girl from her home just outside Jaipur (Rajasthan) and gang raped her over a period of three days. Upon her return to her village, the village's upper caste community threatened to remove her family if they reported the incident. Dalit women are also singled out for other indignities, like being paraded naked, even for petty disputes. These indignities have symbolic significance. For example, on November 3, 2005, a Dalit women in Kishanganj (Bihar) was paraded half-naked by a group of people who wanted to teach a lesson to her family for not relinquishing their claim to a piece of land. According to an another report by The Hindu on 10th October, a 19 year old pregnant Dalit women was allegedly abducted and raped by two youths in Kaithal village of Haryana district. Teltumbde (2012) has exposed the horrifying picture of Dalit women in Haryana state. In just one month, there have been 19 gang rapes of Dalit girls, one more gruesome than the other, in a single month. It has also provided the data to present the complete picture of Dalit women in Haryana. The number of rape cases where Dalit girls/women are the victims has consistently gone up in Haryana from 21 in 2007 to 56 in 2011.

Vulnerability to sexual violence also results from Dalit women's lower economic and social status, leading many Dalit women to turn to prostitution for their survival. Other forms of abuse result from superstitious beliefs, according to which Dalit women may be branded as a "witch", Dalit women are also punished for these mishaps, for example, by being made to eat facces and drink urine and by being beaten severely enough to result in death.

However, rather than ensuring Dalit women's development and in some instances, has directly participated in abusive acts. Cases, documented by India's National Commission for Women, by local and national non-governmental women's rights organisations, and by the press, reveal a pattern of impunity for attacks on Dalit women. However, due to uninterested, ignorance of proper procedure or their own caste biases, the police have failed to register or properly investigate many cases of attacks against women. In all cases of attacks on women documented by Human Right watch the accused state and private actors escaped punishment, in most cases, the attacks were neither investigated nor prosecuted.

Various Issues being Confronted by Indian Dalit Women

- **Police abuse for Dalit Women**

Dalit women are particularly vulnerable to sexual assault and rape by the police. As with sexual abuse of Dalit women by upper-caste men, the sexual abuse of Dalit women by the police is used as a tool to punish Dalit communities as a whole. Dalit women have also been arrested and raped in custody to punish their male relatives who are hiding from the police. Police also routinely sexually abuse Dalit women during police raids as a mean of exerting pressure on their male family members to surrender, give false evidence, retract their complaints, or silence their protests regarding police mistreatment. In many states of India, Dalit women have been beaten, arrested, and sometimes tortured during violent search and raid operations on Dalit villages. Medical personnel often collude in these cases by issuing false certificates that deny sexual assault or by including statements in the medical examination report that cast doubts on the credibility of the victim's complaint.

- **Inadequate development and protection of Dalit women**

The obligation to ensure thc development and protection of certain groups or individual belonging to them is especially relevant for those individuals within the Dalit community who face multiple forms within the Dalit community who face multiple discrimination. Dalit Women face multiple axes of discrimination, with the National Campaign a Dalit Human Rights asserting:

> Dalit women are often described as the oppressed, the violence and oppression on them being more complex, and manifold even compared to Dalit men. There is (an) inseparable relationship between caste status, occupation and discrimination. The Dalit women face triple discrimination because she is an untouchable, a poor and is a women.

- **Lack of Gender Equity**

Dalit women have unequal access to services, employment opportunities and justice mechanisms as compared to Dalit men. In relation to employment opportunities, Dalit women are allotted some of the most menial and arduous tasks and experience greater discrimination in the payment of wages than Dalit men. The employment opportunities of professional Dalit women may also be limited by discriminatory practices that deprive employment opportunities of professional Dalit women may also be limited by discriminatory practices that deprive facilities run by Dalit women of a customer or patient base or require accommodation of request of upper-caste community members. In relation to services, Dalit women have less access to education and health facilities ensuring that their literacy rate, and nutrition and health standards fall for bellow that of Dalit men and non-Dalit men and women . The number of Dalit women in decision-making position is also very low, and in some central services, Dalit women are not represented at all. Benefits of various development programmes for Dalits, such as distribution of land and other productive assets have essentially gave to Dalit males and have not improved the status of Dalit women. Investment in projects targeted to the development of Dalit women is also for lower as compared to those for men.

- **Forced Prostitution Devadasi System**

The practice of devadasi in which a girl, usually before reaching the age of puberty, is ceremoniously dedicated or married to a deity or to a temple, continues in several southern states including Andhra Pradesh and Karnataka. Literally meaning "female servant of God", devadasis usually belong to the Dalit community. Once dedicated, the girl is unable to marry, forced to become a prostitute for upper caste community members, and eventually auction into an urban brothel. The age old practice continues to legitimise the sexual violence and discrimination that have come to characterise the intersection between caste and gender.

While India has adopted measures to abolish the practice and "rehabilitate" devadasis, these efforts have been largely unsuccessful. The societal perception of devadasis as women who are sexually available to men makes it more difficult for devadasis to approach the police with complaints of sexual violence. Moreover, the police themselves have been known to exploit devadasis. President of National Alliance of Women Dr Ruth Manorma (2013) called Devdasi system 'an organised crime against dalit women'. Religion, illiteracy, poverty and superstitions have played a major role in making the Devadasi system an organised crime against dalit women.

Quoting the report on National Commission of Women, Manorma said, "Five lakh girls who are dedicated to temples in Maharashtra – Karnataka borders are all from Dalit communities. The report said, she said, also says that the girls dedicated to temples, are unable to marry and forced to become prostitutes for upper caste members in villages and many eventually are pushed to urban brothels." Though Devdasi system declared illegal by the state government in 1982, the practice is still prevalent in many parts of India.

The joint women programmes for the National Commission of Women has found that devadasis rehabilitation programmes neither address the whole range of problems faced by devadasis, nor target the population they were intended to assist. Further, devadasis find it difficult to earn a livelihood outside the systems because the rehabilitation programmes do not provide adequate means of livelihood and skill development, and because financial assistance is often in the form of a loan which must be repaid. Most devadasis also lack access to a residential house, healthcare, or educational facilities for their children.

- **Failure to prosecute rape cases of Dalit women**

Dalit women, occupying the bottom of both the caste and gender hierarchies, are both uniquely susceptible to violence and particularly vulnerable to the infringements of their right to equal treatment before organs administering justice. Cases documented by the National Commission for Women, Human Rights Watch, local and national women's rights organisations, and the press, overwhelmingly demonstrate a systematic pattern of impunity in attacks on Dalit women. Dalit women are more likely to suffer violence and especially sexual violence, and are least likely to get redress in the courts. They are, in a sense, doubly victimised- first at the hands of their attackers, and then at the hands of judicial system that fails to offer them protection and address.

A Dalit woman who is a survivor of rape will face significant obstacles in bringing her case to the attention of the police and in turn the courts. She will likely face ostracism from her community and family, and she will have difficulty gaining access to the justice system. Further, even if a woman is able to surmount all these obstacles and convince the police to lodge an initial complaint called the First Information Report, she will face new roadblocks at every step of the way. A Dalit woman is likely to be confronted with any of the following impediments to the successful prosecution of her case. Unsympathetic doctors and police officers, difficulty in finding witnesses who are bribed or pressured by the (usually more powerful) attackers, as well as having her case misfiled under more lenient sections of the Indian Penal Code or not being simultaneously filed under the Prevention of Atrocities Act. The combined effect of these hurdles is such that, even if her case is properly investigated a Dalit women will likely find that her attack have been granted impunity.

In fact, statistics from the National Crime Records Bureau demonstrate, conviction in rape cases is not only extremely rare, but becoming rarer- out of the total rape cases in which trial were completed between 1990-1993, in 1990, 41.5 per cent ended in conviction; the figure dropped to 34.2 per cent in 1991 and to 33.8 per cent in 1993. The failing of the prosecutorial claim are further evident in the disproportionately large backlog of rape cases (on an average, 80 per cent of rape cases remained pending for trial in 1994) and the comparatively low levels of conviction of the crime of rape as compared with less serious crimes of burglary and theft.

Certain stokes have provided some compensation to Dalit rape victims. As per the 2002-2003 Annual report on the prevention of atrocities act, during the year 2002-2003, the state government of Madhya Pradesh incurred an expenditure of Rs 28.5 lacks for providing relief to rape victims. While the state of Maharashtra provided financial assistance in the amount of Rs 19.68 lacks. It should be noted that the prosecutorial failure to investigate, file and pursue cases involving rape against Dalit women has an injurious effect not just on the individual woman harmed in each instance of sexual violence but more broadly, on women and Dalit communities in general- prosecutorial failures empower potential perpetrators by signalling that claims against Dalit women will be rewarded with impunity and also further disembowels marginalised communities by eroding their trust in the judiciary. Finally, prosecutorial failures in the context of cases involving rape against Dalit women encourage the use of rape as a tool to punish and silence Dalit communities.

Recommendations

No doubt, government has done a lot to improve the status of scheduled castes and scheduled castes women. But still they are (Dalit women) are far away from the path of progress without any kind of discrimination. Some of the suggestions are given below for consideration to curb the issue and to improve the status of Dalit women.

- Evolve a National Labour Policy for the unorganised sector, and extend social security especially agricultural labour where the majority of Dalit women are concentrated, to protect worker's rights.

- Ensure Dalit women equal access without caste or gender discrimination to healthcare and social security services.
- Ensure that the fundamental rights of Dalit women are protected in all situations, and that swift measures are taken to bring justice to Dalit women whose rights have been violated as per the law.
- Disaggregate all criminal, economic, social and political data on the ground of gender and caste.
- Evolve and implement a comprehensive strategy to address impunity and ensure criminal justice for Dalit women.
- Provide support to establish informal organisations for Dalit women to freely discuss the social, domestic and development issues in their own community and to strengthen leadership within local governance structures.
- Mandate proportional representation of Dalit women elected into parliaments, legislatures and local governance system, including equal distribution of other minority groups, such as Joginis/Badis (India/ Nepal) irrespective of their faith, and to provide adequate budget allocations in this regard.
- Eradicate the practice of manual scavenging and the jogini system and enforce rehabilitation policies and programmes for their alternative livelihood and sustenance.

Implement Laws that Prohibit Bonded or Forced Labour

- Allocate sufficient budget for full primary and secondary level education of all Dalit girls, including funds for staff in schools and infrastructures, and vocational institutions.
- Ensure reduction of pre-natal mortality, infant mortality among Dalit women on a time-bound basis.
- Provide assistance to launch national campaign of caste sensitisation and elimination of caste, class and gender discrimination.

References

1. Acharya Sangmitra. 2002. Healthcare utilisation in rural north India a case of Nirpura district Meerut, study undertaken as part of the monitoring health sector project, centre of social medicine and community health and European

Union project. Unpublished report, Centre of social medicine and community health, School of Social Sciences, JNU, New Delhi.

2. Chandan Mukerjee, Preet Rustagi, Krishnaji, 2001. 'Crime against Women in India, An Analysis of Official Statistics', *Economic and Political Weekly*, Vol.36, No. 43.
3. Human Rights Watch, World Report, 2003. Institute for Human Development, New Delhi.
4. International Labour Organisation.1998. World Employment Report, 1997-98, Geneva (1998a) Decent work, Geneva.
5. Mamta Rajawat, 2005. *Dalit women issues and perspectives*. Anmol Publication Pvt. Ltd, New Delhi.
6. Michael, S.M., 2001. *Dalits in modern India vision and values*. Vistar Publication, New Delhi.
7. National Commission for Women,1996 Women of Weaker Section: Socio-Economic Development of Scheduled Caste Women, New Delhi.
8. S. Dev, V Gayathri, R.P. Mamgain, 2002. Social and economic insecurity in India.
9. Thorat SK and Mahamallik and S Venkatesan., 2006. 'Human Poverty and Socially Disadvantages', Resource Centre, New Delhi.
10. Teltumbde Anand, 2012. '*Haryana's Rapist Regime*', November 3.
11. The Hindu. 2012, October 11.
12. The Indian Express, August 25th, 2013 'An organised crime against Dalit women' IDSN briefing paper: Dalit women, www.idsn.org/caste-discrimination/women key issues/dalit women

Website Links

www.google.com

www.idsn.org

www.populationcommission.nic.in

www.ncrb.nic.in

13

Development Projects at Odisha's Coast and the Silent Spiriting away of Fishing Communities

—***Dr Sunakar Patra***

Abstract

The State's new strategy of ensuring development through the philosophy of liberalisation, privatisation and globlisation seems to have counter-productive results. The fact is that most of the development projects and policies for ports, industrialisation, mining, trade, and transport have deleterious effects on the marginalised and deprived sections. These policies have not only failed to benefit them, but have also increasingly threatened their source of livelihood. In recent times, developmental activities at the 478 kilometers long coast of Odisha has gathered momentum and fishing communities have been impoverished. Such attitude of the State to undermine the significance of life, livelihood and social capital has been the main agenda of debate at different public forums. Thus, the present study attempts to analyse and assess the impacts of such projects upon the livelihood and social capital of fishermen communities of Odisha's shoreline.

Keywords: *development, liberalisation, privatisation, globalisation, fishermen communities.*

Introduction

There is no common definition of what constitutes a coastal region. Most are based on an area within 60 to 200 kilometres of the shoreline and may include coastal floodplains, coastal forests called mangroves, marshes, and tide flats (coastal areas affected by the rise and fall of the tide), as well as beaches, dunes, and coral reefs. The term "coastal regions" also covers marine fisheries because the bulk of the world's marine fish harvest is caught or reared in coastal waters. Odisha is bestowed with a coast line of 480 kilometres which stretches from the river Subernarekha mouth in Balasore district in the north to Bahuda muhan (mouth) in Ganjam district in the south. There are six maritime districts: Balasore (80 km), Bhadrak (50 km), and Kendrapara (68 km), Jagatsinghpur (67 km), Puri (155 km) and Ganjam (60 km), with Puri district covering more than a third of the coastline. These six districts cover 14.5 per cent of the total land area in the state, but nearly 30 per cent of the population (28.35 per cent) in the state resides in the coastal districts, with an average population density more than twice that of the state. The coastal region of the state is quite healthy and progressive so far as the development scenario is concerned. In year 2009 the Government of Odisha signed 14 Memorandum of Understandings (MoUs) for setting up of new ports along its long sea coast during the port conclave organised by the Confederation of Indian Industry (CII), Odisha Chapter. The state government marched ahead with its planning amidst anti-port protests by several human right activists and environment protection activists and vulnerable commons. Priority of the Government of Odisha since last two decades has been to bring quick development through optimum utilisation of its mineral resources and long coast line and thus building of new ports through private investment is a part of the larger context.

Marine Fishermen

Odisha has a total of 220 marine fishing villages. Most of the fishermen households living in these marine villages belong to Scheduled Caste, categories. All the fishermen households can be divided into two broad groups i.e. Odia fishermen and migrant fishermen from the neighbouring Andhra Pradesh and West Bengal. There are for about 335208 fishermen members from 52576 fishermen households live and profess fishing activities in the marine villages at the Odisha's shoreline. Most of the people in these villages live on their own land while there are some households who have built houses by encroaching upon the unused marine land of the government.

Table 12.1: District wise Fisher Population of Odisha's shoreline

Districts	*No. of Households*	*Male*	*Female*	*Total*
Balasore	14422	50566	46527	97123
Bhadrak	5720	17188	13599	30787
Kendrapara	7844	22613	17106	39979
Jagatsinghpur	7402	23336	20426	43762
Puri	10949	38838	34160	72998
Ganjam	6595	25306	25543	50829
Total	**52576**	**177847**	**157561**	**335208**

Source: Odisha Traditional Fish Workers Union, Samudram and Action Aid.

For the fishermen people, sea beach is the cheapest and most effective fish-drying yard, stationing and repair of boats. It is also used as a playground, an open-sky festival area, a people's laboratory to observe their sea and study its nature. In fact, beaches are integral to the existence of the fishermen. The harsh reality is that private land owned by fishermen as well as the land of government (the land encroached by some fishermen households and unused open beaches) are sold off to private enterprises, small, medium and more often large. Port developers with affinity for land are fast turning into the worst adversaries of fisher folk, directly and indirectly capturing their lands, and beaches. The customary rights of traditional fisher people over the natural Common Property Resources is being squeezed without considering its effect on their livelihoods. Moreover, inaction of government machinery to implement pro-people policies for the development programmes and sustainable marine resources development has been jeopardised.

Table 12.2: Location of Marine Fisher Villages

Districts	*Remote*	*Rural*	*Urban*	*Total*
Balasore	12	66	0	78
Bhadrak	2	19	3	24
Kendrapara	5	17	0	22
Jagatsinghpur	9	32	2	43
Puri	1	24	3	28
Ganjam	1	23	1	25
Total	**30**	**181**	**9**	**220**

Source: Odisha Traditional Fish Workers Union, Samudram and Action Aid.

Development Script

To extract minerals from beneath the mother earth and to establish mineral-based industries has intensified in the mineral-rich hinterland of Odisha since last two decades. Scheduled Tribes, Scheduled Castes and other marginal communities are being uprooted from their habitat, livelihood resources taken away, forests and water bodies destroyed. It is worrisome that the same development script has been extended to the coastal region of the state. It is argued by the so called development planners that it would bring huge investment and help in building a vibrant and prosperous Odisha. Thus, development of new ports along the 478 kilometres shoreline of the state stands in support of the logic of a developmental paradigm that has been rolled on by the development planners since the last two decades. No thought is being given to the dark sides of such development projects. No doubt, such ill-thought out development script would result in colossal loss to coastal ecology and coastal communities. In coastal Odisha, the traditional fisher people are now restrained to enter into the sea and use beach for testing their net and boat due to some unwanted restriction for promotion of tourism, ports, industrial activities etc. Forcible acquisition of public as well as private land along the Coast of Odisha has resulted in large scale displacement of fishermen, with many documented cases of inadequate or no compensation The irony is that most of these ports are being handed over to industrial houses and mining mafia who have proven track record of uprooting poor tribes and other marginal sections in the mineral-rich Odisha's hinterland.

Table 12.3: Proposed/MoUs Signed for Ports in Odisha

Sr. No	*Name of Port*	*District*	*Promoter/ Company*	*Status*
1.	Astaranga Port	Puri	Navayug, Hyderabad	
2.	Bahabalpur	Balasore	IL & FS Maritime Company	
3.	Bahuda Mouth	Ganjam	Good Earth, Chennai	
4.	Baliharchandi Port	Puri	Puri Ports Ltd.	
5.	Barunei Muhan	Kendrapara	Proposed	
6.	Chandipur	Balasore	Proposed	
7.	Chudamani	Bhadrak	Essel Mining/ Aditya Birla	
8.	Dhamara	Bhadrak	Adani/TISCO/L&T	Operated
9.	Gopalpur	Ganjam	Odisha Stevedores Ltd.	Ongoing
10.	Inchudi	Balasore	Proposed	

(*Contd*...)

11.	Jatadhari-POSCO	Jagatsinghpur	POSCO, South Korea
12.	Kirtania Port	Balasore	Creative Ports, Chennai
13.	Palpur	Ganjam	Proposed
14.	Talsari-Ichitrapur	Balasore	Jindal Infrastructure Ltd.

Source: Patra, J, Global Assessment Report on Disaster Risk Reduction

Displacement and Impoverishment

Development of ports along the shoreline of Odisha would cause eviction of well settled human settlements. The average population density of coastal districts of the state is quite higher than the national average. The coastal region is quite prosperous in terms of agriculture, industry and also on several other parameters. Establishment of several ports would destroy the traditional livelihood sources of coastal communities. But it is a matter of tragedy that the coming of ports would wipe out the livelihood of lakhs of fishing communities who depend upon the sea shore for fishing activities. Traditionally there has been a fishing hamlet at every two kilometers of Odisha's coast, but such a galloping capital inflow in to coastal infrastructure development will see a port at every 33 kilometers. It is going to produce serious implications over these fishing hamlets and will deprive these communities of beaches on which their lives and livelihood depend (Shidhar, A). Overall, there would be a forcible shift in livelihood resources for which these traditional resource dependent communities are not at all acquainted and trained. The poor and half-hearted track record of resettlement and rehabilitation measures offered by the state of Odisha to the victims of earlier evictions clearly hints at the rehabilitation bounty in its coffer, for the victims of upcoming ports.

Ecological Vulnerabilities

The coastline of Odisha is bestowed with diverse eco-system, which not only maintains natural balance but also provide livelihood and protection to the coastal human settlements. This region is enriched with typical type of mangroves and other vegetation. This diverse vegetation plays a significant role in sediment repository, protection of shoreline from erosion and works as a buffer zone against sea storm surges. It is argued by the environment scientists and meteorologists that the impact of cyclones (Super cyclone of 29th Oct. 1999, Phailin of 12th Oct. 2013 and Hudhud of 12th Oct. 2014) of Odisha were severe due to the destruction of vegetation for different kinds of developmental purposes. The proposed ports would require large scale cutting down of the existing vegetation and thus leading towards furious natural calamities.

Ports are a man-made hazard to natural resources. Port development creates a wide range of impacts on local environments through dredging, construction work, landfills, discharges from ships and waterfront industries, cargo operations, and other port-related activities. The potential adverse effects of port development include water pollution, contamination of bottom sediments, loss of bottom habitat, damage to marine ecology and fisheries, beach erosion, current pattern changes, waste disposal, oil leakage and spillage, hazardous material emissions, air pollution, noise, vibration, light and visual pollution.

River mouths of Baitarani, Bramhani, Devi and Rusikulya are the famous breeding and nesting groundings of the endangered Olive Ridley sea turtles. The irony is that some of the ports have been proposed on the mouth of the rivers and others are not far away from the nesting and breeding zones of the rare turtles. Construction of ports adjacent to this reptile habitat would be a threat to their existence. Every year more than two lakh turtles come to the mouth of these rivers for mating and nesting. Movement of cargo ships from and to these ports would create inconvenience for this globally significant but endangered turtles. Spillage of oil from the ships would pollute the coastal water. Besides, heavy light and loud sound of the ports would add to the problems and ultimately this family of reptiles is more likely to be extinct in a few years.

While the geographical positioning of the state along the Bay of Bengal has many economic advantages, it also puts the entire state and its population at risk to various hydro-meteorological hazards, mostly flood and cyclone. The coastline is undergoing a major change due to port development, with unknown cumulative impacts. The cyclone, the tsunami, sea level rise predictions, all exposes varying vulnerabilities of coastal inhabitants. But the present-day loopholes in law and the investment dreams encased in official MoUs represent ongoing tragedies – the silent spiriting away of commons, property and natural resources.

Some of the major rivers like Mahanadi, Subarnarekha, Brahmani, Baitarani, Vansadhara and Rushikulya flows through the state before draining out in to the Bay of Bengal and hence a large landmass, most of which is used for agriculture, and the population dependent on it for their livelihoods are at constant danger. Similarly, the entire coastal stretch of Odisha has been classified as Very High Damage Risk Zone to Wind and Cyclone Hazard. Construction of ports on the river mouths would multiply the existing problems through the closing of river mouths and water lodging in the coastal delta during monsoon period.

Conclusion

The upcoming of development projects along the Odisha's coast may generate some revenue for the state but socio-ecological concerns would overweight the benefits. Such kind of projects would put severe impacts upon vulnerable fishing communities and coastal ecology while a handful of corporate houses make merry.

References

1. Chakravarty, A., 2011. "Bichitrapur and Kirtania ports will endanger Olive Ridleys", retrieved from http://www.downtoearth.org.in
2. Creel, L., 2003. "Ripple Effects: Population and Coastal Regions", retrieved from http://www.prb.org
3. Das, N., 2008. "Sea level rise and Inundation of Coastal Orissa", retrieved from http://www.blog.siliconindia.com
4. Handbook on Fishery Statics, Government of Odisha (various years).
5. Mahapatra, B., 2013. "Orissa may have to lose its turtle mass nesting grounds for Ports", retrived from http://www.hotnhitnews.com
6. Patra, J., 2013. "Coasts, Ports and Communities: The Emerging Dynamics of Investment-Risk Interactions in Odisha, India, Background Paper prepared for the Global Assessment Report on Disaster Risk Reduction 2013, retrieved from http://www.preventionweb.net
7. Patra, Sunakar, 2010. "The POSCO Project in Coastal Orissa: A Disaster in Making?", Research Link-81, Vol. IX (10), Dec-2010.
8. Ranjana and Nigam, 2012. "Ports: The New Frontiers in the Development War In Odisha", retrieved from http://www.countercurrents.org
9. Roy, S., 2010. "Development State and People's Struggle for land Rights", Mainstream, Vol. XLVIII, No. 29, July.
10. Sridhar, A., 2011. "Harbouring trouble: The impact of ports on commons", retrieved from http://www.infochangeindia.org

14

IT and Gender from Social Exclusion to Social Inclusion

—*Dr Ranjay Vardhan*

Abstract

Women have been traditionally socially excluded from development process and they could not reap the benefit of development due to patriarchal attitude and prevalent orthodoxies. This paper based on primary data is an attempt to study the impact of ICT on women. The paper will conclude that the digital divide that existed in the usage of ICT by gender is minimising between male and female users. Women are being empowered with the spread and usage of as ICT as it is enabling them in education, jobs, income, improvement in family and social status, etc. IT is helping women from social exclusion to social inclusion especially in urban areas. The paper recommends that there is need to popularise IT usage in rural as well as tribal areas so that benefits can reach to all sections of women.

Keywords: *women, ICT, education, rural area, tribal area, empowered.*

Introduction

Women have been traditionally socially excluded from development process and they could not reap the benefit of development due to patriarchal attitude and prevalent orthodoxies. However, among other factors, Information Technology has a deep impact on the society and has been playing an important role in bringing social change. Traditional technologies continue to be important for large numbers of people around the world, particularly in rural areas. However, new technologies have a vast potential for empowerment which needs to be fully exploited. Over the past decade, there has been a growing understanding that these technologies can be powerful instruments for advancing economic and social development through the creation of new types of economic activity, employment opportunities, improvements in healthcare delivery and other services, and the enhancement of networking, participation and advocacy within society. IT revolution has taken its roots in India creating a heavy demand for information professional in the country. Women have not been traditionally associated with technology and are attributed a passive attitude to it. Reality shows despite the existence of persistent barriers that may hinder access to and use of these new technologies by women, the women are adopting new technologies and are becoming empowered. There has been a change in the socialisation patterns, unequal access to education and training and is opening up new avenues for women. Women are being empowered with the spread and usage of as ICT as it is enabling them in education, jobs, income, improvement in family and social status, etc. IT is helping women from social exclusion to social inclusion especially in urban areas. This paper based on primary data is an attempt to study the impact of ICT on women and how IT is helping women from social exclusion to social inclusion.

Information and Communication Technologies (ICTs) comprise a complex and heterogeneous set of goods, applications and services used to produce, process, distribute and transform information. ICT does not mean the Internet alone; it also includes radio, wireless phone, computer connected (or not) to the Internet, electronic brail writer, and a wide variety of software, hardware or tools such as operating systems, databases, e-mails or office productivity applications, networks, etc. They are not to be used instead of other tools, but complement what exists to achieve a goal, be it better food distribution or health care access, or e-learning, entertainment, etc. In today's world, the most prevalent ICT device is the mobile phone, with almost 3.5 Billion users around the world. Information and communication technologies (ICTs) permeate every aspect of our lives; from community radios in the most rural parts of the globe to cellular phones in the hands of women and men in every community on earth, to computers in almost every medium to large organisation. The advancement of ICTs has brought new opportunities for both knowledge sharing and knowledge gathering for both women and men. To the extent that the global community can reach to unconnected individuals, families, and populations to better understand their needs and challenges, ICTs can provide unlimited opportunities for economic development and social engagement through new innovative thinking and tools.

Traditional technologies continue to be important for large numbers of people around the world, particularly in rural areas. However, new technologies have a vast potential for empowerment which needs to be fully exploited. Over the past decade, there has been a growing understanding that these technologies can be powerful instruments for advancing economic and social development through the creation of new types of economic activity, employment opportunities, improvements in healthcare delivery and other services, and the enhancement of networking, participation and advocacy within society. ICT also have the potential to improve interaction between governments and citizens, fostering transparency and accountability in governance. IT applications have brought a big change in the total scenario of information storage, access and dissemination. Advancement of telecommunication and networking technologies has facilitated faster methods of information access and delivery. The developments of Internet and World Wide Web have made a big impact on whole of the society. It has truly shrunk the world into a global village.

However, despite such advances, ICT usage is not neutral to gender. The dramatic positive changes brought in by these information and communication technologies (ICTs) have not touched all of humanity. Existing power relations in society determine the enjoyment of benefits from ICTs; hence these technologies are not gender neutral. Access to new ICTs is still a faraway reality for the vast majority of people. The countries of the South, particularly rural populations, have to a significant extent been left out of the information revolution, given the absence of basic infrastructure, high costs of ICT deployment, unfamiliarity with ICTs, dominance of the English language in Internet content and indeed – lack of demonstrated benefit from ICTs to address ground-level development challenges. These barriers pose even greater problems for women, who are more likely to: be illiterate; not know English; and lack of opportunities for training in computer skills.

Domestic responsibilities, cultural restrictions on mobility, lesser economic power as well as lack of relevance of content to their lives, further marginalise them from the information sector. Inequality between men and women subsists in that respect and is significantly high in the less developed countries, which should be taken into account by all analyses of development possibilities. Such differences are barriers that widen the already existing gap. Women have not been traditionally associated with technology and are attributed a passive attitude to it. Reality shows the existence of persistent barriers that may hinder access to and use of these new technologies by women. Such obstacles have to do with socialisation patterns, unequal access to education and training - that are usually less technology-oriented and frequently link up men's image to ICTs.

Illiteracy and low language training levels are obvious barriers for access to information. A predominance of contents in English is a great hurdle for Hindi/Regional language-speaking women. Overcoming such obstacles calls for the development of applications like multilingual databases and graphic interfaces for illiterate women, and automatic translation programmes. Another obstacle faced by women on entering the world of ICTs is their more limited access to financial resources for covering the costs of the equipment required. Technological changes affect the quantity and quality of female work. The benefits afforded by the new technologies to employment come hand in hand with higher health and environmental costs. The employment problems of women that work with these technologies have more to do with their contractual terms, heavier workloads, wages, health and security. Some international organisations and civil society groups are engaging with issues that concern the democratisation of the ICT arena - from the digital divide and the right to communicate, to cultural diversity and intellectual property rights. Gender equality advocates have also been pushing for addressing the gender dimensions of the information society: integrating gender perspectives in national ICT policies and strategies, providing content relevant to women, promoting women's economic participation in the information economy, and regulating violence against women and children connected to pornography on the Internet.

Theoretical Background

A Theoretical Background Mainstream view of technology often take it to be a technical tool that society can use, but not something that in itself is influenced by society. They also ignore the differential influences of technology on the various sections of society. As such, technology is seen to be gender neutral. However, feminist scholarship has pointed to women's exclusion from science and also from the creation, design and use of technology. The more recent critiques point to the dangers of putting technology ahead of people and of an uncritical acceptance of modern technology as something that works everywhere and provides immediate solutions to development challenges. The gendered approach argues that technology is not neutral, but depends on culture and women's exclusion from technology is due to the gender division of labour. Marxist approach views technology as reflecting male power as well as capitalist domination. Eco-feminist approach shows that technology, like science, is part of the masculine project of the domination and control of women and nature. It gives value to "feminine" knowledge and skills arising from women's biology and presumed closeness to nature. The relationship between gender and technology is seen as the core issue.

Studies indicate digital divide in the use of ICT across the world. The digital divide is not simply an issue of access, but also of obstacles to Internet use. Even once the difficulty of access to ICT is achieved; gendered social, cultural and financial factors impede women's use of information technologies. For women, gendered roles and culture limit both their access and use of ICT especially the internet. Three large North American national surveys concluded that "women's domestic responsibilities, particularly raising children, limit the use they make of internet (Kennedy, Wellman, Clement, 2003). Women's multiple roles limit the time they have available to access and use ICT. This is compounded in developing countries like India where home access to ICT is comparatively less and women must travel to access that too at public places. They have limited time at disposal and the limitations on their time also restrict their investment in development of skills necessary for using ICT effectively. Apart from location and income, language is another determinant of the digital divide. The predominance of English on the Internet is a barrier for most users globally.

Speakers of non-European and indigenous languages – including a large proportion of women – tend to be left out of the information loop. Even among the educated, proficiency in the dominant European language of a region may not be such that the user feels comfortable in using the Internet for training or involvement in List Serves (Huyer and Mitter, 2003).

The gender divide within the digital divide can be seen in the lower numbers of women users of ICTs compared to men. One illustration of this is the number of women Internet users. The majority of the world's women do not use the Internet. They are excluded from the World Wide Web. The digital divide within countries broadly reflects the gender divide. Women are in the minority of users in almost all developed and developing countries. The trend for differentiation in use starts early, as seen in the United States where boys are five times more likely than girls to use home computers and parents spend twice as much on ICT products for their sons as they do for their daughters (UNDP, 1999: 62). It is extremely difficult to get data on use by gender by country for developing countries (Hafkin and Taggart, 2001).

In India, in the well known "hole in the wall" experiment it is shown that the aggressiveness of the boys pushed away girls from using the computers (Hafkin and Taggart, 2001). Further, in India there is difference in the literacy levels of males and females. Looking at the literacy data, it is expected that there is likely to be difference in the use of ICT by gender. The mobility of women (both in the sense of access to transport and ability to leave the home) is also more limited than that of men. In Seelampur and Sitakund in India, where there are community ICT training centres, Muslim women cannot travel or use public spaces without socially acceptable reasons, and girls from the community are not allowed to move unaccompanied outside the confines of the city centre (Slater and Tacchi, 2004). A major cultural variable that affects women's ability to go to information centres or cyber cafes is the norm governing men and women gathering in public places. Frequently, they are located in places that women may not be comfortable frequenting or culturally inappropriate for them to visit. The tendency of young men in internet public access points to view pornography deters many young women for frequenting such sites. In India and many other places as well the internet café manager is usually male who frequently surfs pornographic content; he helps his friends in doing so, and the café serves as a hangout for them (Gurumurthy, 2004). Class and education levels are also concerns that keep women away from public access ICT centres. Particularly in India, the poorest often fear that ICT and ICT centres are not places for people like them for reasons of caste, illiteracy and gender. They often assume that these centres are only for educated people.

The confluence of culture and computers can also constrain women from accessing and using ICT when the traditional cultures view women and computers negatively or put an economic burden on their families. This is a situation that young Muslim women in Seelampur have confronted. Girls in Seelampur have been rejected in the process of spouse selection in the arranged marriages on the ground that they know computers and so will not adjust in the marital family. Similar instances have also come to light about the boy's kin making greater demands from the girls' family if she is computer literate (Maindiratta and Maindiratta, 2004). There is a general perception that the use of computers and Internet are not easy for most women and technophobia is common, particularly among poor, rural women with little education. Women are often disinterested in technologies, until they see how ICT are useful to them. However, marital status can be a factor in the use of ICT as in a study "Single Women: A Study of Spinsters", done in Chandigarh city Vardhan (2008) found that single women are techno savvy women and are enjoying Electronic Salad of I-Pods, DVDs, Computers, Mobiles, Laptops, MP3 payers and other things. They are frequent users of the internet and had no inhibitions on its use.

Methodology

The present study has been conducted in different cities two each in Punjab and Haryana and the city Chandigarh itself which is fast emerging as a new IT destination with setting up of IT Park and coming of big IT companies in the city. The data was collected through structured interview schedule from randomly selected sample of 150 males and 150 females in the age group of 18-35 years selecting 30 males and 30 females each from Chandigarh, Yamunanagar, Kurukshetra, Patiala and Ludhiana which were purposively selected. Before the preparation of an Interview Schedule, area was visited and attempt was made to talk to people in a natural and free environment. Everything that was heard or observed was recorded. This field experience helped in constructing the interview schedule. Review of literature also helped in identifying the variables concerning Information Technology. An interview schedule was made to seek information with regard to these variables. This interview schedule was administered to the respondents in the areas covered in the study. The respondents were interviewed at their place of residence, work and educational institutions. The respondents were even asked to demonstrate their practical knowledge on laptop which was fully utilised for the study.

Findings

The analyses of socio-economic and demographic characteristics of the respondents show significant variations. Though the percentage of respondents based on gender was same but differences were observed in other characteristics. Seventy three per cent of male respondents were below 26 years of age whereas 64 per cent female respondents belonged to these age groups. As compared to females, higher percentage of males were having higher education as 58 per cent males were graduates and above whereas 43 per cent of females were graduates and above. Income-wise distribution of the respondents shows that large majority of respondents belonged to middle income categories. Majority of respondents were staying in nuclear families and belonged to upper caste and had the knowledge of computers. There were gender gaps in knowledge of computers as compared to 74 per cent of males, 53 per cent females had the knowledge of computers which is almost similar to gender gap in literacy in these areas. More than two third of male respondents in upper caste had knowledge of computers whereas only half of the female respondents in upper caste category had knowledge of computers. In middle and lower caste category, the proportion of female respondents was comparatively higher as compared to male respondents. The data reveal that majority of respondents have formal training in computers which helped them in their education, employment and other activities. Higher percentage of males had formal training in computers which indicate gender divide in the usage of computers and attitudes of the family towards computer education of boys and girls. The data reveal that the respondents were using computers for various purposes. Both males and females were using it more for getting information, making projects and internet, the difference was in their percentage which favoured males in these categories. Higher percentage of females was using it for pass time as compared to males. As compared to 60 per cent of males, only 31 per cent of females were using Internet. This analysis show a deep divide in gender-wise usage of Internet. Thirty per cent of males were spending per month Rs 250 and more on Internet whereas only 10 per cent of female respondents were spending equivalent amount. The data show significant differences in the reaction of the family towards computer/internet use by gender as compared to two-third of the male respondents, only one-third of the female respondents reported approval by their family.

The data revealed that two-third of respondents said that males can better use computers. Comparatively higher percentage of male respondents (57 per cent) reported help by computers in their life as compared to female respondents. Majority of respondents had an e-mail account but male respondents having e-mail account was higher as compared to female respondents. The data show that large majority of the respondents reported that ICT is essential and it should be made compulsory for all as it is simple and greatly helps in life. It not only increases employability but also brings a change in outlook of the individuals and instills confidence in them. The data show that majority of the respondents were interested in ICT training by government. However, as compared to 50 per cent of females, 63 per cent of males showed interest in training by government. The data collected indicate that internet is being used for various purposes in these cities. However, there exists a digital divide if the data is analysed on the basis of gender and ICT as wide disparity exists among the male and female users. Income was a significant factor in the usage of internet and so was the factor of accessibility of internet at home. The users used internet for content, communication and services but communication was the highest usage and content was the lowest usage.

Discussion

The low and declining proportion of women in computing has been widely noticed and much lamented (Cohoon and Aspray, 2006;

OECD 2007; Kirkup *et al.*, 2010; Misa, 2010). The entry of women into ICT education and employment has not only stalled, but has gone into reverse, in the sense that their representation in certain areas of computing education and computing work has begun to decrease in some countries. In the discussion of ICT and gender, it must be remembered that women have multiple identities – for example, of class, ethnicity, caste, race, age – and that these interplay with gender to define women's access to technology. Strategies for addressing unequal gender relations will therefore need to hinge on an understanding of the complex intersections of gender and other social identities. For instance, while it may not be difficult for an upper class, urban woman to have easy access to the Internet, it may be unthinkable in feudal rural contexts for a poor, low-caste man to access such facility. While such realities of particular contexts are at the heart of the relationship between gender and technology, it needs to be remembered that women and men from the same social context may not enjoy equal access to ICTs. Women's rights groups working in rural areas point to how access to household assets is affected by gender. If the household has one television, it is most likely to be used by men. Women may not have the leisure time for television, nor may be allowed to join others for recreation and even social interaction. The fact that technology has remained a male preserve historically, suggests that the appropriation by women of technology is in itself a political project. And, as active agents of change, women have been engaged in the process of claiming technology. However, we cannot assume that all women relate to technology in the same way. This will result in over-generalised approaches to redressing gender imbalances in access. We also cannot ignore the fact that gender power operates within institutions in many insidious ways. Therefore, women's empowerment in the information society requires a constant examination of how gender relations as a dynamic cultural process are being negotiated and contested, in relation to the technology environment. The claiming of technology by women for communicating their concerns started well before the advent of new ICTs. The underside of history is full of examples of women negotiating their spaces in private and public domains.

In the recent years, through the implementation of various ICT related projects, various states are successful. By seeing its growth in this sector, the potential work force in the state, various foreign agencies, Government of India and other non-governmental agencies are seriously involved for the further development of this sector. Their mission is to reach where no one had reached before. There are also many projects for the greater involvement of women and more particularly poor and rural women. The main object is to make the women both economically and socially strong. The use of ICT helps to bridge the gap between people's opportunities for self-employment in the informal economy and the high growth sectors of the world economy. It can be concluded that the women of various states have empowered with the information and communication technology. It has changed their position from the past. It has also taken several steps and implemented various plans and policies along with Government of India to eradicate poverty and bring the women into the IT-related industry. NGOs working in the field, multinational agencies and other private agencies have also extended their help to promote IT among the women. The development of IT has enabled the women section to participate in the daily affairs of the state, which range from the household work to local governance.

Inclusion through Entrepreneurship

Gothoskar (2000) in an interview with women tele-workers in Mumbai, got responses ranging from welcoming the freedom to fulfil family commitments to dislike of the lack of access to public and social spaces and reinforcement of the role at home. Tele-centres can solve these problems by combining home work with social spaces and organisation. One way to do this is to move to Entrepreneurship on the internet. The Internet can offer great assistance to Entrepreneurship by women. It offers databases, put together by women's groups, from which women can find relevant links, connections, resources and information and develop partnerships, not just for their services, but also for financing, mentoring and business coaching. It can even mitigate the effect of lack of access to capital. Support groups can be formed through electronic bulletin boards. Thus, the internet itself can help to organise and build solidarity with and between people working from home offices. It can break down isolation, aid job-related concerted action, or just increase information, opportunities and interaction. Rural women in developing countries may be able to sell their products directly without going through middlemen. One of the most powerful applications of ICT in the domain of knowledge networking is electronic commerce (E-commerce). E-commerce refers not just to selling of products and services online but to the promotion of a new class of ICT savvy women entrepreneurs in both rural and urban areas. E-commerce initiatives can link producers and traders directly to five markets at national, regional and even global levels, allowing them to restructure their economic activities and bypass middlemen and the male dominated and exploitative market structure. In Gujarat, women producers use the Dairy Information System Kiosk (DISK) which manages a database of all milk cattle and provides information about veterinary services and other practical information about the dairy sector.

Challenges of ICT use for Women's Social Inclusion

Women face enormous challenges to use ICT for their own economic empowerment. Using and benefitting from ICT requires education, training, affordable access to the technology, information relevant to the user and a great amount of support to create an enabling environment. Access to affordable services and availability of infrastructure is without doubt a major requirement if ICTs are to be used for women's economic empowerment. Availability of electricity, transport and security may also influence the use of ICT. Radio and television, as the widest form of communication, provide one way of solving information dissemination. In addition to being used as effective ICT for development, radio and television should be considered and used as a means of educating the population on the benefits of ICT for development. Radio and Television programmes can be developed to educate women on various development issues, including the various uses of ICT, thus increasing awareness and knowledge of ICT's uses. When possible, such programmes should be developed and conducted by women and their content should reflect a gender perspective. Even when infrastructure is available, affordable access is a concern in most developing countries. Universal access policies aim at developing solutions that provide community access at affordable prices. Expansion of public telephone and ICT access points are examples of these solutions. Tele-centres, however, do not guarantee affordable access because most tele-centres are run as business ventures that need to be sustained and therefore charge for services according to their costs. Lack of local and community-related content in local languages continues to be a major barrier in women's use of ICT for economic empowerment. To make ICT more useful and meaningful, particularly for rural and poor women, relevant information and tools need to be provided to address women's needs and demands. Multimedia can be developed to provide information both in spoken and written language. The challenge is to develop content that is relevant and useful to communities in their own language.

Training Women for the IT Workplace

Although women have made some gains in employment in the IT workforce, they are employed predominantly in low-level data processing work in much of the world. Even in the industrialised world, women's participation in skilled IT employment remains much lower than men's. Women generally lack access to technical and skills training that would allow them to move into more technical and cognitive jobs. Technical and vocational training can redress the inequalities women experience with respect to skills training and IT-employment. Such training can provide IT skills to women for IT based employment, as well as for use in the running of a small business, and other income generating activities such as food processing and agriculture among others. The India Technician Education project assists industrially and economically underdeveloped and geographically remote regions in India to improve the quality and efficiency of technical education to meet local economic needs. The project aims to increase access to technical education and training for some disadvantaged sections of society, including women, scheduled tribes, and rural youth. The eighteen project polytechnics develop close links with local communities to train rural artisans, the educated unemployed, and school dropouts, and help transfer appropriate technologies to villages. The project covers a total of twelve existing and six new polytechnics in the eight project states, and has the following components: developing and expanding capacity to provide increased access to technical education; enhancing the quality of education to produce better trained technicians; improving efficiency through better planning, administration, and use of the system; and increasing the responsiveness of education to emerging labour market needs. Key policy and institutional reforms supported by the project include:

- Creating opportunities for technical training of women and tribal communities to increase their earning capacity.
- Introducing structural and academic flexibility in all programmes offered by polytechnics to make them responsive to market demands, and to offer services as needed by industry and community.
- Promoting self-employment by developing entrepreneurial and communication skills in students through curricular interventions; and developing human resources capacity for key areas of economic growth including IT (World Bank, 2000).

Recommendations

It is evident that not enough research has been done on the feasibility, efficiency, and reach of various strategies for using ICT for education, particularly with respect to gendered distribution of benefits. Therefore, sex-disaggregated data needs to be collected at every level of implementation. Support and encouragement for increased participation of women and girls need to be present at every level of scientific and technical education, to motivate them to continue their education past primary levels and increase the recruitment and retention of girls at higher levels. More women teachers and role models, alternative schools with flexible schedules, and culturally appropriate facilities are some of the ingredients for success. It is important to generate curricula which address the interests and perspectives of women and girls, and do not include gender stereotypes. In this area, the Bank could work with clients and operational colleagues to expand the focus of its technology curriculum to include science education that emphasises hands-on activities and application to everyday life, society, and the environment. Programmes to introduce computers in schools should take into account differences in access between girls and boys. Steps to take include structured and monitored computer access; addressing girls' domestic obligations; and providing training in use and understanding of computers so that girls may feel comfortable using them. Distance learning programmes using ICT should ensure that women are involved in setting up and implementing projects that target men and women equally. In this context, sequential use of predecessor tools, beginning with low-tech solutions and moving gradually up to new technologies, is a tested and proven solution. To increase the successful participation of women in the IT workforce, education must help to demystify technology, while carrying on the task of training and retraining. Costs of ICT in education should be carefully assessed before technologies are implemented. Although there is no substitute for school in basic education, the new technologies, when properly implemented in a larger national strategy, with resources for ongoing project support, can contribute substantially to the quality of learning and teaching at all levels, and for men and women equally.

This study suggests the need of direct action by the government and NGOs to provide free computer education and access to internet to the people especially to the females to popularise the internet usage and bridge the digital divide. Internet communication will become a critical factor, in future, to enhance their life opportunities in the cities and for that matter in India, hence requires immediate attention of planners, policy-makers and society at large. Women should not wait for policymaking alone to bridge the 'digital divide' but rather take action through ICTs to access information sources and engage in the communication processes to achieve their socio-economic development goals. The paper concludes that women are being empowered with the spread and usage of as ICT as it is enabling them in education, jobs, income, improvement in family and social status, etc. IT is helping women from social exclusion to social inclusion especially in urban areas. The paper recommends that there is need to popularise IT usage in rural as well as tribal areas so that benefits can reach to all sections of women.

References

1. Braga, Carlos A Primo, 1995. *The Impact of the Internationalisation of Services on Developing Countries*, World Bank. 2002.
2. Green, Lyndsay and Lawry Trevor-Deutsch, 2002. *Women and ICTs for open and distance learning: Some experiences and strategies from the Commonwealth*, Vancouver: Commonwealth of Learning.

3. Gajjala, R., 2002. Interrogating identities: Composing other cyber-spaces. International and Intercultural Communication Annual, 25.
4. Gothoskar, S., 2000. "Teleworking and gender: emerging issues" *Economic and Political Weekly* 35(26): 2293-2298.
5. Gurumurthy, A., 2004. Bridging the Digital Gender Divide: Issues and Insights on ICT for Women's Economic Empowerment, New Delhi: UNIFEM.
6. Haffkin, Nancy and Nancy Taggart, 2001. *Gender, Information Technology and developing countries*, Washington D.C., Academy for Educational Development.
7. Kalia, H.L., 2005. *Women, Work and Family*. Jaipur: Rawat Publications.
8. Jain, Atul, 2010. *Computer in Education*. Delhi: Isha Books.
9. Jhunjhunwala, Rajiv R., 2007. *Human Rights Governance*. Delhi: Indian Publishers Distributors.
10. Kanter, Jerome, 2009. *Managing with Information*, New Delhi: PHL Learning Private Limited.
11. Kapoor, Sradh, 2011. *Management; Information Systems for the Information Age*. Delhi: Swastik Publications.
12. Kotwal, Pradeep, 2011. *Community Work and Social Action*. New Delhi: Aadhayan Publishers and Distributors.
13. Kumar, Girija, 1998. *Sociology of Information Management*. New Delhi: Har-Anand Publications Pvt. Ltd.
14. Kumar, Akshay, 2000. *Information Technology: An Info Guide*. Delhi: Authors Press.
15. Ono Hiroshi and Zavodny Madeline, 2003. 'Gender and Internet', *Social Science Quarterly,* Vol. 84, No.1, pp. 111-121.
16. Plant, Sadie, 1996. 'On the Matrix: Cyberfeminist Simulations, in Rob Shields' (ed.): *Cultures of Internet: Virtual Spaces, Real Histories, Living Bodies*. London: Sage, 170-183.
17. Raju, M.V., 2011. *Global Information Society and Human Rights*, Delhi: Swastik Publications.
18. Rao, Amruta, 2000. *Sex Discrimination*. Delhi: Indian Publishers Distributors.
19. Slater, D., and Tacchi, J., 2004. Research: ICT Innovations for Poverty Reduction, http://cirac.qut.edu.au/ictpr/downloads/research.pdf.
20. UNESCO Chair Symposium on *Gender Issues in the knowledge based Information Society from the perspective of NGOs/Academia*, 24 June, 2005, Seoul, Korea.
21. Vallikkad, Santhosh, 2009. *Information Communication Technology for Teacher Education*. New Delhi: Kanishka Publishers Distributors.

22. Vardhan, Ranjay, 2009. *European Union Manifesto and other Essays*. New Delhi: Indian Publishers Distributors.
23. Vardhan, Ranjay, 2008. *Single Women: A Study of Spinsters*. New Delhi: Indian Publishers Distributors.
24. Weiser Eric B., 2000. Gender Differences in the Internet Use Patterns and Internet Application Preferences: A Two Sample Comparison, Cyber Psychology and Behaviour, 3(2), 167-178.

15

Gender Discrimination: The Status of Girl Child

—*Dr Mona Arora*

Abstract

Short changing girls are not only a matter of gender discrimination; it is bad economics and bad societal policy. Experience has shown, over and over again, that investment in girls' education translate directly into better nutrition for the whole family, better healthcare, declining fertility, poverty reduction and better overall economic performance. Despite the remarkable progress in efforts to enable girls fully enjoy their rights; there is still a great deal of work to be done in order to achieve the objective. There are still many unresolved issues of discrimination, inequality, neglect, exploitation and violence against girls and women. With this background the present paper aims to determine the status of girl child in society.

Keywords: *Girl child, neglect, abuse, deprivation, violence.*

Introduction

Discrimination against the girl child occurs in every strata of society – rich or poor – having different forms of manifestations, but it is more visible in poverty stricken families or in families under financial stress. One of the crudest forms of discrimination is the one which takes place subtly and is sanctioned in the name of culture. A girl is made to fit in culturally defined roles – be it is at home or outside. Traditions have portrayed girls as less important than boys, less deserving of the basic qualities of life and girls themselves have endorsed their second class status. As a result, the girl child does not enjoy the rights of childhood for the reasons extraneous to her.

Discrimination and neglect in childhood initiates a lifelong downward spiral of deprivation and exclusion from the mainstream. The girl child often faces discrimination from the earliest stages of life, through childhood and into adulthood. Her low status is reflected in the denial of fundamental needs and rights and in such harmful attitudes and practices as a preference for sons, early marriage, female genital mutilation, domestic abuse, incest, sexual exploitation, discrimination, less food and less access to education.

There are two main inequalities as pointed out by Amartya Sen : educational inequality and health inequality. These are the indicators of a woman's status of welfare. In India, irrespective of the caste, creed, religion and social status, the overall status of a woman is lower than men and therefore a male child is preferred over a female child. A male child is considered a blessing and his birth is celebrated as opposed to a female child where her birth is not celebrated and is considered more of a burden. Therefore, education and healthcare of the female child in India is an important social indicator to measure equality between men and women. According to the 2001 Indian census, overall male-female ratio was 927 females per 1000 males. However, the 2011 Indian census shows that there are 914 females per 1000 males. During the last decade the number of female children to male children in the youngest age group fell from 945 per 1000 males to 927 per 1000 males. As per the data available there seems to be gender disparity depending on the location, as the Northern states (particularly Punjab, Haryana, and Himachal Pradesh) seem to be more biased than the Southern states. The sharpest decline for the age group of zero to six years is observed in the Northern States particularly in Punjab (793 per 1000 females) and Haryana (820 per 1000 females). These new figures point out that the use of new technology contributes to the gender composition. Furthermore, the availability of and access to new technologies provides new ways for parents to achieve such goals of sex determination before birth. Due to the widespread use of this technology the Indian Government banned the sex determination before birth. In spite of these bans imposed by the government, the law is not widely followed.

Despite progress in advancing gender equity from a legal standpoint, in practice many women and female children still lack opportunities, and support for the socio-economic advancement. Historically, the inclusion of young girls and women in education has helped challenge gender stereotypes and discrimination. This suggests that providing space for young girls to develop leadership skills, through education and healthy living is important. This can shape attitudes towards women's capabilities as leaders and decision-makers especially in conventionally male domains and male-dominated cultures. Because of the sex preference of male children in India, female children are deemed of resources in the areas of health and education.

Health

It has been found that girls are given less food and healthcare than boys, especially in Northern India. Girls are breastfed for shorter periods, given less medical attention, fewer consultations and visits to the doctor, and are often taken very late to the hospital in an emergency.

Because of some culturally assigned duties, many girls miss out on the chance to improve their overall health. Miller calls this as an extended infanticide, since life sustaining necessities like food, nutrition and healthcare are denied to the female child. Female children are given less food, both in quality and quantity, and therefore are undernourished compared to male children. This in turn leads to health issues like anemia and intrauterine growth restriction during pregnancy. If a woman gives birth to a female child while malnourished, then the child's survival issues and salon nutritional issues increase.

In times of diminished food resources, girls and their mothers are often last to be fed, resulting in a diet low in calories and protein. An estimated 450 million adult women in developing countries are stunted as a result of childhood protein-energy malnutrition. Iodine and iron deficiencies also have significant consequences for pregnant women and their offspring.

There has been an alarming increase in the number of girls infected with the HIV virus. Adolescent girls are at high risk of contracting HIV because their low social status often pressures them into situations where they are forced to have unprotected sexual intercourse with men.

Education

The female child in India is often deprived from her right of an education. The number of girls dropping out of school far exceeds the boys because girls are expected to help at home, either with household work like washing and cooking or with taking care of younger siblings. Since girls spend more time performing domestic duties and this increases the gap between female and male equality in rural parts of India, it perpetuates the myth that education is of no help to the girl and her primary job will be to look after the household work, get married early, have children and then raise them. If this is the job she has to do, then education is of no importance to her and it is not imparted. Also, even with education and financial independence, women might not get the same rights and liberties which a man may have. It is through education in the early days of a child that we can bring about behaviour changes and open doors to opportunities that will enhance their confidence, personality, and career.

Some studies have shown that educated mothers are far more "efficient" in discriminating against their daughters than uneducated mothers. Other studies have shown that though higher levels of maternal education decreases infant mortality for both boys and girls, the effect is larger for girls. Thus, higher levels of maternal education decrease gender differentials in child mortality. However, in the past 20 years, high female literacy has not stopped Delhi, Gujarat, and Rajasthan from showing increased discrimination against girls.

Violence against Girls

Violence against girls as well as women remains a persistent problem that takes many forms, including sexual exploitation and abuse, rape, incest, prostitution, child pornography, trafficking, and harmful traditional practices such as female genital mutilation.

Statistics reveal the urgent need for action. According to the United Nations Population Fund, it is estimated that between 85 and 114 million women and girls, most of whom live in Africa, the Middle East, and Asia, have undergone female genital mutilation. Trafficking in women and children, most often for commercial sexual exploitation, is estimated to generate up to $8 billion each year according to the International Organisation for Migration (IOM).

Equal Rights for Girl

Girls are often treated as inferior to boys, both within the home and by society-at-large. They are socialised to put themselves last, which in turn undermines their self-esteem and their ability to reach their full potential as human beings. When a girl is prevented from going to school or is too exhausted to pay attention in class because of her workload at home, she is being denied her right to education. When a girl carries the bulk of responsibility for the housework while her brother studies, plays or attends to his interests and hobbies, she is being discriminated against. To help promote girls' rights, a number of initiatives have been developed.

Legislative Provisions Regarding Girl Child

In a country like India, a caring and protective environment for a girl child does not develop easily. Failure to ensure protection of the girl child entails their promotion and rehabilitation. However, many initiatives have been developed and legislations does exists in theory to protect girl child.

Some exemplary and district administrations have taken a lead in combating this problem e.g. in Haryana, the Ladli scheme for girl child was drawn by the state government to provide incentatives to the family NGO's have also organised the companies, rallies and programmes to raise awareness about female foeticide around the country.

Discrimination against girl children, female foeticide and girl infanticide are in direct violation of both the UN Convention on the Rights of the Child (UNCRC) and the international Convention on the Elimination of all forms Discrimination against Women (CEDAW).

The United Nations Convention on the Rights of the Child provides for instance for the right to non-discrimination (Article 2), for the right to life (Article 6) and development in a context where the girl child is protected from abuse, exploitation or neglect.

The Convention on the Elimination of All Forms of Discrimination against Women (CEDAW) is considered to be equivalent to an international bill of rights for women, defining what constitutes discrimination and providing an agenda for action. It states the negative consequences of female discrimination and seeks full equality between men and women, in all fields of political, economic, social and cultural life.

The Constitution of India guarantees:

Equality before the law and equal protection of laws to each and every person in the country (Article 14).

Prohibits discrimination on grounds of race, caste, sex, place of birth or residence (Article 15).

The main law for prosecuting persons who are engaging in sex selective abortion is the Pre-Natal Diagnostic Techniques (Regulation and Prevention of Misuse) Act, 1994. This Act provides for the prevention of misuse of such techniques for the purpose of prenatal sex determination leading to female foeticide.

On 17 January 2003, India amended its Pre-natal Diagnostic Techniques (Regulation and Prevention of Misuse) Act, 1994 that was renamed Pre-Conception and Pre-Natal Diagnostic Techniques Act (PCPNDT) of 2003.

Apart from this Law, the relevant sections from the Indian Penal Code can be used to prosecute for Female Foeticide and Female Infanticide.

Conclusion

The female child's status is the product of general societal attitude towards women at large in India. Girls in India face higher risks of malnutrition, disease, disability, and retardation of growth and development. They have no access to or control over the resources because their work toward raising a family and in the household chores is undervalued. A popular Telugu saying from Andhra Pradesh says, "Bringing up a daughter is like watering a plant in another's courtyard." Due to this understanding, she is considered a liability and outside commodity and is deprived of good food and nutrition. According to a global study, India is the fourth most dangerous country for a female child in the world.

It has been found in India, girl child is discriminated against, ranked unequally lower and prevented from realising her full potential. A wide gap continues to separate the girl child from her male sibling. Overall, the situation that emerges is that India still has a long way to go before the human rights of the girl child are enforced. Certain social trends have in fact made the situation worse, as borne out by the fact that the girl child is discriminated even before her birth in the form of foeticide and after birth in the form of infanticide, and numerous other forms of violence and parental neglect. The third Article of UDHR says that everyone has the right to life, liberty and security of person. However, in India the girl child is denied these basic human rights. The government admits that gender discrimination continues to be a daunting challenge and that it will continue to pursue all measures, in a concerted manner, to eliminate discrimination against women and girl child.

References

1. Anandlakshmi, S., 1991. 'The female child in a family setting', *The Indian Journal of Social Work*, LII (1) Jan: 29-36.
2. Arnold, F. and E.C.Y. Kuo, 1984. 'The Value of Daughters and Sons: A Comparative Study of the Gender Preference of Parents', *Journal of Comparative Studies*, 15(2).
3. Bhogle, S., 1991. 'Child rearing practices and behaviour development of a girl child', *The Indian Journal of Social Work*, LII (1), Jan: 61-69.
4. Bandewar, S., 2003. 'Abortion Services and Providers Perceptions: Gender Dimensions', *Economic and Political Weekly*, XXXVIII (21):2075-81.
5. Chhabra, Rami, and Sheel C. Nuna, 1994. *Abortion in India: An Overview*. New Delhi: Ford Foundation.
6. Lahiri, S., 1974. 'Preference for sons and ideal family size in urban India,' *Indian Journal of Social Work*, 34(4).
7. Rothman, Barbara, 1986. *The Tentative Pregnancy: Prenatal Diagnosis and the Future of Motherhood*. New York: Viking.
8. Rahman, M., and J. Davanzo, 1993. 'Gender Preference and Birth Spacing in Matlab, Bangladesh,' *Demography*, 30: 315-332.
9. Srikantan, K., B.K. Narayan, and D.V. Rao, 1978. 'Female and Child Work Participation in the Integrated Development of a Common Area' cited in Vinaya Prabha V. Baligar (1999) *Mother and Girl Child*. Jaipur: Rawat Publications.

16

Social and Economic Status of the Marginalised Community in Dugri Village of Rupnagar Districts of Punjab with Special Reference to Scheduled Castes

—*Amrit Kaur*

Abstract

The Scheduled Castes is considered as one of the marginalised section of Indian Society. According to 2011 census, the scheduled castes constitute about 16.2 per cent of the population in India. Majority of Scheduled Castes population are living in rural area and their population are 80 per cent and their main occupation is agriculture. In the state of Punjab the scheduled castes population according to 2011 census was 28.9 per cent. Castes system is a very rigid system in rural Punjab. The objective of the paper is to answer these questions: Are Scheduled castes being able to compete with the changing scenario? What will happen with their occupations? Are they able to get quality education? What changes Reservation and education system has brought into their lifestyles? Is there any social, occupational, cultural mobility among them or are they stagnated?

Keywords: *Caste System, Scheduled Caste, Socio-economic, Discrimination, Inequality, Social Mobility, Marginalised Section.*

Introduction

Since the drawn of history, the less privileged in Indian society have suffer from diverse type of social disabilities. Some of the most unsocial and unscrupulous social inequalities and disabilities were centred around the institution of caste. There are many castes and sub-castes in Indian society who are placed one above the other. Among these castes, one of the caste named Ravidasia (Scheduled Castes) was also deprived of their basic, legitimate human rights as untouchables to live with dignity. The majority of marginalised sections in India are of Scheduled Castes. According to 2011 census, the scheduled castes constitute about 16.2 per cent of the population in India. Majority of Scheduled Castes population are living in rural area and their population are 80 per cent and their main occupation is agriculture. In the state of Punjab the scheduled castes population according to 2011 census was 28.9 per cent. Caste system is a very rigid system in rural Punjab. There is less mobility among the marginalised section of Punjab. But the various government policies have made some efforts for the upliftment of marginalised section and they are being able to improve their social, economic and political status. After Independence there has been a growing awareness and concern for the degraded socio-economic condition of the Scheduled Castes.

For this, efforts are being made in collaboration with different organisations and institutions to inculcate and encourage them to merge with the socio-economic fabric of the country. In turn, they have experienced a modicum of social mobility and there has been an unprecedented rise in the political consciousness among them. Scheduled castes as community has tried to build a new identity and founds a ways of moving upward in the terms of socio-cultural, economical as well as political level.

The term "Protective Discrimination", was adopted by the Government of India as applied to the laws reserving seats in legislature, government employment, places in the schools and universities, as well as provisions for certain financial assistance for Scheduled Castes. The Constitution of India has taken special care to uplift certain marginalised communities in India, those who were oppressed for a long period of time. The policy of positive discrimination towards scheduled castes groups is one such measure. These days due to reservation and other facilities provided by the government to the people of Scheduled Castes are helpful to arise their level of standard life. The Reservation Policy was introduced with a view to achieve equal social status to a section of population which has been opposed, exploited and socially degraded to a large extent for centuries together. Reservation seems to be perhaps the best practical strategy for the eradication of inequality in Indian society. The Constitution provides certain special provisions for the depressed classes to protect their educational and economic interests.

Yogendra Singh, in his book "Social Stratification and Change in India" has argued that there are two kinds of social movement which directly influence the status or position of scheduled castes. One is of integrative orientation and other is related with the alienating orientation. In integrative orientation the scheduled castes made an effort to sanskrities themselves. The motive forces for the backward and the scheduled castes to sanskritise was just to ventilate their deprived feelings of status and position which were denied to them for centuries. By imitating the local dominate caste they find a position as that of upper caste but they were not succeeded in their efforts because there is no legitimate acceptance by the upper caste. The movement aims to reform the caste system in order to put an end to the problem of untouchability. This movement was arrived out during different periods in India i.e. Bhakti movement, neovedantic movement, sanskritisation movement. The alienating movement aims to create an alternative cultural environment by conversion to, another religion.

Caste system carries a unique characteristic of rigidity, and domination. One of the well known Indian authorities on the subject, G.S. Ghurye described the caste system in his book "Caste and Race in India" (1932). In this book he draws attention to its six main features of caste and considered that each caste was separated from one and another in a hierarchical order. The six main features of caste were as follows:

- Segmental division of society.
- Hierarchy of groups.
- Lack of unrestricted choice of occupation.
- Restriction on feeding and social intercourse.
- Restriction on Marriage.
- Civil and religious disabilities and privileges of the different sections.

Scheduled Castes

The Scheduled Castes is a political-legal term. For this term Sudras, Panchamas, Antyajas, Chandalas and a few other names were frequently used. Gandhi ji called them Harijans (The people of God). During the colonial period, the term "Exterior Caste" and 'Untouchables' were commonly used for them. Dr Ambedkar termed them as Depressed Class, which referred to those classes or categories of persons who were poor and exploited, and socially and ritually degraded. The term "Scheduled Castes" was first coined by the Simon Commission (1927), after the recommendations of Simon Commission the term 'Scheduled Castes' was adopted in the Government of India, Act, 1935. In April 1936, the British Government issued the Government of India Order, specifying certain castes in the list of depressed classes as Scheduled Caste. 'Scheduled Castes' means such castes, races or tribes, parts or group within such castes, race or tribes as are deemed to be the Scheduled Caste under Article 341 of the Constitution of India.

Social Status of Scheduled Castes in Rural Areas

Social status of a person in the society is determines by caste, class, occupation and income etc. In the category of Scheduled Castes there is majority of service provider castes. But these days the social status of a person is determines by the education, wealth and types of Government Private Jobs. These days due to reservation, impact of globalisation, urbanisation and other facilities provided by the government to the people Scheduled Castes are helpful to arise their level of standard life. When I asked to my respondents that how they feel about their social status in the village and how they were treated by the people of upper caste in the village, most of them answered that they were treated indifferently. Very few of them answered that they were treated badly by the people of upper caste in the village. Thus, we concluded that most of people among the Scheduled Castes were treated indifferently by the people of dominant castes.

Objectives of Study

In the present study the basic thrust has been to understand the Socio-economic status among Scheduled Castes. For this, the following objectives are being formulated:

- To access the Socio-economic status of scheduled castes.
- To study their educational and occupations levels and their linkages to social mobility.
- To examine whether inter-caste marriages and religious conversions have taken place and helped them in social mobility.

Research Methodology

The present study attempts to assess the Socio-economic status and mobility among Scheduled Castes of Dugri villages in Rupnagar Districts of Punjab, India. Proper care was taken to collect information with the application of both primary and secondary sources. Accordingly, an interview schedule was prepared and questions were framed both open ended and close ended, for the purpose of data collection through primary source. Apart from that, a few secondary sources of data collection like observation of respondents and their family background, informal talks with the family members of the respondents, focused group discussion (FGD) were held for the purpose of getting supplementary information regarding the study. Hundred respondents have been taken as a sample size "Snow Ball Sampling Method" was used for collection of data.

Village Profile

The study was carried out in the Dugri villages of Rupnagar, District of Punjab. As far as, the demographic profile of the village is concerned, there are about 2998 households in the village. There are pucca houses for every family unit in the village. Mostly people are small business man for e.g. – tailor, Confectioner shop, Vegetable Vendors, government officer etc. There is one government senior secondary school at the entrance of Dugri village. Apart from that, there are for about four places of worship to meet the religious and spiritual requirements of the residents. In Dugri village, there is Separate Temple and Gurudwara for Scheduled Castes people.

Data Discussion

After collecting the data, the information collected was coded and tabulated on the basis of the responses given by the respondents, in order to generalise the responses of the respondents.

Table 16.1: Distribution of the Respondents According to their Sub-Castes

S.No.	*Caste*	*Frequency*	*Percentage*
1.	Ravidasia	15	15
2.	Ramdasia	85	85
	Total	**100**	**100**

It is important to state that 38 sub-castes have been listed in the Scheduled Castes Category in Punjab. The Sub-Caste distribution of the Sampled Respondents indicated that the major Sub-Castes in the village are Ravidasia and Ramdasia. Out of the total Respondents Ramadasia constitute 85 per cent and Ravidasia constitute 15 per cent.

Table 16.2: Distribution of the Respondents According to their Religion

S.No.	*Religion*	*Frequency*	*Percentage*
1.	Hindus	38	38
2.	Muslims	0	0
3.	Sikhs	62	62
4.	Christians	0	0
	Total	**100**	**100**

The Table 16.2 shows that out of the total respondents 62 per cent are Sikhs and 38 per cent are Hindus. Thus, we can say that majority of our respondents are of Sikh community in the village.

Table 16.3: Distribution of the Respondents According to their Educational Qualification

S.No.	*Qualification*	*Frequency*	*Percentage*
1.	Illiterate	16	16
2.	Primary	24	24
3.	Secondary	27	27
4.	Higher Secondary	18	18
5.	Graduate	15	15
	Total	**100**	**100**

The Table 16.3 shows the level of education of the respondents. It shows that the 16 per cent respondents were illiterate, 24 per cent respondents were Primary, 18 per cent respondents were Higher Secondary and the majority of our respondents (27) were educated up to Matric level and 15 per cent were graduate. It also shows the mostly head of families were educated.

Table 16.4: Distribution of the Respondents According to their Present Occupation

S.No.	*Occupation*	*Frequency*	*Percentage*
1.	Wood cutter	12	12
2.	Mason	32	32
3.	Retired from Government jobs	11	11
4.	Daily Wagers	36	36
5.	Government Jobs	9	9
	Total	**100**	**100**

The Table 16.4 showed that majority of our respondents were Daily wagers (36 per cent), 32 per cent of them were Mason, and 12 per cent were involved in the occupation of woodcutting, 11 per cent were retired from different government jobs and hardly 9 per cent were in government sector (army, men's, drivers in roadways and railways, and some were working at telephone exchange etc).

Table 16.5: Distribution of Respondents who had Changed their Occupation

Occupation	*Previous*	*Change*
Wood Cutting	3 per cent	12 per cent
Mason	6 per cent	32 per cent
Retired	6 per cent	11 per cent
Daily Wagers	6 per cent	36 per cent
Government Jobs	3 per cent	9 per cent
Weavers	80 per cent	0 per cent
No change	2 per cent	0 per cent

It is interesting to observe that Ramdasia sub-caste is not following their traditional work named, weaving. Majority of them had changed their occupation and adopted the other occupations. Due to impact of globalisation and education in their lifestyle they changed their occupations. It was revealed that lack of input in their previous traditional business forced them to change their occupation. There was only two per cent of responded who never changed their occupation.

Table 16.6: Distribution of the Respondents According to Ownership of Resident

S.No.	*Ownership of Residence*	*Frequency*	*Percentage*
1.	Own house	100	100
2.	Rented house	0	0
	Total	**100**	**100**

The Table 16.6 shows that 100 per cent respondents have their own houses and no single respondent lives in rented home in village.

Table 16.7: Distribution of the Respondents According to their House Type

S.No.	*House type*	*Frequency*	*Percentage*
1.	Pucca	75	75
2.	Kacha	0	0
3.	Semi- Pucca	25	25
	Total	**100**	**100**

The Table 16.7 shows that there was no signal respondent who had kacha house. Out of 100 Respondents, 25 per cent had semi-pucca houses. Apart from this 75 per cent respondents lived in their own pucca houses.

Table 16.8: Distribution of the Respondents According to Family Type

S.No.	*Family type*	*Frequency*	*Percentage*
1.	Joint Family	90	90
2.	Nuclear	10	10
	Total	**100**	**100**

The pie chart gives the analysis of type of the family of respondents. It showed that majority of our respondents (10 per cent) were belonged to joint family and 90 per cent of respondents were belonged to nuclear family. So, it showed that the joint family structure still prevails in the Indian villages.

Table 16.9: Factors Responsible for Change in the Lives of the Respondents

Factors	*Percentage*
Education	11
Social	16
Economic	32
Psychological	10
Communication	14
Media	6
Transportation	8
Awareness	3

The Table 16.9 showed that out of 100 respondents 32 per cent thought that Economy had changed their life, 9 per cent of the respondents felt that education had improved their lives. 16 per cent were reported that the change had come in their lives due to the social contact with other communities. Ten per cent due to media, 14 per cent due to communication, 9 per cent due to transportation and 7 per cent due to awareness.

Table 16.10: Distribution according to Ownership of Households Assets

Assets	*Percentage*
Cycle	90
Car	5
Telephone	90
Television	100
Refrigerator	98
Ceiling Fan /Table Fan	100
Room Cooler	85
DVD	90

(*Contd...*)

Washing Machine	50
LPG	100
Chula	100
Mobile	100
Motor Cycle	68

The Table 16.10 showed that 100 per cent of respondents had television, ceiling fan and table fan, LPG, Chula, mobile phones appliances, 98 per cent of them had Refrigerator, 90 per cent had DVD, Telephone and Cycle. 85 per cent of them had room cooler. 68 per cent respondents had motor cycle, 50 per cent had washing machine.

Table 16.11: Relationship with Upper Caste People towards Scheduled Castes

S.No.	*Upper Caste relationship with Scheduled Castes*	*Frequency*	*Percentage*
1.	Treated badly	15	15
2.	Treated good	85	85
	Total	**100**	**100**

The Table 16.11 shows the Relationship of upper caste people towards Scheduled Castes. When we asked them how they were treated by the people of upper caste in the village. Most of them i.e. 85 per cent answered that they were treated equal, good and 15 per cent answered that they were treated badly by the people of upper caste in the village.

Table 16.12: Socialisation and Mobility among the Respondents

Age group	*Vertical mobility*	*Horizontal mobility*	*Total*
20-30	8	10	18
31-40	14	55	79
41-50	5	7	12
Total	**28**	**72**	**100**

The Table 16.12 shows that in (31 – 40) age group are more mobile vertical that other. Fifty respondents are horizontally mobile in this age group. Thus, 79 out of 100 are mobile in this age group. This indicates that the age group of (31 – 40) is more favourable for mobility.

Table 16.13: Feelings of Schedule Castes for taking Food and Water by Higher Caste People

S.No.	*Sharing of Food and Water*	*Frequency*	*Percentage*
1.	Favoured	65	65
2.	Disfavoured	35	35
	Total	**100**	**100**

In the Table 16.13, 65 per cent respondents out of 100 were felt that the higher caste people were now in favoured of taking food or water from Scheduled Castes and 35 per cent respondents were not in favour of taking food or water from them. Thus, we can say that due to availability of education and modern occupations the SCs were taking off their traditional unclean occupations, most of the people of upper and middle strata were in favour of taking food or water from the lower castes people. So we concluded that the restriction and bondage of caste system are broken due to the globalisation, westernisation, modernisation, education and availability of legal provisions by government.

Table 16.14: Attitude of Respondents towards Education

S.No.	*Attitude towards Higher Education*	*Frequency*	*Percentage*
1.	Favourable	90	90
2.	Unfavourable	10	10
	Total	**100**	**100**

The Table 16.14 reveals that 90 per cent of respondents were in favour of high education, only 10 per cent of the respondents were not in favour of high education. They feel that good and higher education would mobile them in social ladder. Higher Education will change their status and position.

Table 16.15: Respondent's Views about to Change their Caste

S.No	*Change of Caste*	*Frequency*	*Percentage*
1.	Want to Change	15	15
2.	Not want to change	85	85
	Total	**100**	**100**

The Table 16.15 shows that 15 per cent of respondents want to change their caste but 85 per cent of them don't want to change their caste. They were happy in their own castes.

Table 16.16: Respondent's Views about Inter-Caste Marriage

S.No.	**Inter-Caste Marriage**	**Frequency**	**Percentage**
3.	Favoured	66	66
4.	Disfavoured	34	34
	Total	**100**	**100**

The Table 16.16 reveals that 34 per cent respondents were not in favour of inter-caste marriage but 66 per cent were in favour of inter-caste marriage.

Table 16.17: Distribution according to Infrastructure

S.No	*Infrastructure*	*Frequency*	*Percentage*
1.	Old	12	12
2.	New	88	88
	Total	**100**	**100**

The Table 16.17 shows that 88 per cent of respondents had new infra-structure and 12 per cent had old infrastructure. They had used lots of new things in their home like tiles in rooms/kitchens, chine's ports, sink in verandas, wooden doors, etc.

Summary and Conclusions

Result shows that majority of respondents are of Ramdasia community, have considered education and occupation is one of the most important factor for their social mobility, they are getting information through TV and Radio about new schemes launched by government and most of them are a waling. They used telephone for message convey and large number have personal Transportation facilities. The majority of the respondents were living in a nuclear type of household. The trends are now becoming very common in rural areas too, which was once known for a traditionally joint family system. While studying the occupational patterns of the respondents, it was revealed in this study that the large numbers of respondents were working on daily wages and very few of them were employed in government/private services. It is interesting to observe that Ramdasia sub-caste is not following their traditional work named weaving. Majority of them had changed their occupation and adopted the other occupations due to global trade. These respondents changed their previous occupation due to heavy loss. They started occupations other than their traditional occupation. It was observed that all of the respondents had their own houses and majority of them resided in pucca houses. It was also noticed that they had all kinds of luxury assets in their houses like TV telephones, DVD, sitting pots, motor vehicles, marbled houses and well furnished furniture and infrastructure. Education, communications, media, transportation, psychological mind and social contacts with other communities found major factors of changes in the scheduled castes people in rural areas. In the end it was also found that majority (90 per cent) of scheduled castes people were in favour of higher education.

The forces of globalisation, urbanisation are likely to change the life style and cultural practice of the people, since the world is going to be a global village. The value system of the people is becoming more and more individualistic and materialistic. The association between the life styles and the impact of globalisation was examined and found to be statistically significant. It was observed that the respondents with low change in their life styles had perceived high impact of globalisation as compared to the respondent with high change in their life styles.

It was found that majority of the respondents did not experience untouchability and most of them said that their relationship with the other caste was good and quite a large number of them had said that their social status was improved during the past few years.

Upper caste people started accepting food from lower caste people. Both upper caste and lower caste people participate in social interactions. In spite of all these cordial relations many a times they felt that upper caste behave indifferently with them.

References

1. A.R. Naronakar, 2003. *Untouchability and Caste System in India*, New Delhi: Anmol Publications, India.
2. B.R. Ambedkar, 1948. *The Untouchables: who were they and why they became Untouchables?* Delhi: Amrit Book Company.
3. Bhai. P Nirmala, 1986. *Harijan Women in Independence India.* New Delhi: B.R. Publishing Corporation.
4. B.K. Nagla, Indian Sociological Thought, Jaipur: Rawat Publications.
5. D'Souza, Victor, 1962. 'Changing status of Scheduled Castes', *Economic and Political Weekly*, XIV (48):1853-1855.
6. G.K. Ghosh and Shukla Ghosh., 1997. *Dalit Women.* New Delhi: APH publishing co-operation
7. Ghuman, Paul A.Singh, 1936. *British Untouchability : A study of Dalit Identity and Education.* Ashgate Publishing Limited Wey Court East, Union Road, Farnham, Surrey, GU97PT, England.
8. Gursharan Kaur, 2002. *Pattern of Employment and Social Mobility among SC Women (A study of Ludhiana City*, M.Phil Thesis, Submitted to Department of Sociology, Panjab University, Chandigarh.
9. J. Everett,1981. *Women and Social Change in India*. Jaipur : Rawat Publications.
10. Jagan Karade, 2009. *Occupational Mobility among Scheduled Castes*. Tyne United Kingdom: Cambridge Scholars Publishing.
11. Joyce P. Jacobsen., 2007. *The Economics of Gender*. Australia: Blackwell Publishing.
12. Karade Jagan, 2009. *Occupational Mobility among Scheduled Castes.* Tyne United Kingdom: Cambridge Scholars Publishing.
13. K.K. Das and D.R. Sharma, 1971. *Study of the utilisation of government resources by Scheduled Caste Communities.* New Delhi : Blackwell Publishing.
14. N.K. Bose, 1970. *Scheduled Castes and Tribes: Their Present Condition, Man in India*. New Delhi: 50:319-349.
15. P.C. Jain and Sashi Jain, 1986. *Scheduled Caste Women*. Delhi: Perfect Book Agency.
16. R.L. Chatterjee, 1989. *Social Decision of Scheduled Castes in India.* New Delhi: Intellectual Publication House.

17. R Trivedi Harshad, 1976. *Scheduled Caste Women: Studies in exploitation with reference to superstition, ignorance, and poverty.* New Delhi: Concept Publication House.
18. Suma Chitnis, 1972. 'Education for Equality: Case of Scheduled Castes in higher education', *Economic and Political Weekly*, 3 (31):75-81 .
19. S. Desai, '*Caste in* 21st *century India:Competing Narratives', India Human Development Survey Working.*

17

Empowerment and Political Participation of Dalit Women in Local Self Governance

—*Poonam Sharma*

Abstract

Dalits discrimination is based, first, on their birth into specific 'untouchable' castes, and secondly, on their traditional 'polluting' work. As a result, although almost one in five Indians is a Dalit, half of whom are women, their political participation as a large minority Dalits in India, officially termed scheduled castes, form the largest discriminated community. Looking specifically at Dalit women, the current Indian Lower House of Parliament has only 12 Dalit women MPs, only 2.2 per cent of Parliamentarians. In its consideration of the Government of India's report in 2007, the Committee on the Elimination of Racial Discrimination noted its concern over the under-representation of Dalits in all levels of government. The Committee went further to state that: "Dalit candidates, especially women, are frequently forcibly prevented from standing for election or, if elected, forced to resign from village councils or other elected bodies or not to exercise their mandate, and that many Dalits are not included in electoral rolls or otherwise denied the right to vote..." I want to just take the example of Dalit women's political participation in local governance institutions in India called the panchayats. The simple reason is that this is the largest political space open for Dalit women today to participate in public affairs. Moreover, at this level, there are separate quotas for Dalit women, aside from quotas for Dalits and women in general, meant to facilitate their inclusion in local governance.

Key words: *Dalit women, discrimination, participation, panchayat.*

Introduction

Women's participation in mainstream political activity has important implications for the broader arena of governance in any country. Direct political participation of Dalit women in local governance is a central human right in itself and enables the realisation of a host of other human rights. Political voice and decision-making power concerning basic services, economic development and social justice are critical factors in challenging and transforming structural caste-class-gender discrimination, and enabling Dalit women to realise their fundamental rights. Political participation also demands accountability from state and non-state actors to guarantee and respect these women's equal political voice and development.

This requires a transformation of power relationships both within institutions of governance and in the women's social environment. Recent legal and policy reforms in India to ensure the representation of marginalised social groups in decentralised governance, including Dalits and specifically Dalit women, through constitutionally mandated reservations in Panchayati Raj institutions bring these issues to the fore. They demand analysis to determine, that the way Dalit women are enabled to claim their right to political participation in local governance, and the extent to which this participation is an effective tool for empowerment and realisation of human rights for excluded social groups.

Panchayati Raj Institution

The Panchayati raj is a South Asian Political system mainly in India, Pakistan, Bangladesh and Nepal. The word "Panchayat" literally means "assembly" of five wise and respected elders chosen and accepted by the local community.

Panchayati Raj is not a new phenomenon in the country. Its illustration in history goes back to more than 1000 years. Panchayati Raj Institutions have always been considered as a means to good governance and 73rd Constitutional Amendment was effected in the hope that it would lead to better governance and provide political space to the disadvantaged section of the society like scheduled castes, schedule tribes and women. Bringing women into power is not only a matter of equity, of correcting an unjust and unrepresentative system political restructuring is the key to economic growth with justice.

Panchayati Raj is a system of governance in which gram panchayats are the basic units of administration. Mahatma Gandhi advocated Panchayati Raj, a decentralised form of government. This system was adopted by state governments during the 1950s and 60s as laws were passed to establish panchayats in various states. It is found backing in Indian Constitution with the 73rd Amendment in 1992 to accommodate the idea. Currently, the Panchayati Raj system exists in all the states except Nagaland, Meghalaya and Mizoram and the all Union Territories except Delhi.

Issue of Women's Empowerment

The importance of women as an important human resource was recognised by the Constitution of India which not only accorded equality to women but also empowered the State to adopt measures of positive discrimination in their favour. The status of women in India has been subject to many great changes over the past few decades from a concept of welfare in the seventies to development in eighties and the current phase of full empowerment. The Tenth Plan continued with the major strategy of "empowering women" as agents of social change and development. The vision or philosophy of empowerment for the Eleventh Plan is inclusive and integrated economic, social and political empowerment with gender justice. Women have been identified as key agents of sustainable development and women's equality and empowerment are seen as central to a more holistic approach towards establishing new patterns and processes of development that are sustainable.

Despite efforts, women in India still continue to be discriminated and their current status still causes concern. Although the constitution provides legal equality for men and women but social and economic equality is yet to achieve. This is the fact why Indian women continue to be recipients' of welfare and remain at a lower status with low literacy and poor access to resource and facilities. The problem persists despite the vibrant resistance by the women's movement to this over the past several decades. In most parts of India today, women constitute a disproportionate share of the chronically poor population.

Indian women face gender discrimination throughout their life within the family, society and at workplace that runs common across the country along all class, caste and religion with varying degrees. Gender division of labour prevails in all sectors of employment. Gender discrimination starts from the foetus, in terms selection of sex, child-rearing, feeding, education, employment, control over property and resources, participation and influencing decision-making in public and political spheres etc. Women need self-confidence to fight against all the atrocities against her and to live self-confidence and self-esteemed life. Hence, boosting the morale and self-confidence of the women, is the key to eliminate their inferior complex. Women also have all the potential and empowering women will help to use her full capability with decision-making aptitude, education and employment will make the society to accept the women as a equal gender like male.

As per Human Development Report, the question of gender equality related to the power and space of women in the society. Power may be defined/measured in terms of access to and control over resources (resources include physical wealth and income and also human capital i.e., the literacy and education levels and status of health) and the role in decision-making process. Freedom to decide and choose extend from matters pertaining to her own body and life, her education and career, her matrimonial status, job options, and ability to migrate, sexuality and fertility. It goes further to her right to represent in economic activity, the politics and become members and leaders in business enterprises, corporate entities, states legislature and Parliament.

The 2006 World Development Report says, "Gender equality does not necessarily mean equality of outcomes for males and females; it means equal access to the opportunities that allow people to pursue a life of their women choosing and to avoid extreme deprivation in outcome"- that is gender equality in rights, resources and voice.

The Government of India declared 2001 as the "Year of Women Empowerment" and the national policy for the empowerment of women came into force from 2001. Internationally, with the onset of the new millennium, world leaders pledged with great fanfare, to boost standards by achieving Millennium Development Goals (MDGs) – covering poverty, health, education, gender and environment by 2015. Out of these eight goals, although the third one named as, "Promoting gender equality and Empowering Women", is directly targeted at women issues, but MDG 4 titled "Reduce child mortality" and MDG 5 as "Improve Maternal health" are also related to improvement in the plight of women in society. SAARC also followed path and India being its leading nation is committed to reduce social and institutional vulnerability of women and children.

However, as per the UNDP Human Development Report 2009, India's GDI (Gender Development Index) with a value of 0.594, ranks 114 out of 155 countries.

Taking note of this reality a number of exclusively targeted programmes for women upliftment have been launched in India. To name a few, Swayam Sidda, Swawalamban, National Maternity Benefit Scheme, single girl child scholarship, girls hostels in educationally backward blocks, Kasturba Gandhi Balika Vidyalayas, Janni Suraksha Yojana are all schemes to educate women, to provide healthcare, to impart skills to earn a livelihood, to give old age pension and support. For example, Support to Training and Employment Programme (STEP), for women seeks to provide updated skills and new knowledge to poor women in 10 Traditional sectors for enhancing their productivity and income generation. The concept of gender budgeting is also about earmarking or demarcating the extent of social expenditure which is specifically aimed at women empowerment. The 73rd Amendment in our Constitution in 1993, giving one-third reservations to women representatives in Panchayati Raj Institutions is a major landmark in empowerment of women in India. The bill ensuring 30 per cent representation in Parliament is long pending and needs early legislation.

Surveys and findings from as diverse a set of countries as Bangladesh, Brazil, Ghana, Indonesia and South Africa show that when women are the direct users of credit rather than men, the impact of credit on several measures of household welfare is greater. When women have more schooling, the returns flow not only to themselves but to the next generation as well. And when they have greater control over resources in the family, they are more likely than men to allocate more resources to food and to children's health-care and education.

The whole issue of allocating more resources towards women's development boils down to the right kind of economic choice, in which social surplus is generated i.e., the output is much more than the costs involved. It is called SMART ECONOMICS in the words of Mayra Burimic (Sector Director for Gender and Development at the World Bank) and Elizabeth M. King, Research Manager in World Bank's Development Economics Research Group. For a nation, so as for a family or that matter for a society it is the right choice, the Wise Rational Economic Choice.

Dalits

Dalits are a pan-Indian category. Heterogeneity is a marked feature of them. They belong to 'the most oppressed bottom' collectivises in the hierarchical society. They are part and parcel of village communities all over Indian subcontinent, except few north-eastern states. They are found not only in India but they are found in Pakistan, Bangladesh, Sri Lanka, Nepal and other neighbouring countries. They share common features across the country and states and even sometime they are found in more than one state known by synonyms such as Mahars and Holeyas or Chalwadis in Maharashtra and Karnataka respectively. Similarly, the caste called Malas in Andhra Pradesh; Paraiyas in Tamil Nadu are one and the same as Holeyas and Chalwadis in Karnataka state. Madiga caste, another untouchable community, that exist by the same name in Karnataka and Andhra Pradesh states and Mangs in Maharashtra is synonym of Madiga in Karnataka State. The matrimonial alliances take place between them across the state boundaries and it is very common in border areas of more than one state.

Obstacles in the Way of Dalit Women in Rural Areas

Caste-affected women in rural settings face a number of serious challenges, including lack of access to resources, land, basic services and justice. In India, Dalit rural women face serious challenges in carrying out their multiple productive and reproductive roles within their families and communities, in part due to lack of rural infrastructure and lack of access to essential goods and services. They have the highest poverty levels, are landless and depend on the dominant caste for employment, wages and loans. Their access to resources or even their efforts to access them are often met with violence.

Due to the intersection of caste, class and gender, Dalit women are subjected to direct and structural violence. Specifically, the structural violence and lack of access to resources perpetuate their poverty and undermine their dignity.

Dalit rural women have very limited access to and control over land, which in turn leads to food insecurity. They also lack access to water and other communal resources; when those resources are in non-Dalit areas, the women are attacked for attempting to use them. When it comes to infrastructure and resources in Dalit communities, the government often overlooks those areas and does not allocate the necessary funds to ensure equality of access to resources. Further, Dalit women lack employment options and other livelihood opportunities, more so than their male Dalit counterparts.

The increasing encroachment of land, forest and water at the community level as well as privatisation has made the lives of Dalit women residing in rural communities more difficult.

The situation of Dalit women, who have less access to ownership of land, households and livestock, is significantly worse than that of Dalit men. When the effects of caste and gender discrimination are combined, Dalit women end up at the bottom of the socio-economic scale. Dalit women are continually met with violence, discrimination and subjugation from every group.

Contribution of Various Sociologists and Anthropologists

Indian villages have been perceived by the Sociologists and Social Anthropologists as an integral part of Indian civilisation and without proper understanding of villages the study of Indian society is incomplete. Therefore, the study of village communities has been carried out by scholars across the disciplines. Initially the study of Indian villages was commensurate with the study of caste / chaturvarna, joint family and social hierarchy as an ideal type by Indologists and other Indian scholars mostly Dwijas. This was purely a 'book view' of Indian society. In contrast to this the field-based empirical studies carried out by sociologists and social anthropologists have greater relevance in understanding inter and intra- caste relations, between various social categories, patron-client relation, organic solidarity based on agrarian social network, hegemonisation of certain castes despite resistance and coercion applied for strict compliance and so on. This interpretation of Indian society was the 'field view'.

Mid-1950's and 60's the orientation and outlook of sociologists changed drastically from 'ideal types' based on the 'book view' to more 'pragmatic and empirical research' based on the field view. The impact of Marxian and democratic egalitarian perspective played a pivotal role. Sociologist perceived the villages as breeding centres of communalism and casteism. Further the notion of 'patria-potesta', male dominance, led to the discrimination based on gender in Indian village communities.

The third category of research investigations were of recent origin which were popularised in the mid-1980. The affected collectivities try to locate themselves in the hierarchical social structure by conducting empirical studies on their own castes and their relation with others. This attempt was mainly to locate their position in the hierarchical society and assert for new identities in the contemporary Indian society.

Firstly, the village studies have described the agrarian relations and the problems and prospects of the peasantry. Series of studies have been undertaken by the sociologist and social anthropologist to study the agrarian social structure, political structure, economic relations, vis-à-vis organic solidarity between the various castes and pace of social transformation. Srinivas (1955), Beteille (1974), Kroeber and Red Field (1965), Shanin (1987), etc., have tried to study the villages, joint family and caste system. Srinivas's India's villages (1955), M. Marriot 'Villages in India', 'Rural profiles' by D.N. Majumadar (1955) and S.C. Dube's 'Indian Villages' are some of the important research works on Indian villages. As part of their studies, the location of untouchables and their relation with other communities, patron-client relations in the agrarian economy, their problems and over all life situations of Dalits have been focused by these scholars.

Secondly, another set of scholars have conducted research on Indian villages and produced the 'monographs'. Dube (1955), Majumdar (1958), and Lewis (1958) are important. Further, studies on Indian village communities have identified the caste system as essentially a hierarchical order and the study of caste is important than the study of village communities (Dumont and Pocock). Majumdar (1958) pointed out the differential attitude, settlement patterns and lifestyle within the village communities despite living together. Beteille identified the element of unity in physical sense and not in social sense.

Thirdly, Lewis and Bailey have noticed that the element of conflict that exists in the caste system and organic solidarity is achieved due to the coercion by the landowning peasant communities despite resistance by the untouchables (Lewis, 1958) and (Bailey, 1960).

Fourthly, these studies, however scientific in their approach, lack the consistency as the researchers belong to the upper strata and their inaccessibility with untouchable communities due to social restrictions and contempt have rendered their studies on the lower strata suffers the accuracy of data and later interpretation. The upper caste bias is other important limitations of village studies particularly with regard to the location and position of untouchables. There is virtually no reference to the idea of the village being a site of exploitation in the village studies. It was only in the 1970's and more importantly in 1980's the caste began to be looked at from a Dalit perspective.

Dalit Women's Participation in Politics

The position of women has always been a rather ambivalent one in our culture. A woman is a symbol of sacrifice and blossom of life. She prepares herself for life ahead and lives in a daze with an unexplained smile. One side, she was raised to the status of divinity and on the other side she was exploited in every aspect. There is invisibility and underestimation of women's economic contribution. Though they contribute nearly one-third of India's GNP, it is undervalued and invisible. Yet she continues to be in a disadvantaged position. The problems of inequality of status and freedom, sexual harassment, lack of economic independence, lack of health facility, lack of access to credit, training, decision-making positions which prevent women to participate in formal and informal social organisations. A number of research findings indicate that women are the disadvantaged gender in both rural and urban areas of the country.

Women, in many societies, are often restricted to the roles inside the house, those of wife and mother. While major changes have occurred in the status of women in some parts of the world in recent decades, norms that restrict women to the home are still powerful in defining the activities that are deemed appropriate for women and they exclude political life, which by its very nature takes place in a public forum. Caste has played an instrumental role in raising issues related to the more marginalised among women. In a highly hierarchical society, women belonging to the lower castes have lesser access to public fore, which is compounded by their gender. This exclusion makes it difficult for these women to represent and articulate the voices of their constituencies and their demands are often overlooked or subsumed by the dominant sections of the society. Women's empowerment is one of the objectives of the third generation Panchayat in India. Women in India are awfully underrepresented in political institutions. The political power, access to decision-making and authority are the critical prerequisites for women's equality in the process of nation building. The 73rd Amendment has mandated representation of at least one-third women through election instead, of the earlier token one or two women nominated by government or co-opted by the predominantly influential, powerful male membership/leadership of these panchayats. It is a significant step in political history of independent India. It offers at once a challenge and an opportunity for women generally and Scheduled Castes and Scheduled Tribes women in particular to make an impact at the policy planning and programme administration level in each and every locality of our vast country.

Suggestive Measures

It is evident that men's attitude towards women's entry into politics has begun to change from that of total rejection to limited encouragement and in some cases even to active encouragement. This trend needs to be strengthened through orientation courses and training programmes for officials and elected representatives, both men and women. Besides there is a need to train the women leaders at regular intervals to enable them to manage the responsibilities assigned to them in the Panchayat at all the levels. Since the hard up women members found it difficult to forgo their wages for attending training programmes, these must be organised at their doorstep and some of the articulate Panchayat leaders should be involved as the trainers.

Another important effort required for real empowerment of Dalit women is to bring about an attitudinal change in both men and women. The feeling that women are meant for household activities and rearing children needs to be transformed into a feeling of equal partnership of women and men. To inculcate this they should be imparted education for bringing about social and political awareness among both. It is not enough that women are motivated, but the whole household and the community, especially men need to be made aware and be convinced and hence they too support the women in their effort for an integral development. Studies on women in politics have emphasised that contact with outside world makes women more alert and also active in the political process. There could be two ways of doing it.

Firstly, interaction between enlightened rural women and illiterate elected one's should be encouraged. Secondly, these women could be taken out to the urban areas and their interaction with educated urban elected women representatives be arranged. The women should also be encouraged to organise themselves. The Mahila Mandals in the village can be effectively used as instruments to mobilise them for this purpose. Some successful women's organisations can also act as catalytic agents for encouraging the women's participation in social and political activities. The government should provide finances and infrastructure to some of the deserving and successful women organisations to take up the responsibility of encouraging the women elected representatives.

Incentives play a vital role in ensuring the participation of elected representatives in decision-making. It has been noticed that there are certain very active and enlightened women leaders at all the levels of Panchayat, who have been successfully implementing the developmental schemes and have ensured overall development of their constituencies. Such leaders need to be encouraged by publicising their leadership qualities and honouring them in public meetings. It will certainly encourage other women representatives and their success stories and good practices will get replicated. The media both print as well as electronic can play an important role in creating awareness in the rural society. It can act as an agent of political socialisation for inculcating the values of gender equality and gender justice.

All the members may not have the same calibre and expertise, the group developers should identify the inefficient members of the group and impart proper training to them in order to make them competent. The training of Dalit women Panchayat members should be based on their own local experiences and elicit their involvement in preparing a framework that will enable them to analyse and understand their roles and responsibilities in accordance with the 73rd Constitutional Amendment.

Conclusion

Local self-governance is not a new phenomenon in the country. Its illustration in history goes back to more than 1000 years. Panchayath Raj Institutions have always been considered as a means to good governance and 73rd Constitutional Amendment was effected in the hope that it would lead to better governance and provide political space to the disadvantaged section of the society like schedule castes, schedule tribes and women. Dalit women face discrimination, exclusion and violence as a result of both their caste and gender. Dalit women's participation in the panchayath is necessary so that they can think about Dalit women's issues. In as much as Dalit women's participation is required, they also need to be given support and guidance. Then only can they become capable representatives. The government, NGOs and donor community need to understand and address this situation right from the start. Crucial aspects to the development of Dalit women's potential is training and other empowerment activities that lead to Dalit women being financially independent.

References

1. Hazal, D'Lima, 1983. "*Women in Local Government*", New Dehli: Concept Publishing House.
2. Hazra, Anupam, 2010. "Gender Budgeting and Development: The Indian Scenario", *A Journal of Social Focus,* 1(2).
3. Hazra, Anupam, 2011. "Protection of the Rights of Girl Child", *Social Welfare*, 57 (1).
4. Hazra, Anupam, 2009. "Gender Disparity in Education." *Yojana,* 53.

5. "How Equal?" United Nations, http://www.un.org.in/wii.htm.
6. "Info Change Women: Background and Perspective", http://www.infochange-india.org/
7. Jain, S.P., 1970. Panchayti Raj in Punjab, A case study, National Institute of Community Development, Hyderabad.
8. Jain, L.C., 2005. *Decentralisation of Local Governance*, Essay for George Mathew, New Delhi: Orient Longman Pvt. Ltd.
9. Jayapalan, 2001. "*Indian Society and Social Institutions.*" Atlantic Publishers and Disrtibutors.
10. Jena, K.N., 2009. "*Globalised India and Development Issues*", Delhi: Abhijeet Publication.
11. Jharta, Bhavana, 1996. "*Women and Politics in India*", New Delhi: Deep and Deep Publications, p. 53.
12. Johri, J.C., 1994. "*Indian Government and Politics*", New Delhi: Vishal Publications.
13. Judge, Paramjit Singh. "*Interrogating changing Status of Dalits of Punjab*' in Harish K.(ed.), Op.cit; pp. 100-131.
14. Kabeer, N., 1999. "Resources, Agency, Achievements: Reflections on the Measurement of Women's Empowerment." *Development and Change,* 30(3).
15. Kahlon, Prabhjot Kaur (ed. 2004). "The Impact of 73rd Amendment and Women's Empowerment: A study of Panjab" cited in Surat Singh *Decentralised Governance in India: Myths and Reality.* New Delhi: Deep and Deep Publications.
16. Kahlon, Prabhjot Kaur, 2004. "73rd Amendment and Women Empowerment: A Study of Punjab," *Punjab Journal of Politics*, xxvii (1), January– June :101 -121.

18

Constitutional Prerogatives in Mainstreaming of Dalit in India

—*Dr Gobinda Chandra Sethi*

Abstract

Dalit community is excluded from enjoyment of social, economical, educational and political opportunities. It has long history of struggle to fight against caste discrimination. Constitutional provisions have enabled Dalits to have their greater access to services, resources and development opportunity. Reservation policy of the government is an affirmative step in mainstreaming Dalits. Dalit's lobby and regular sharing of the situation of Dalits has gained support and solidarity from international donor community including UN agencies. This process was started from later 1990s and got momentum from mid of the last decade. It is still continued. The gap between the upper and lower strata still exists, despite of the constitutional provisions and the efforts of the government by making some remarkable measures. It has sparked multiple challenges engulf us to think a step ahead.

Key Words: *Dalit, Deprivation, Strata, Self-Identity, Constitutional Provisions.*

Introduction

Dalit means all those people of different castes and sub-castes among the depressed classes who were traditionally subjected to invidious discriminations on grounds of untouchability, and categorised as the untouchables, downtrodden, exterior classes, depressed classes or Scheduled Castes. The organisational or institutional efforts made by Dalit leaders for the liberation of the downtrodden masses could be termed as Dalit movement. It is a movement of protest against untouchability, casteism and superstitions. It aims at the uplift of the Dalits to the level of non-Dalits. "Negatively speaking, it stands for rejection of the old traditional Hindu social order based on untouchability, socio-economic inequality, casteism, unscientific and irrational religious beliefs and customary servitude. Positively speaking, it stands for acceptance of a new social order based on equality, liberty, and social justice, scientific and rational religious or moral principles and social, economic, cultural and political development of the Dalit." It is the movement to regain self-respect and equal human status in the society.

Dalit Identity

It is the result of the consciousness of Dalits of their own identity as human beings, equally equipped with physical and mental capacities as other human beings, and equally entitled to enjoy all the human rights "without any infringement, abridgement or limitations." Double folded issues are directed towards Untouchability and its Eradication. Untouchability, as indicated above, has always been considered as social evil. Since long efforts had been made to eradicate it. Religious and social, reformers like Buddha, Ramanuja, Ramanand, Chitanya, Kabir, Nanak, Tukaram and others, made great efforts to eradicate it as far as possible. The Brahmo Samaj and the Arya Samaj, and other social organisations by propaganda, education, and practical measures, did much to secure the social, religious and cultural equality to them.

Vision of Dr Ambedkar

Among the depressed classes also rose intellectuals, distinguished of whom was Dr Ambedkar, who struggled to secure for them the social recognition and human rights. The all-India Depressed Association and the All India Depressed Classes Federation, the principal organisations of these classes, initiated a movement to improve their conditions. They aimed at improving their miserable economic conditions, and to spread education among them. They worked to secure for them the rights to draw water from public wells, admission to the schools, and to the use of roads; and enter the public temples. The Mahad Satyagrah for the right of water led by Dr Ambedkar was one of the outstanding movements of the untouchables to win equal social rights.

Constitutional Prerogatives

India has attempted many different strategies in mainstreaming Dalits by using the Constitutional Prerogatives or Safeguards. Some of the provisions are relating to uplift the downtrodden enumerated in the constitution, the supreme law of the land. Some of the provisions with its dimensions are discussed below:

Directive Principles of State Policy

Article 46 is a comprehensive article comprising both the developmental and regulatory aspects. It reads as follows: "The State shall promote with special care the educational and economic interests of the weaker sections, of the people, and in particular, of the Scheduled Castes and the Scheduled Tribes, and shall protect them from social injustice and all forms of exploitation."

Social Dimension

Article 17. "Untouchability" is abolished and its practice in any form is forbidden. The enforcement of any disability arising out of "Untouchability" shall be an offence punishable in accordance with law. To give effect to this Article, Parliament made an enactment. Untouchability (Offences) Act, 1955. To make the provisions of this Act more stringent, the Act was amended in 1976 and was also renamed as the Protection of Civil Rights Act, 1955. As provided under the Act, Government of India also notified the Rules, viz., the PCR Rules, 1977, to carry out the provisions of this Act. As cases of atrocities on SCs/STs were not covered under the provisions of PCR Act, 1955, Parliament passed another important Act in 1989 for taking measures to prevent the atrocities. This act known as the Scheduled Castes and the Scheduled Tribes (Prevention of Atrocities) Act, 1989, became effective from 30.1.1990. For carrying out the provisions of this Act the Government of India have notified the SCs and the STs (Prevention of Atrocities) Rules, 1995 on 31.3.1995. These acts helps dalits a healthy social protects from social life.

Dimension of Human Trafficking, Article 23

Article 23. Prohibits traffic in human beings and beggar and other similar forms of forced labour and provides that any contravention of this provision shall be an offence punishable in accordance with law. It does not specifically mention SCs and STs but since the majority of bonded labour belongs to SCs/STs this Article has a special significance for SCs and STs. In pursuance of this article, Parliament has enacted the Bonded Labour System (Abolition) Act, 1976. For effective implementation of this Act, the Ministry of Labour is running a Centrally Sponsored Scheme for identification, liberation and rehabilitation of bonded labour. Article 24 provides that no child below the age of 14 years shall be employed to work in any factory or mine or engaged in any other hazardous employment. There are Central and State laws to prevent child labour. This article too is significant for SCs and STs as a substantial portion, if not the majority, of child labour engaged in hazardous employment belong to SCs and STs.

Religious Dimension, Article 25(2)

Article 25(2) (b) provides that Hindu religious institutions of a public character shall be thrown open to all classes and sections of Hindus. This provision is relevant as some sects of Hindus used to claim that only members of the concerned sects had a right to enter their temples. This was only a subterfuge to prevent entry of SC persons in such temples. For the purpose of this provision the term Hindu includes Sikh, Jaina and Buddhist.

Educational and Cultural Dimension

Article 15(4) empowers the State to make any special provision for the advancement of any socially and educationally backward classes of citizens or for SC and ST. This provision has enabled the State to reserve seats for SCs and STs in educational institutions including technical, engineering and medical colleges and in Scientific and Specialised Courses. In this as well as in Article 16(4) the term 'backward classes' is used as a generic term and comprises various categories of backward classes, viz., Scheduled Castes, Scheduled Tribes, Other Backward Classes, Denotified Communities (Vimukta Jatiyan) and Nomadic/Seminomadic communities.

Political Dimension

Article 330 provides for reservation of seats for SCs/STs in the Lok Sabha. Article 332 provides for reservation of seats for SCs/STs in the State Vidhan Sabhas (Legislative Assemblies).

Article 334 originally laid down that the provision relating to the reservation of seats for SCs/STs in the Lok Sabha and the State Vidhan Sabhas (and the representation of the Anglo-Indian community in the Lok Sabha and the State Vidhan Sabhas by nomination) would cease to have effect on the expiration of a period of ten years from the commencement of the Constitution. This article has since been amended four times, extending the said period by ten years on each occasion. This provision was to expire in January 2000 but not ceased off. The reason behind indicates that the government realise the need of its continuation.

Dimension of Reservation and Service

Article 16(4) empowers the State to make "any provision for the reservation in appointments or posts in favour of any backward class of citizens which, in the opinion of the State, is not adequately represented in the services under the State." Article 16(4A). "Nothing in this Article shall prevent the State from making any provision for reservation in matters of promotion to any class or classes of posts in the services under the State in favour of the Scheduled Castes and the Scheduled Tribes which, in the opinion of the State, are not adequately represented in the services under the State." Article 335. "The claims of the members of the Scheduled Castes and the Scheduled Tribes shall be taken into consideration, consistently with the maintenance of efficiency of administration, in the making of appointments to services and posts in connection with the affairs of the Union or of a State." Article 320(4) provides that nothing in clause (3) shall require a Public Service Commission to be consulted as respects the manner in which any provision under Article 16(4) and 16(4)A may be made or the manner in which effect may be given to the provisions of Article 335.

Statutes and Legislations

There are a number of laws, both Central and State, which provide for safeguards to SCs/STs. Some of these emanate from the various

Constitutional provisions. An illustrative list of such laws is given below:

- The Protection of Civil Rights Act, 1955.
- The Scheduled Castes and the Scheduled Tribes (Prevention of Atrocities) Act, 1989.
- The Bonded Labour System (Abolition) Act, 1976.
- The Child Labour (Prohibition and Regulation) Act, 1986.
- Acts and regulations in force in different States to prevent alienation of land belonging to SCs/STs. In some States such provision exists in the Land Revenue Code.
- Acts in different States for restoration of alienated land to SCs/STs.

The Position of Dalits in India Today

According to the 2001 census, scheduled castes comprise 16.2 per cent of the total population of India, that is, they number over 17 crore. Scheduled tribes comprise 8.2 per cent of the population, that is, they number over 8 crore. Both together constitute 24.4 per cent of the Indian population, that is, they together number over 25 crore. The six states that have the highest percentage of scheduled caste population are Punjab (28.9), Himachal Pradesh (24.7), West Bengal (23.0), Uttar Pradesh (21.1), Haryana (19.3) and Tamil Nadu (19.0). The twelve states that have the largest number of scheduled castes are Uttar Pradesh (351.5 lakhs), West Bengal (184.5 lakhs), Bihar (130.5 lakhs), Andhra Pradesh (123.4 lakhs), Tamil Nadu (118.6 lakhs), Maharashtra (98.8 lakhs), Rajasthan (96.9 lakhs), Madhya Pradesh (91.6 lakhs), Karnataka (85.6 lakhs), Punjab (70.3 lakhs), Odisha (60.8 lakhs) and Haryana (40.9 lakhs). It has earmarked positive note in the last census report. The dimensional shift in the social, political and economic aspects of the Dalits are better in comparion to the previous census. Though not mainstreamed but in the track to be mainstreamed, if the circumstances and situations go side by side.

Findings

Ensuring access to education for the Dalits of India has been the greatest challenge for the Indian government in diminishing the social effects of the caste system, which still remain entrenched in

Indian society. There have been many different reasons proposed as to why the Dalits suffer from low rates of literacy and primary education enrollment, but the most realistic one describes history and unequal access as the causes.

Suggestions

Reservations: All the backlogs in reserved seats and posts and in promotions for Dalits which includes SCs, STs and OBCs must be filled forthwith with special recruitment drives. A comprehensive legislation covering all aspects of reservation for SCs/STs in employment and education both public and private institutions should be enacted. A National Commission should be set up to assess the real position of Dalits including reservation in proportionate with population. The state level commissions should be set up to oversee the implementation of all schemes connected with the SCs including reservation. Infrastructure development in the scheduled caste areas like road, water, health, culture and other needs has to be given proper importance by aimimg at Rooting out Untouchability in all its forms which is deep-rooted in Indian society. Strengthening the relevant laws, ensuring their strict implementation for the protection against from Atrocities, which is vibrant in the major pockets of the country. The Central Government should amend and strengthen the SC and ST (Prevention of Atrocities) Act 1989, providing for special courts with judges, investigating officers and public prosecutors unburdened by any other work. Social and economic boycott and blackmail should be included as substantive crimes. Full economic rehabilitation of victims and their survivors must be ensured. The commercialisation of education should be stopped since the massive fee and donation structure of private educational managements is something that socially and economically backward students cannot afford. For this, the central government must increase its own outlay on education to six per cent of the GDP. Steps should be taken to universalise primary education and expand secondary education. Special measures to curb the drop-out rate among SCs should be undertaken.

Agricultural Workers: The Minimum Wages Act for agricultural workers must be stringently implemented throughout the country. The National Rural Employment Guarantee Act must be strictly implemented all over the country by involving the people, their mass organisations and the panchayati raj institutions. It should be extended to all districts and also to urban areas of the country. The public distribution system must be universalised to ensure food to all. Until this is done, BPL ration cards must be issued to all Dalits. Ensure total liberation and full rehabilitation for scavengers (safai karamcharis), ban engagement of contract labour in safai services and other services where SC and ST numerically predominate and instead introduce necessary improvements by involving such Karamcharis; and reactivate the Central Monitoring Committee for Liberation and Rehabilitation of Safai Karamcharis and State, Municipal and District Level communities. Inter-caste marriages should be encouraged by giving special subsidised housing and other facilities to married couples immediately after their marriage. We should consciously try to uphold such inter-caste marriages and make them an event of big social participation and sanction.

Conclusion

Dalits are the marginalised in India but Dalit among the Dalits should get their due space in the society. Elimination of Creamy Layer and preference should be given to the unprivileged among the unprivileged. The other important argument may be put forth that there should be an elite class among the Dalit to carry forward the community. It can create a vista of clear cut vision for their community can be proved to be a boon in mainstreaming the Dalits in India.

References

1. AIR 1964 SC 737.
2. Prasad, Dr Anirudh, 2007. Outlines of legal language in India, p. 414.
3. Extempore speech by Hon'ble Mr. Justice S.H. Kapadia, Judge, Supreme Court of India on the occasion of the Eighth Justice J.K. Mathur Memorial Lecture on 13-12-2008 at Lucknow.

   Surendrasingh, 2005. "Dr Ambedkar Contribution to Social Justice" Edt. By Prof M. Shabbir, Jaipur: Rawat pub., pp. 78-81.
4. Nazeer, H.Khan, "B.R. Ambedkar on federalism, ethnicity and under justice" Deep and Deep Pub. New Delhi, p. 151.
5. John Rawl's "Theory of Justice" Universal Law Pub. Delhi, 2002, pp. 44 and p. 336.

6. Friedman, W. "Legal Theory" 5th Edn, Universal Law Pub. Delhi, 2002, pp. 336-37.
7. Friedman, W. "Legal Theory" 5th Edn, Universal Law Pub, Delhi, 2002, p. 338.
8. Krishna Iyar, "B.R. Ambedkar Centenary, Social Justice and the Undone vast Justice" B.R. Pub. Delhi, 1991, p. 141.
9. Merunandan K.B, Naveed Ahmed. "An Introduction to the Constitution of India" Merugu Pub. Bangalore, 2006, p. 226.
10. Mohamed Shabbir (2005). Ambedkar on Law, Constitution and Social Justice. Rawat : Jaipur.
11. Venugopal P. (1998). Social Justice and reservation" Emerald Publications: Chennai.
12. D.C. Ahir (1990). The Legacy of Ambedkar" B.R. Publications: Delhi.
13. J.S. Narayana Rao and A. Somashekar "B.R. Ambedkar is relevance today" Shakthi Publications: New Delhi.
14. Dr Ambedkar on women's emancipation, Dr B.R. Ambedkar series Pub of Ambedkar Peeta, KSOU, Mysore, 2005, p. 5.
15. Purohit B.R, Sandeep Joshi (2003). "Social justice in India" Rawat : Jaipur.
16. B.R. Ambedkar on "Pakistan or Partition of India" Vol. 8, p. 225.
17. B.R. Ambedkar on "Pakistan or Partition of India" Vol .8, p. 226.
18. Dr Baba Saheb Ambedkar writings and Speechs. Vol. 17, part-3, p. 283.
19. Mohamed Shabbir (2005). Ambedkar on Law, Constitution and Social Justice" Rawat: Jaipur.
20. Many amendments were suggested by the members of Constituent Assembly, viz., Sri L.N. Sahu, Patabi Seeta Ramaiah, Smt. G. Durga Bai, Pandith Thakurdas Bhargava, Dr B.V. Keshkar, T.T. Krishnamachari, M. Ananthasham Iyengar, K. Shantharam, Aututal Chandra, Upendranath Bhraman and Professor K.T. Shah.
21. Mohamed Shabbir (2005). Ambedkar on Law, Constitution and Social Justice. Rawat: Jaipur.
22. CAD Vol. X-XII, pp. 456.
23. Mohamed Shabbir (2005). Ambedkar on Law, Constitution and Social Justice" Rawat : Jaipur.
24. CAD Vol. VII, p. 661.
25. CAD Vol. VII, p. 662.
26. Article 37 of the Constitution of India.
27. Minerva Mills Vs Union of India, Air, 1980, SC 1789.
28. Article 38 of the Constitution of India.
29. Article 39 of the Constitution of India.
30. Article 38A of the Constitution of India.

31. Article 41 of the Constitution of India.
32. Article 42 of the Constitution of India.
33. Article 43 of the Constitution of India.
34. Article 43A of the Constitution of India.
35. Article 44 of the Constitution of India.
36. Article 45 of the Constitution of India.
37. Article 46 of the Constitution of India.
38. Article 47 of the Constitution of India.
39. Purohit, B.R, Sandeep Joshi (2003). Social justice in India. Rawat: Jaipur.
40. Mahbal Ram (2003) Changing Economic Scenario and Social Justice on India, Dominant Publication: Delhi.
41. Wodeyer, D. Hegade (2005). "Job reservation for Dalits and Backward classes in Private sectors issues and strategies" Center for human development studies, Mysore, p. 46.
42. Ambedkar, B.R. 1916. *Castes in India: their Mechanism, Genesis and Development*, Writings and Speeches, Vol. I, Bombay, Govt. of Maharashtra, 1979.
43. 1918 *Mr Russel and The Reconstruction of Society,* Writings and Speeches, Vol. I, Bombay, Govt. of Maharashtra, 1979.
44. 1936 *Annihilation of Caste,* Writings and Speeches, Vol. I, Bombay, Government of Maharashtra, 1979.
45. Ambedkar, B.R. 1945. *What Congress and Gandhi have done to the Untouchables*, Writings and Speeches, Vol. I, Bombay, Govt. of Maharashtra, 1979.
46. 1987 Philosophy of Hinduism, Writings and Speeches, Vol. 3, Bombay, Government of Maharashtra, 1987.
47. 1989 *Away from the Hindus*, Writings and Speeches, Vol. V, Bombay, Government of Maharashtra, 2003 Writings and Speeches, Vol. I7.3 Bombay, Govt. of Maharashtra.
48. Arjan de Hann (2008). Social Exclusion : Towards a Holistic Understanding of Deprivation, Critical Quest, New Delhi.
49. Das, Bhagwan (1979). *Thus Spoke Ambedkar*, Vol. I and II, Jullandur: Bheem, Patrika Publications.
50. Satyapal, P.D. (2010). *From Culture of Reservations to Culture of Representations: Phule-Ambedkarite Agenda for Social Inclusion in India* in V. Subrahmanyam (ed.) Social Exclusion, Integration and Inclusive Policies Jaipur : Rawat Publications.
51. 2010a *Dr B.R. Ambedkar's Exhumation of Cultural Capital and its Dynamics in Indian Society* in G. Bhadru Naik (ed.) Economic Philosophy of Dr B.R. Ambedkar an relevance in the Contemporary Society, Warangal.

19

Politics of Religious Exclusion: Status of Sehajdhari Sikhs in the Sikh Panth

—***Kanwar Deep Singh***

Abstract

'Sehajdhari Sikhs' have continued to participate in Sikh life right up to modern times and have associated themselves with Sikh institutions and organisations. The Sehajdhari Sikh Party has been contesting a legal battle in the Punjab and Haryana High Court for the voting right of Sehajdhari Sikhs in the SGPC elections which was existing since 1959 and was disfrenchised in 2003 by a notification. Akali Dal and other panthic groups have been consistently opposing the inclusion of 'Sehajdharis' among voters, and the recent intervention of the Punjab and Haryana High Court has complicated the matters and has implications for Shiromani Akali Dal (SAD) in Gurdwara politics. Ignoring 'Sehajdharis' and distorting the definition of `Sikh` has divided Sikhs into another sub-minority and nearly 80 per cent of Sikhs have been thrown out of the mainstream of the religion. This issue of Sikh identity has significant implications for elections to the Shiromani Gurdwara Prabhandhak Committee (SGPC). It's a big identity crisis within the Sikh Community.

This paper is an attempt to examine and analyse the contemporary status of 'Sehajdhari Sikhs' in the Sikh 'Panth', on the basis of their historical origin and evolution. The paper will focus on the political dynamics behind the resulting explorations in context to the religious status of 'Sehajdhari Sikhs', who form a significant part of Sikh Community.

Key Words: *Sehajdhari Sikhs, religion, identity, voting right, identity crisis.*

Introduction

The Sehajdharis share with the main body of the Sikhs all of their religious and social customs and ceremonies and join their congregations in the *Gurdwaras*. The population in the Punjab of Sehajdhari Sikhs according to 1891 Census was 397,000 (20 per cent of the total Sikh population); according to 1901 Census, 297,000 (13 per cent of the total Sikhs); according to 1911 Census, 451,000 (14.9 per cent of the total Sikhs); according to 1921 Census, 229,000 (7 per cent of the total Sikhs); according to 1931 Census, 282,000 (6.5 per cent of the total Sikhs). Outside of the Punjab, the North-West Frontier Province and Sindh had considerable Sehajdhari populations. Consequent upon the partition of India in 1947, Sehajdharis became widely dispersed in the country. Their India-wide forum was *Sarab Hind (All-India) Sehajdharis Conference* which rotated from town to town for its annual sessions.

Sehajdharis have continued to participate in Sikh life right up to modern times and have associated themselves with Sikh institutions and organisations such as the Shiromani Gurdwara Prabandhak Committee, Chief Khalsa Diwan, Shiromani Akali Dal, and the All-India Sikh Students Federation. The Singh Sabhas used to have seats on their executive committees reserved for the Sehajdharis. Among their own societies, confined prior to the migrations of 1947, mainly to north-western India, were the Sehajdhari Committee of Multan, Guru Nanak Sehajdhari Diwan of Panja Sahib and Sri Guru Nanak Sehajdhari Jatha of Campbellpore. The Sehajdhari Diwan of Panja Sahib attained the status of their central forum.

'Sehajdhari' is a compound of two words *sahaj* and *dhari*. In Sanskrit and other Indo-Aryan languages, the word *Sehaj* means: *spiritual state of equilibrium* and *dhari* means adopter. A *sehajdhari* believes in all the tenets of Sikhism and the teachings of the Sikh Gurus but has not put all of them into practice. The reasons can be many, including not being disciplined enough to maintain the 'Khalsa' code of conduct or due to personal reasons of them not believing they have enough commitment to become a 'Khalsa Sikh'. In the Sikh community, these reasons are considered valid, as to renege upon them or break the 'Khalsa' code of conduct.

According to the *Shiromani Gurdwara Prabandhak Committee*, the 'Sehajdharis' are ones "*who have expressed their desire to adopt Sikhism slowly and gradually, its doctrines, ethics and tenants with belief in Shri Guru Granth Sahib and the 10 Gurus.*" SGPC further adds that, "*A Sehajdhari Sikh is a person who performs ceremonies according to the Sikh rites; who does not use tobacco, kutha (halal meat) in any form, who is not a Patit and who can recite mulmantra.*" SGPC also clarifies: "*Once a Sahajdhari becomes a Keshdhari Sikh, he, under no circumstances by cutting or trimming hair, beard, eyebrows in any manner, can claim to be a Sahajdhari Sikh.*" Thus, *Shiromani Gurdwara Prabandhak Committee*, describes 'Sehajdhari Sikh' as a person: (i) *who performs ceremonies according to Sikh rites; (ii) who does not use tobacco or kutha (halal meat) in any form; (iii) who is not a patit; and (iv) who can recite Mool Mantar.*

Politico-Religious Exclusion of Sehajdhari Sikhs

Every few years, Indian courts receive petitions from some mischief makers and some apparently aggrieved people questioning the definition of a Sikh. Shiromani Gurdwara Prabandhak Committee (SGPC) has reiterated that 'Sehajdhari Sikhs', who shave, cut or trim their hair, cannot be recognised as Sikhs for the purpose of grant of electoral rights in SGPC elections and only 'Keshadhari Sikhs' should have the right to vote. The submission to this effect was made before the Punjab and Haryana High Court by Mukhtar Singh on behalf of SGPC in an ongoing case challenging the notification (dated October 8, 2003) issued by the Union Government. By way of issuing this notification, Ministry of Home Affairs, Government of India had amended sections 49 and 92 of the Sikh Gurudwara Act, 1925, also barring 'Sehajdhari Sikhs' from casting their votes in SGPC elections. A memorandum in this respect was presented by Professor Kirpal Singh Badungar, President of SGPC to the then Indian Home Minister, L.K. Advani on March 3, 2002. SGPC claims that certain vested interests, had from time to time sought to misuse the statutory provisions to induct into the electoral rolls non-Sikhs under the garb of 'Sehajdhari Sikhs'. The committee also confirms that a large number of such persons, some with fake names and addresses, were sought to be included with a view to dilute the electoral rolls, which essentially should consist bonafide Sikh voters. *The line of questioning is disturbing for the term 'Sehajdhari Sikh' has practically been removed from the statue in the elections to the general house of the Shiromani Gurdwara Parbandhak Committee. All votes registered in separate forms for the so-called Sehajdhari, voters, running into lakhs, were rendered null and void.*

Politicisation of 'Sehajdhari Sikh' Identity

The 'Sehajdhari Sikh' voting issue was very first taken up by the SAD (Mann) through its General Secretary Jagmohan Singh and former SGPC Member Bharpur Singh, who filed a petition in the Punjab and Haryana High Court in 2001 for debarring the Sehajdhari Sikhs to participate in SGPC voting. The Sehajdhari Sikh Party previously known as the Sehajdhari Sikh Federation jumped into the fray and requested the Court to implead it as a necessary party as the lakhs of 'Sehajdhari Sikhs' were to be effected by the decision of the Court. The High Court then impleaded the Sehajdhari Sikh Federation as a necessary party and meanwhile the Union Government issued a notification on October, 8th, 2003 debarring the 'Sehajdhari Sikhs' and this case was admitted by the Court. It is mentionable here that the said notification of the Union Government was challenged by the Sehajdhari Sikh Federation in 2003. The petitioners had mainly challenged the Centre's notification "where by Sehajdharis Sikhs are not being considered as Sikhs in view of the impugned amendment in Section 49 and Section 92 of the Gurudwara Act." The petitioner had submitted that the original Act declared 'Sehajdhari Sikhs' as qualified electors for the SGPC elections, and the Apex court had in numerous judgements held that the state cannot regulate the definition of religion. It was argued by the petitioner that state authorities cannot fetter the definition of Sikhs in general and 'Sehajdhari Sikhs' in particular when religion is not within the bounds of any kind of legislation. Sehajdhari Sikh Federation was formed on 13 April 2001, when resolutions were passed by SGPC to disfranchise the voting right of Sehajdhari Sikhs in SGPC elections by group of individuals, especially those Sikhs who were born in Sikh families. Firstly the organisation was registered under the Society Act at Ludhiana and then on November 4, 2001, the Federation held a large congregation of thousands of Sehajdhari Sikhs before Akal Takht at Amritsar and held 'Ardaas' by turning the Sehajdhari Sikh Federation into a political outfit and named it as

Sehajdhari Shiromani Akali Dal. Later, the Election Commission has approved the change of name of the Party as *Sehadhari Sikh Party* (SSP). The Party has been contesting a legal battle in the Punjab and Haryana High Court for the voting right of 'Sehajdhari Sikhs' in the SGPC elections which was existing since 1959 and was disfrenchised in 2003 by a notification.

A pertinent issue of distinct Sikh identity has implications for elections to the Shiromani Gurdwara Parbhandhak Committee, Shiromani Akali Dal, and other panthic groups which have been consistently opposing the inclusion of Sehajdharis among voters, and the recent intervention of the Punjab and Haryana High Court has complicated the matters and has implications for SAD in gurdwara politics.

Under contemporary social and political scenario, Gurdwaras assume a significant legitimising social space for the diverse community of Sikhs in India. While the exclusion of Dalits among Sikhs has found dissenting expression in the construction of "caste" gurdwaras in Punjab and abroad, the Sikhs in Haryana, Himachal Pradesh and Rajasthan may over the years press for claims of their own Gurdwara Parbandhak Committees. After all gurdwaras always had the shared function of the community's participation, and the demand of Haryana Shiromani Gurdwara Prabhandhak Committee (HSGPC) seems like a legitimate disenchantment against almost a century old hegemony of Shiromai Akali Dal (SAD) over Sikh shrines on which the Sikhs of the neighbouring states have little say. The Sehajdhari Sikhs in Haryana voted against the Congress and Akalis as they felt betrayed during the formation of Separate Shiromani Gurdwara Management Committee in Haryana. The Hooda Government had changed the definition of 'Sikh' in the HSGM Act 2014 by considering only Keshdharis as Sikhs which has sided the Sikh Minority into a further sub-minority, thereby removing a vast majority of Sikhs from their religion.

Conclusion

The definition of 'Sehajdhari Sikh' has no religious sanction as far as the fundamental tenets of the Sikh religion are concerned. One is either a Sikh or not a Sikh. This nomenclature was added to the Sikh Gurdwara Act, 1925 under a particular set of circumstances, which too are questionable, but without going into the details of those times, the circumstance ceases to exist.

Given the enlargement of the community beyond the shores of Punjab, given the rise of apostasy amongst the community and particularly its youth, given the lack of knowledge amongst the religious leaders running the SGPC affairs in handling such issues, given the lack of adherence to the requirements of unshorn hair by Sikh boys and girls, such questions are likely to arise and the situation is likely to take an ugly turn when some individuals want to reap the benefits of being a Sikh –say admission into institutions where nearly 85 per cent of Sikh population of the World are of the non-baptized Sikhs, who are born in Sikh families and have no other religion except Sikhism and believe in Guru Granth Sahib only. Stating and recognising such non baptized Sikhs as 'Patit' or non-Sikhs shall create a wedge between the Sikh Community worldwide. However, it is an established historical fact that all 'Khalsa Sikhs' were 'Sahajdhari Sikhs' at one point in their lives because no-one is born a baptized Sikh – 'a Khalsa'. According to Sikh Governing Institutions, 'non-keshdharis' born in Sikh families are legally left without any religion. They are not Hindus and do not belong to any other religion, and legally they cannot claim to be Sikhs. It's a vital identity crisis within the Sikh Community which could have crucial religious and political implications.

References

Adiraju, V.R. 1991, *Sikhs and India: Identity Crisis*, Satya Publications, Hyderabad.

Ahluwalia, Jasbir Singh 1983, *The Sovereignty of the Sikh Doctrine*, Bahri Publications, New Delhi.

———1987, *Sikhism Today- The Crisis Within and Without*, Published by Guru Gobind Singh Foundation, Chandigarh.

———2003, *Liberating Sikhism from The Sikhs - Sikhism's Potential for World Civilisation,* Unistar Books, Chandigarh.

Alcoff Linda Martin and Eduardo Mendieta (eds) 2003, *Identities-Race, Class, Gender, and Nationality*, Blackwell Publishing Ltd., USA.

Bedi, Harchand Singh (ed) 2001, *The Sikhs in the New Century,* published by Khalsa College, Amritsar.

Dhanoa, Surain Singh 2005, *Raj Karega Khalsa*, Sanbun Publications, New Delhi.

Gayer, Laurent 2000, "The Globalisation of Identity Politics: The Sikh Experience", *International Journal of Punjab Studies*, Vol. 7, July-December 2000, pp. 223-262, available at http://www.sciencespo.fr/ceri/sites/sciencespo.fr.ceri/files/artlg_0.pdf, accessed on 23/07/2014.

Ghuman, Ranjit Singh, "The Sikh Community in Indian Punjab: Some Socio-Economic Challenges", available at http://www.global.ucsb.edu/punjab/journal/v19_1/5-Ghuman Sikh Community_ 19_ 1.pdf, accessed on 23/09/2014.

Grewal, Gurdev 2006, *The Searching Eye: An Insider Look at the Punjab Crisis,* Rupa Publications, New Delhi.

Grewal, J.S. and Indu Banga, 2002, *Khalsa Itihaas Ate Vichardhara* (in Punjabi), GNDU, Amritsar.

Grewal, J.S. 1990, *The Sikhs of the Punjab*, Cambridge University Press.

———1998, *Contesting Interpretations of the Sikh Tradition*, Manohar Publishers, New Delhi.

———2009, *The Sikhs- Ideology, Institutions and Identity,* Oxford University Press, New Delhi.

———2011, *Recent Debates in Sikh Studies-An Assessmen*t, Manohar Publishers, New Delhi.

Gupta, Dipankar *et.al.* 1988, "Punjab: Communalised beyond Politics", *Economic and Political Weekly*, Vol. 23, No. 33, Aug. 13, 1988, pp. 1677-1684.

Jodhka, Surinder S. 1997, "Crisis of the 1980s and the Changing Agenda of Punjab Studies", *Economic and Political Weekly*,Vol. 36, No. 2, Feb. 8-14, 1997, pp. 273-279.

———2001, "Minority Status for Sikh in Punjab: What does it mean?" *Economic and Political Weekly,* Vol. 36, No. 8, May 5-11, 2001.

Judge, Paramjit Singh 2004, "Religion, Identity and History", *Economic and Political Weekly* Vol. 39, No. 32, Aug. 7-13, 2004, pp. 3605-3608.

———2010, "The Politics of Sikh Identity: Understanding Religious Exclusion", *Journal of the Indian Sociological Society*, Sept. Dec, 2010.

———(1998), "Sikh Fundamentalism", *Journal of the American Oriental Society*, Vol. 118, No. 1, January – March, 1998, pp. 15-27, available at http://www.jstor.org/discover /10.2307/ 606295?uid=2134&uid=2&uid=70&uid=4&sid=21104853633231, accessed on 16/11/2014.

Patil, Sharad 1994, "Real Challenge before the Sikhs", *Economic and Political Weekly,* Vol. 29, No. 39, Sept., 1994.

Hall, Stuart and Paul Du Gay (eds) 1996, *Question of Cultural Identity,* Sage Publications, London.

Hawley, John Stratton and Gurinder Singh Mann (eds) 1993, *Studying The Sikhs: Issues for North America*, Published by State University of New York Press, Albany.

Jacobsen, Knuta and Kristina Myrvold (eds) 2011, *Sikhs in Europe,* Ashgate, Surrey, England.

Kaur, Gurdeep 1990, *Political Ideas of the Sikh Gurus,* Deep and Deep Publications, New Delhi.

Kaur, Nikky Gurinder 2011, *Sikhism:An Introduction,* I.B. Tauris, London.

McLeod, W.H. 1989, *Who is a Sikh? The Problem of Sikh Identity,* Oxford University Press, New Delhi.

———1995, *The Evolution of the Sikh Community: Five Essays*, Oxford University Press, New Delhi.

———2003, *Sikhs of the Khalsa – A History of the Khalsa Rahit*, Oxford University Press, New Delhi.

Robinson, Rowena (ed) 2012, *Minority Studies,* Oxford University Press, New Delhi.

Sandhu, Devinder Pal 1992, *Sikhs in Indian Politics: Study of a Minority*, Patriot Publishers, New Delhi.

Shackle, Christopher *et.al.* 2001, *Sikh Religion, Culture and Ethnicity,* Curzon Press, Surrey.

Singh, Ganda 1967, *Hukam-Name,* Punjabi University, Patiala.

Singh, Ajmer, *Vihvin Sadi Di Sikh Rajneeti* 2012 (in Punjabi), Singh Brothers, Amritsar.

Singh, Gobinder 1986, *Religion and Politics in the Punjab*, Deep and Deep Publications, New Delhi.

Singh, Gopal (ed) 1994, *Punjab Past, Present and Future,* Ajanta Publications, Delhi.

Singh, Gurdev (ed) 1986, *Perspectives on the Sikh Tradition*, Siddharth Publications, Patiala.

Singh, Jasbir and Harbans Singh 1989, *Advanced Studies in Sikhism*, Sikh Community of North America.

Singh, Jaspal 1997, *Sikh Dharm Ate Rajneeti,* (in Punjabi) Navyug Publishers, New Delhi.

Singh, Mohinder 1988, *The Akali Struggle: A Retrospect,* Atlantic Publications, New Delhi.

Singh, Pashaura and Gerald Barrier (eds) 1999, *Sikh Identity Continuity and Change,* Manohar Publishers, New Delhi.

Singh, Pashaura 2011, *Sikhism in Global Context,* Oxford University Press, New Delhi.

Singh, Tarlochan 2001, *Religion and Politics in Sikhism: The Khalsa Perspective,* Singh Brothers, Amritsar.

———2001, *The Turban and the Sword of the Sikhs-Essence of Sikhism,* Singh Brothers, Amritsar.

Singh, Teja 1990, *Essays in Sikhism*, Siddharth Publications, New Delhi.

Singh, Devinder 2008, "Controversy over Sehajdhari Sikh- But Who is a Sikh?", *Understanding Sikhism - The Research Journal,* Institute for Understanding Sikhism, Laval, QC, Canada, December 2008, available at http://www.iuscanada.com/journal/articles/sehjdhari.pdf, accessed on 25/11/2014.

Singh, Gurtej 1996, "Sikh Identity in the Context of Resurgent Modern India", *Abstract of Sikh Studies*, Jan-March: 68-89.

"Plea against voting rights of Sehajdhari Sikhs dismissed" (2013, November 11), *The Hindu*, available at http://www.thehindu.com/news/national/plea-against-voting-rights-of-sehajdhari-sikhs dismissed/article5402543.ece, accessed on 12/11/2014.

20

Political Marginalisation in Punjab Villages: A Nexus of Corruption, Factionalism and Political Distrust

—*Gunjan Setia*

Abstract

Marginalisation, an effect of exclusion, is a phenomenon that prevents or limits the enjoyment of certain rights; it manifests itself in all social relations including politics. Globalisation, the current economic crisis and recent developments of welfare policies have been claimed to give rise to new cleavages between 'winners' and 'losers' in terms of social risk positions and in terms of political attitudes and party sympathy[1]*. The paper puts forward the changing attitudes, experiences and beliefs of the rural folk after the green revolution in Punjab. It tries to deal with the issue of political marginalisation and political reality as perceived by the inhabitants at village level. The conclusions were derived on the basis content analysis of various focus group discussions carried with farmers, Panchayat members, farmer unions, labour unions and women groups across five villages in the Malwa belt thereby grasping the total picture of social perception related to local political processes. It was found that political distrust towards the village government and State agencies was the dominant belief of the people. Corruption was rampant and was explicitly accepted, talked about social evil whereby marginalised groups felt insecure and helpless. Another aspect was factionalism at village level which had two major basis; that of caste and another of class whereby inter-group rivalry was a dominant factor. This factor was a major deterrent to the functioning of development projects in villages and for the collective organisation of the masses to address their commonly faced social issues.*

Introduction

The term 'Marginalisation' generally describes the overt actions or tendencies of human societies whereby those perceived as being without desirability or function are removed or excluded (i.e., are "marginalised"...) from the prevalent systems of protection and integration, so limiting their opportunities and means for survival. The term marginalisation is generally used for the minorities and tribals in Indian context but in the realm of research the term is synonymous to social exclusion where the later being a larger, complex concept which includes both marginalised and the process of marginalisation and its forms.

It is generally accepted that the term social exclusion originated in France in the early 1970s first to describe various categories of people (the mentally and physically disabled, the aged, abused children, single parents, marginal, asocial persons, 'misfits' and so on comprising 10 per cent of the French population) who were excluded from the employment based social security system. The term was continually redefined to encompass new problems and social groups. It was used in the 1980s to refer to various types of social disadvantage related to social problems arising from economic crises and crises of the welfare state – long-term unemployment, ghettoisation, growing instability of social bonds including among family members, in neighbourhoods, trade unions, etc. but also of the lack of integration of immigrants, especially Muslims. Exclusion was seen as the result of the rupture of social and symbolic bonds between individuals and society and the failure of the state, reflecting the French emphasis on the organic and solidaristic nature of society. Social policy was directed towards 'insertion' or integration of the excluded to ensure social cohesion or social solidarity (Silver, 1994-6; de Haan, 1998)[2], as there was also increasing concern with social rights of citizens. So, marginalisation, an effect of exclusion, is a phenomenon that prevents or limits the enjoyment of certain rights; it manifests itself in all social relations including politics. Globalisation, the current economic crisis and recent developments of welfare policies have been claimed to give rise to new cleavages between 'winners' and 'losers' in terms of social risk positions and in terms of political attitudes and party sympathy.[2]

For the present paper, political processes acting at local level had been gauged by using social perception of villagers as an indicator of the political atmosphere prevalent in rural Malwa Punjab. Social perception was chosen to be an indicator as it leads to social construction of reality and in it plays dominant role in creating every political wave and it also shapes the expectations of the masses from political parties.

The study was conducted in two Districts of Malwa Punjab namely, Bathinda and Sangrur; these were selected by simple random sampling. Further one block from each District was selected on the basis of social backwardness in terms of low sex ratio, cancer deaths and farm suicide cases. The information was gathered from Block Development Officers on socially backward villages. Two villages from each block were thus selected. So villages Bhundarh and Chauke from District Bathinda and Bhutal Khurd and Chottian from District Sangrur were studied. Focus group discussions across various sections of society namely, farmers, labourers, youth, females, village elderly were conducted and interviews of panchayat members were taken in person. The collected information was substantiated with personal observations. Content analysis of the collected data in the form of emerging coherent themes was done whereby a coherent picture of public perception was charted out.

Major Findings

People were usually dissatisfied and frantic about government functioning; as they frequently stated that all politicians and officers were corrupt, bribery was the only way to get any work done. Two major issues related to politics emerged through various discussions. First was insensitivity of officials and second was discrepancy between dictated rules and problems in implementation at grass root level.

Sarpanches from different villages shared that the ways of government were unjustified, as government provides only the infrastructure or equipment for any project to be launched at village level but the responsibility of functioning of the project and collection of grant for its administration was left with the panchayat. Sarpanches were unhappy with such an approach as it leads to intra-village rivalries and disputes. For example, the water works in two of the visited villages were non-functional due to lack of funds and pending electricity bills as sarpanches were helpless to collect money from villagers as even the rules of collection were not clear. Another issue was the panchayat had a need to employ security guards to protect the machineries but such appointment was not sanctioned and the responsibility was put on sarpanches. One of the sarpanch remarked that "The ways of government functioning were beyond comprehension as on one hand government provides free electricity to farmers for tube-wells and on the other hand they demand charges for the electric motor being installed for drinking water for the whole village."

Personal observations too validated the above facts, as a local female was seen with her five year old son amidst hot '*loo*' (local hot breeze) in afternoon visiting panchayat members to enquire if her card was brought from town when she got a negative response, on hearing this she softly spoke "*ek do din ch lea di bhai*" (get it in one or two days brother) and went away calmly. After she went, the official explained that according to the new government rules some identity proof was necessary for the wards to get admission in government schools and officials were accepting only ration cards, as it has residence address on it and no other proof was being accepted. A sarpanch explained "This is the only problem with officials they cannot understand ground realities. They make laws sitting in air-condition rooms, on the other hand he gave the example of the lady who just visited him, that she came one km on foot in such scorching heat with her child and yet went away patiently after knowing that her work was not done, how can any official understand this?" he further remarked:-

> "*jehra banda tang hai ji, ohnu tangi da pta, dujje nu ni pta*"
> (Only the wearer knows where the shoe pinches)

Factionalism

The kissan unions were very strong in all the villages; their work included carrying out of *Dharnas* (agitations) against any atrocity towards farmers by the government and for their rights. They also acted as mediators during any tiff between kissan (farmer) and money lender they also unite and stand against the police arrest of defaulter farmer of bank loan. In case a farmer is unable to pay back his debts unions don't allow his land to be auctioned. They fought for many problems that a farmer had to face which ranged from high input and low output cost, inflation, water logging, debt and no rights available to farmers for the rate of their own produce. The kissan union activists demanded loan waivers and not only subsidies. The kissan unions gave emotional support and sympathy to suicide victim families and raise their issue during agitations. They go to the DC (District Collector) office to lodge complaints regarding any atrocity faced by the farmers. Kissan Union members revealed that there were many farmer and labour unions active in the village such as BKU (Ugraha), Kissan Union Sidhupura, Punjab Kheti Majdoor Union etc. As I enquired about the reason behind the emergence of as many as 13 unions in villages, it came to light that the demands of all unions were same and was for the betterment of masses though they had varying ideologies. There were few Unions like Lakhowal, Ugraha, Sidupura, Rajewal who had played dominant role for the betterment of masses at different times. Rajewal and ugraha had good support in the region and its members were also educated and pro-masses. The major factor that has led to factionalism was greed for leadership though these unions did unite on major issues to pressurise the government. There was political segmentation as many labour and farmer unions had been active in the villages like the Labour union, Palledar union, Ugraha group, Rajewal, Dakonda, Sidupura, Lakhowal, Takhatpura etc. Villagers said that these unions were independent and were not connected to any political party rather and they unite for specific common issues, as recently they collectively protested against the acquisition of land for factory in village Gobindpura. Such parties in all the villages help the villagers by putting pressure on moneylenders to decrease the rate of interest to some optimum level and also don't allow the banks and moneylenders to capture farmers' lands.

Such factionalism on one hand had weakened the strength of the pressure groups and on the other had created hindrance in development works as all groups tried to avail maximum proportion of available government facilities or subsidies.

Corruption

Corruption had become the order of the day and was an accepted open fact. Villagers expressed dissatisfaction over work of government officials especially the Patwaris and nambardars. People reported that they had to bribe Panches to get their names into the lists for various form of pensions like widow pension, old age pension and pension for differently able; despite the fact that they were genuine beneficiaries. Union activists shared that even people owning huge kothis had been allotted BPL cards while on the other hand actual beneficiaries are left behind if they are unable to bribe the Panches who usually charge Rs 400. On the other hand poor can avail their due government benefits only if they have cordial relations with politically active villagers. Another factor that makes government grants and subsidies out of reach of the actual beneficiaries was the friction among various political groups, who by hook or crook would like to channelize largest possible share of grants towards their family, friends and supporters. So many actual beneficiaries are left at God's mercy for survival.

Further it came to light that in one of the villages, no beneficiary had received pensions from last three months as the *panchayat* members including two woman *panchs* were behind bars due to embezzlement of pensions under different categories, especially "*marre bandiyan di pension kha gye*" i.e. they kept receiving old age pensions of the beneficiaries who have died, by forging their thumb impressions. Secondly as most of the beneficiaries being illiterate or/and helpless, are incapable of keeping a check on public servants. A nexus between some of panchayat members and anganwadi workers via whom the money was being distributed had emerged but as the scam came to light they all were arrested. To verify the truth in the issue, as revealed by the activists many other sources were also mobilised who too nodded to the misdeeds prevalent in the village and the persons who were out on bail in the same case were also met.

A possible reason behind corrupt attitudes of panchayats could be seen in the expenditures they incur during elections. Once any candidate spends beyond his means then automatically he/she would try to embezzle grants or indulge in malpractices to recover their spent money. This issue was discussed with Sarpanches and they openly agreed to it. An ex-sarpanch from Bathinda disclosed some incidents to explain how things work at ground level; he started with his own experience of panchayat elections. He narrated that politics today is all a game of money, though villagers insisted him to contest the elections independently against the candidate of ruling party yet he had to spend a lot. He revealed that he had sold three acres of land during his term as sarpanch and explained how everything happened. The election cost was 13.5 lakhs; contestants have to provide all addictives which people consume for votes though he won the elections but further after much tussle for the seat of sarpanch for a few months finally he had to buy the vote of a female *panch* for 3.5 lakhs, to bear all these expenditures he had to sell one acre of his ancestral land. He explained that the system had become so problematic that people would vote for the party not for the candidate. Even during vote counting there was no transparency the officers stopped showing the numbers midway and then they had to raise their voice and after re-counting he was declared winner. So such malpractices were linked both with corruption and political marginalisation where in a so-called democracy poor could not even think of contesting any election.

The sarpanch told that it is a well known fact in the area that whosoever becomes a sarpanch had to sell his land, as after meeting election costs one requires money to maintain the standard of a sarpanch and none is saved from it even not the sarpanch allied to a ruling party, in fact the ones allied to ruling parties have higher links and more expenditures, they sell more of their lands. After being a sarpanch one needs a car for transport, needs good clothes as had to visit officials, even has to construct a few new rooms or office in his house as villagers/ activists/party workers keep visiting him which further leads to increase in household consumption expenditures.

A similar picture was put forward by a sarpanch from Sangrur who belonged to scheduled castes and had a kriyana shop in the village that if anyone belongs to the party of state government he has more political powers, as the sarpanch revealed that he was declared a looser by six votes, but he had an eye on the counting process, so he raised an alarm, then the electoral committee got the booth vacated for recounting of votes and declared him a winner by 167 votes. When the sarpanch later grieved in front of the counting officer that 'I had risked everything I owned for the election and I am in such a state of bankruptcy that I would have to leave the village if I had lost; why did you manipulate the numbers?' then the officer replied that he had pressures from above so was helpless. Later after the recounting, the officers apologised for their mistake (here one gets a peep into the mode of functioning of government authorities).

As I asked about the election expenses incurred by him; the sarpanch revealed that he had an prior estimate of 3-4 lakhs but the expenses rose to Rs10 lakhs, though many villagers, relatives and friends had contributed to it voluntarily but he has to repay those relatives and villagers who themselves are poor. Someone spent 20000 other spent 50000 to make him win; it's now after the elections are over that they all told him about the expenses incurred, though he was forced by fellow villagers to contest the elections but later he was trapped, as the opposition was buying votes so even he had to spend money in order to win.

Another factor highlighted by another Sarpanch was that it was not easy for any panchayat members to embezzle grants, the one having political links can survive in the system as then no one would catch him but others have to give records of every penny used from government grants. Another thing shared was that every official has fixed shares as J.E asks for 10 per cent, BDO for 2-3 per cent of the grants and secretary takes Rs 5000, so finally what can a sarpanch earn? Even a sarpanch allied to ruling party can't embezzle grants as opposition keeps a check on him so finally it's the officials only who earns. Moreover, the one with political links can still survive after doing misdeeds as he has political links but a normal man would be caught.

Such discussions threw light on the declining value system, individualism whereby everyone eyes on ones' own benefit and the inescapable role of money in politics. The narrated incidents further highlighted the grasp of greed for money among rural folk which may go to the extent of being insensitive and irresponsible while holding positions of power. Further villagers shared that they never had any educated Sarpanch earlier so the village didn't progress.

Conclusion

It could be concluded that under the pressure of economic forces especially after Globalisation, economy has become the base of society and human relations is no exception. A picture of degrading social integration, lack of goodwill and political malpractices of corruption, factionalism were observed. All these processes being gelled together had led to widespread feeling of political marginalisation among lower strata of the society which includes poor, lower castes and women which contrarily form the largest chunk of village populace. Many other social evils especially rampant drug addiction, farm suicides, lower sex ratio, dowry had been innately linked with such political atmosphere. So it could be judged that such social construction through political processes is affecting the whole gamut of social fabric, which in turn is based on changed economic structure. Village life could be seen to be trapped in a vicious circle where people though aware of such malpractices but at the same time could not get rid of them.

Social inclusion, the converse of social exclusion, is affirmative action to change the circumstances and habits that lead to (or have led to) social exclusion. The World Bank defines social inclusion as the process of improving the ability, opportunity, and dignity of people, disadvantaged on the basis of their identity, to take part in society (World Bank, 2013). In the present scenario such dignity could only be achieved through transparency in all political process which could be achieved by frequent gram sabha meetings, use of technology for e.g. using cameras during vote counting and a strict check on panchayat election expenditures could provide some immediate relief to the masses.

Notes

1. Kriesi, 2006.
2. *Ibid.*
3. Cited at http://www.adityaanupkumar.com/files/The Concept Of Marginalisation. pdf
4. Labourer employed in grain market for filling/weighing/stacking or loading bags of grain.
5. The story was covered by leading papers like Jagran to be cited at http://post.jagran.com/punjab-farmers-to-protest-against-land-acquisition-for-govindpura-thermal-plant-1312207513; Sanhati to be cited at http://sanhati.com/excerpted/4080/; Magazine down to earth to be cited at http://www.downtoearth.org.in/content/now-land-acquisition-stir-punjab.

References

1. Barrentors, S and S. Smith (2006). The ETI Code of Labour Practice: Do workers really benefit?', Summary Report, London: Ethical Training Initiatives.
2. G. Jehoel-Gijsbers and C. Vrooman (2007). *Explaining Social Exclusion; A Theoretical Model tested in The Netherlands*. The Netherlands Institute for Social Research/SCP. ISBN 978 90 377 0325 2: cited online.
3. Jagran to be cited at http://post.jagran.com/punjab-farmers-to-protest-against-land-acquisition-for-govindpura-thermal-plant-1312207513.
4. Kriesi, H *et.al.* (2006), Globalisation and the transformation of the national political space: Six European countries compared. European Journal of Political Research, 921-956.
5. World Bank (2013). New Frontiers of Social Policy. Inclusion *matters: The foundation for shared prosperity*: Washington DC.

21

Are Dalits Part of Inclusive Policy of India? An Overview

—*Navneet Kaur*

Abstract

Hindu religion with its various castes and sub-castes is the most dominating religion in India. The status of caste in hierarchy of Varna system also determines the class. Dalits in India, on the basis of caste and class were discriminated for centuries. There is no doubt that in the contemporary Indian society, the democratic values are set up by the Indian Constitution for the progress of Nation. This paper is, therefore, an attempt to give an answer to the issue of decline of caste-based discrimination in the present scenario. The hypothesis taken is that the democratic progress has really led to the decline of casteism. The paper has tried to raise the issue of upliftment of dalits and through the observation method, has raised several doubts on the sincerity of governments for the welfare of this section.

Key words: *Caste, class, dalits, constitutional objectives, doubts.*

Introduction

2014 Lok Sabha elections are won by the Indian Prime Minister Mr Narender Modi by focusing on the agenda "*Acche Din Aaney Waley Hai*" (good days are about to come). A big difference between Congress and Bharatiya Janata Party (BJP) is that the former believes in ideology of secularism and favours the special provisions on the basis of caste, religion and gender. However, the latter has a strong faith in the promotion of '*Hindutava*' (Hindu religion) and is not in favour of special caste and religion-based provisions. One cannot deny the fact that the Prime Minister Mr Modi has his roots in Rashtriya Swayam Sewak Sangh (RSS) which has strong belief in Hinduism. The focus of elected 'Modi' government (named after Narender Modi) is on collective development of the Nation but the irony is that with the strong faith in 'Hindutava', the issue of collective development seems in doubt.

Brahmanical Structure of Indian Society

In India, the prevalence of Hindu religion is unchallenged. The brahmanical ideology which forms the very basis of Hindu religion has given birth to another ideology named as 'Casteism'. In India, the caste-based discrimination is an issue of serious concern. The casteism is an ideology which divides the Indian society on basis of caste and enriches one section of society with facilities and opportunities whereas the other section is made deprived. It is based on the notion of superiority and inferiority. The man born in high caste believes himself dominant and the lower caste believes their duty to be dominated. This is an ideology framed by the people and the role they provided to society also determines according to caste. On the basis of caste, the Indian society was divided into four Varnas. The highest Varna consisted the Brahmins and because they were at the highest position, therefore, they propagated that they were close to God. The society needed a ruler to frame laws and army to maintain its territories. This function was performed by the Kashatriyas. This was the second highest Varna in the Varna system. The Vaishyas considered at third position. They were inclined towards earning and therefore, they had their own business. The fourth Varna was that of Shudras which was indulged in the service sector like farming etc.. The 'Untouchables' or Ati-Shudras were kept out of the Varna system. The people belonging to this section was kept away from society and also deprived from basic necessities. They were meant to provide services to the higher Varnas. This impure category (Untouchable) mainly consisted of butchers, hunters, removers, cremators, hangmen, sweepers, drum beaters in funerals and festivals, grave diggers and manual scavengers etc. The people belonging to this section were forced to live out of the localities of the four Varnas and thus faced social ostracism. In a nutshell, this section was the most deprived section of Indian society. During the

Feudal System, these people were forced to work in the fields of their feudal lords. Neither the proper wages were given to them nor did they offer proper food. The feudal lords were dominant on this section because they were afraid of losing their control on them. They tried their level best to keep this section away from education and basic amenities. They did not want these people to become conscious of their rights. This was the reason behind that with the change of rulers and the ruling conditions in the Indian history, the caste based professions did not change and atrocities to this particular section continued. The other reason behind these atrocities was that the King granted large landholdings to the Brahmins which strengthened their (Brahmins) position in the society. The upper castes particularly the Brahmins and Kshatriyas were active enough to mould the society according to their benefits. They wanted to remain at the higher positions without any conflict and therefore, on the name of spreading education and providing defence to the society, they maintained the Brahmanical order. Thus, the structure of hierarchy based on occupational and endogamous castes was completely legitimised by the dominant religious categories of *Samskara, Karma* and *Dharma.* The foundation of this structure was entirely sanctified by the dominant Brahminic religio-cultural system.

During the early phase of the colonial period, the Britishers did not take any step for the upliftment of downtrodden. They knew if they interfered into the division of Varnas particularly in context of Untouchables, they will have to face the opposition from the upper strata of society. This could make their (colonial rulers) rule weak. In 1813 and 1854 the Charter Act and Wood Dispatch were adopted respectively to gain the sympathy of dalits and their leadership. Jyotiba Phuley was the first among them who started providing education to this section in a small room against the norms of society. Further, the Princely rulers like Maharaja of Mysore in south, Chatrapati Shahu Maharaj of Kolhapur and Maharaja of Baroda took various efforts for educating the Untouchables. For the first time in the Indian society, these rulers raised the issue of representation of this section in the Indian jobs. The representation was opposed by the higher Varnas because they did not want the brahmanical structure to be disturbed. Later, the issue of representation of Untouchables in jobs at par with upper castes was raised before many committees framed by the colonial rulers. Due to the sincere efforts of various princely states the Mysore became the first state where seats were reserved for the deprived (Untouchables) in the government services in India. However, under a great pressure from the leadership of the deprived section (later known as dalit), the Government of India Act 1919 was introduced.

During this period, Bal Gangadhar Tilak and Mahatma Gandhi were among those leaders who openly supported the Hindu Varna System and did not want any change in the *Varna Vyavstha* and Dr BR Ambedkar was the only leader who spoke in favour of dalits. He took the issue of dignity of the downtrodden section at the platform of three Round Table Conferences. His objective was to make untouchability and caste based discrimination legally prohibited and he finally convinced the colonial rulers to make a law providing the special provisions for upliftment of this section. As a consequence, the colonial rulers were convinced to adopt the separate electorate for this particular section in the Government of India Act 1935. This led to the emergence of conflict between Ambedkar and Gandhi. Gandhi demanded sharing of power with deprived section of society and fought for this till the end. A concrete example of this can be seen when the colonial rulers provided the Separate Electorate for dalits and in its opposition Gandhi went to hunger strike. However, in order to protect the law and order in the society, Dr Ambedkar had to change his stand against his own wishes. Dr Ambedkar and the Dalit community took it as discrimination to them on the name of political rights. This could be the reason behind that Dr Ambedkar had adopted Buddhist religion during the end days of his life because he knew that within Hindu religion a dalit cannot liberate himself from the rigid and discriminatory norms.

Caste in Contemporary India

In 1978, the Government of India appointed a Commission related to Other Backward Classes (OBCs) to look into and recommend ways to investigate the extent of educational and social backwardness among these classes and to give its recommendations on the ways in which this backwardness could be ended. The Commission was popularly known as Mandal Commission after the name of its Chairperson,

Bindeshwari Prasad Mandal. Though the Commission gave its report in 1980 but the recommendations of the report were implemented in August, 1990 by the National Front Government. The focus of the report was on reserving 27 per cent seats for the Other Backward Castes (OBCs) in educational institutions and government jobs. With the implementation of this report the entire political scenario was changed. The decision sparked agitations and violent protests in many cities of north India. The students in large number set themselves on fire against this implementation. The Congress party took its support back from the ruling party and as a consequence, the government lost its majority. During 1990-92, the Bhartiya Janata Party (BJP) also raised the issue of '*Hindutva*' intentionally. Hindutva literally means 'Hinduness'. It was believed in the case of India that Hindu culture alone can provide strong and united national culture. During this period, BJP along with Vishva Hindu Parishad (VHP) and RSS (Rashtriya Sweayam Sevak Sangh) convened a series of symbolic and mobilisational programmes. The BJP, in order to generate a massive support in its favour, took a massive march called the *Rathyatra* from Somnath in Gujarat to Ayodhya in Uttar Pradesh. One cannot deny the fact that the leadership was not interested to grant reservation because they were afraid of losing their control in the political, service and educational spheres. Further, the regional parties took reservation only as their vote bank.

Though dalits have been provided the rights and opportunities by the Constitution of India but the stigma of caste-system in society is still visible in human interaction of Indian society. In states like Bihar, Jharkhand, Chhattisgarh, Tamil Nadu, Orissa, Rajasthan, Punjab and Haryana, the *beggar* and human trafficking can be seen. A large number of dalits become victims of this. In brick kilns, stone quarries, beedi manufacture, carpet weaving, construction projects and sericulture processing industry, majority of poor dalits are working as bonded labourers. In the rural areas, the dalits are forced to work in the fields of rich higher caste landlords without any proper wages and when they demand their wages, they are beaten-up. In many backward areas, the caste stigma is still visible in shop of barber, tailor, washerman and tea-shops. In Punjab, Haryana, Rajasthan, Uttar Pradesh, Dalits are still living outside the village of upper-castes. In few states of southern

India, the dalits are debarred from entering into the temples. Though the Constitution of India has provided reservation to this section in the Gram Panchayats but once this section get elected, they do not have any say in the decision making. One cannot deny the fact that the feeling of superiority exists in higher caste and the lower castes are still serving these higher castes through their manual work. Why not the Brahmins work as cleaners in hotels as the dalits? Why the dalits are mostly poor as compared to higher castes?

Due to the spread of technology, the mechanisation of agriculture, the forced labour and inappropriate wages to dalit workers, they have been forced to migrate to cities in search of jobs. However, the condition of dalits in urban cities is satisfied to the extent that they are living as the neighbour of upper castes in the same locality. At workplaces dalits work with the upper castes because they have common dependency on resources, high literacy rate and belief in democratic values. But does this means that caste in urban cities has been declined? It is true that dalits working in the hotels of urban cities have to face the caste-based discrimination. They are forced by their hotel managers to hide their castes. Similarly, dalits who entered in offices through reservation also experience the caste-based discrimination with themselves. The upper castes call these people (dalits) as 'Quotawalas' (those who enter the services through quota) and feel themselves the victims of *Reverse Discrimination.* The caste-based superiority and inferiority builds the stressful relations between the people of upper castes and dalits. One cannot deny the fact that dalits generally lag behind in the flow of their work, building their strong background and personal contacts. This is because of their late entrance into the education system and mainstream of society as compared to the upper castes. As a consequence, very few dalits could manage the higher posts and the bureaucracy is seemed to be more dominated by the upper castes. The struggle of dalits for proving themselves in the society has to go a long way ahead. Due to the stigma of their low castes and superiority of upper castes in the society, dalits feel themselves inferior and as a result, they try to adopt the culture, dress and language of higher castes. This *Sanskritisation* has positive as well as negative effects too. In the former sense, it leads to the adoption of high culture and high standards that encourages the upliftment of people living at lower level.

But the negative impact is that this leads to the loss of their (dalit) 'own' identity. Though the people of urban cities are educated but a large section of educated society still keep themselves away from inter-caste marriages. Very few inter-caste marriages are taken place only where the generation does not have faith in casteism. In rural areas, the inter-caste marriages are considered as stigma. One can easily see the unity of people on the name of castes against each other. Even the State governments and its policies cannot yield any result in favour of dalits if the higher caste provide a strong opposition to their decisions and policies. The clashes on the name of caste and appeasement of the upper castes are common in India.

No doubt, various welfare policies have been introduced by the Indian Prime Minister Mr Narender Modi in co-ordination with state governments within his 100 days tenure after election. But a lot has still to be done. The focus of the government should be on the downtrodden section of society particularly the poor dalits. It is important because the welfare policies are framed by all Central and State governments do not reach to this section because of corruption and non-sincerity of the administrators. The stigma of casteism also plays very important role in this. The Modi government should not adopt Hindutva in its agenda because the notion is based on division of humanity in the society. For this, it will be a great challenge to him to how to keep away from the pressure groups like RSS and Bajrang Dal etc.. The inclusive development of any State is possible only when the entire humanity is progressing. To achieve this objective, Modi has to build his image as a leader not favouring a particular religion. There is no doubt that dalits in India are still in fear that BJP notion of *Hindutva* will make Hindus more powerful particularly in context of caste system. Therefore, a large number of them (dalits) can be seen opposing the BJP at many occasions. The challenge before Modi is, therefore, to bring inclusive development of each section of society particularly within the dalits and to deal with *Hindutva* tactfully. The struggle of the downtrodden for their identity should be recognised and whole of bureaucracy, legislature and people at large should be sensitised about the plight of Dalits and collective endeavours should be made to elevate the condition of this deprived section of society.

References

1. Aloysius, G. (1997). *Nationalism without a Nation in India*. Delhi: Oxford University Press.
2. Government of Punjab (2005). Manual of Reservation of Scheduled Castes and Backward Classes in Services-Part V. Department of Welfare (Reservation Cell).
3. Illaiha, Kancha (2003). *Main Hindu Kyun Nahi Hoon*. Delhi: Arohi Book Trust.
4. Iverson, Vegard and Raghavendra P.S. (2007). What the Signboard Hides: Food, Caste and Employability in Small Indian Eating Places. Sage Publication.
5. Jaiswal, Suvira (2000). *Caste: Origin, Function and Dimensions of Change*. Delhi: Manohar Publishers and Distributors.
6. Judge, Paramjeet S. and Gurpreet Bal (2008). 'Understanding the Paradox of changes among Dalits in Punjab', *Economic and Political Weekly,* Vol. 43, No. 41(Oct.11-17), pp. 49-55.
7. Nirula (2009). *Dalits- A Bruised Dignity- Recasting Caste (Vol. II).* New Delhi: APH Publishing Corporation.
8. Rao, Parimala V. (2009). 'Gandhi, Untouchability and Post Colonial Predicament: A Note', *Social Scientist*, Vol. 37, No. 1/2.
9. Rath, Prabodh Kumar (2010). 'Gandhian Sarvodaya', *Orissa Review,* 36-39.
10. Shah, Ghanshyam (1985). 'Caste, Class and Reservation', *Economic and Political Weekly*, Vol. 20, No. 3 (Jan.19), pp. 132-136.
11. Shah, Ghanshyam (2008). *Caste and Democratic Politics in India*. Delhi: Permanent Black.
12. Somashekharappa, C.A. (2010). *Dalit Employee: A Sociological Study of Inter-Personal Relations at Work Place.* New Delhi: Prateeksha Publication.
13. Thorat, Sukhadeo (2004). Marginalised Groups and the Common Minimum Programme. *Social Scientist.*

22

Ageing and Social Exclusion: The Gauntlets and Requisite Bucklers for the Elderly in 21st Epoch

—***Rupinder Aulakh***

Abstract

The perception of social exclusion and marginalisation limits the opportunities and keys to living for the people who belong to such group. They are regarded as passive thespians in the participatory process of development of nation. India, like many developing countries is grappling with the population ageing which is an inevitable process. The vulnerability among the aged is not only due to disability and the probability incidence of illness but the economic dependence upon their off springs, spouses and the other younger family members are also the prominent perspectives. Apart from the basic needs, health care of aged which is often accompanied by multiple illness and physical ailments and moreover the drivers regarding the changing patterns of living, women participation in economic pursuits are the various root causes increases the risk of exclusion from main stream of the society. Its ramification has signs of twinges and sighs of sorrows as a grey side of the societal frame work. The study of fountainheads of such social exclusion in multiple spectrums becomes substantial for ensuring quality life to gargantuan reservoir of traditional values, norms and culture.

Keywords: *Social Exclusion, Ageing, Vulnerability, Deprivation, Social Insecurity, Multiple Exclusion, Bucklers, Human Rights, Institutional Inclusion.*

Introduction

Social exclusion is about the inability of our society to keep all groups and individuals within reach of what we expect as a society...[or] to realise their full potential.[1]

The global population of elderly has constantly been proliferating during the second half of last century due to easy availability of life saving drugs, control over communicable diseases, technological advancements, health facilities and nutrition, awareness among the people and overall better standard of living.[2] India: a Nation with umpteen values, aesthetically strong norms and folkways where aged have been considered as pivot and the value based magnanimous and colossal joint families have been a privileged institution for serving the elderly population for ages. It is also witnessing pronto ageing of its population at enormous pace. Ageing which is a natural, substantial, undesirable, inevitable and integral process occurs in human life cycle often regarded as evening of life and brings with a host of challenges in the life of the elderly, which are mostly engineered by the changes in their body, mind, thought process and living patterns. They constitute a value store of such human resources as gifted with knowledge of past learning, experiences and deep insights. It is acknowledged that the present population of India is approximately 1.27 billion and it has around 100 million elderly at present and the number is expected to soar to 323 million constituting 20 per cent of the population by 2050 i.e. the population of aged would shoot up by 360 per cent as compare to 60 per cent of rose in total population.[3] The population of geriatrics has shown a tremendous change after 1961. With the mushrooming population; the patterns of their living, their status, role in the family, community and society is also changing with the passage of time. The cultural values, standards of behaviour and the outlook towards aged is also drifting from the original track on the basis of dynamic particles i.e. changing aspects of societal patterns. This paper is an attempt to comprehend the prevalence of the gauntlets before aged, the fountainheads and the ramification on aging population, the realities in terms of their gratification with living arrangements, strategies and initiatives of the Government to ensure their persistence in the existing framework of society.

Table 22.1: Proportionate Growth of Old Age Population to Total Population in India after Independence

Period	*Population(in millions)*	*Proportionate growth*
1951	20.19	5.6 per cent
1991	55	6.8 per cent
2001	77	7.4 per cent
2025	177.7 (Projected to rise)	12.4 per cent (Projected to rise)

Source: http://www.censusindia.gov.in/
http://mospi.nic.in/

The population grew after 1951 and in 1991 it rose to 20.19 million to 55 million and the growth rate of aged in proportion to the total population rose from 5.6 per cent to 6.8 per cent. later in 2001,the population of aged was 77 million constituting 7.4 per cent and which is said to rise up to 12.4 per cent i.e. 177.7 million in the terms of population by the end of 2025.

So as the dependency ratio of aged to the total population of the country which is gradually creeping at snail's pace.

Table 22.2: Dependency Ratio for Aged to the Total Population in India

Period	*Proportionate growth*
1961	10.5 per cent
1991	11.8 per cent
2021	16.1 per cent (Projected to be)

Source: http://www.yojana.gov.in/

The dependency ratio for aged to the total population was 10.5 per cent in 1961, 11.8 per cent in 1991 which is projected to hike upto 16.1 per cent by the 2021.

Conceptualising Ageing and Social Exclusion: Both of these aspects prevail simultaneously in society. They mushroom being intertwined as the human being proceed towards ageing the aspect of social exclusion comes to existence in many unfair ways.

Ageing: Ageing is the gradual process of growing older representing the accumulation of changes in a person with the passage of time. Ageing is an imperative part of all human societies depicting the biological, cultural as well as societal conventions. Old age is the most unexpected of all things that can happen to a man.[4] Ageing is now recognised as a "global phenomenon" and called as the largest known risk factors for most human diseases.[5] In India, the piecemeal but non-identical transformations have become the platform of bouleversement in the society which directly and indirectly leads to mushrooming problems for ageing population. There are some puissant factors which are responsible for decomposition of cavernous institutional ties such as westernisation, globalisation, industrialisation, education advancement, hedonism, economic pursuits, and women participation in working spectrum as well as open the threshold to the counterbalance in the various aspects of equipoise societal framework. They have marked the beginning of erosion and degradation of traditional values, norms, cultural aspects and institutional setup. Thus, the process of ageing is always accompanied by a decline in the wellbeing of the human beings that results in the rising economic, health and social insecurity among the aged. The aged generally suffer from economic dependency, physical immobility and insecurity in the form access to health care and also from social isolation.[6] with the increase in old age the aged people experience more multidimensional social exclusion.

Social Exclusion: Social exclusion is a multidimensional process of progressive social rupture, detaching groups and individuals from social relations and institutions and preventing them from full participation in the normal, normatively prescribed activities of the society in which they live.[7] as per the domain of public policies; social exclusion is exclusion from social justice also in terms of social isolation. In other words, it is the process in which individuals and the entire communities of people are systematically blocked or denied full access to various rights, opportunities and resources that are normally available to the members of a different group and which are fundamental to social integration within that particular group.[8] it is more often called detachment from the main domain of the societal setup in terms of:

(a) Exclusion from social relationships

(b) Exclusion from cultural activities
(c) Exclusion from civic activities and access to information
(d) Exclusion from decent housing and public transport
(e) Exclusion from financial aspects (pension and property)
(f) Exclusion from common consumer goods (denial to wear and consume certain products).[9]

Multidimensional Aspects of Social Exclusion with Respect to Ageing: (Figure 1)

Thus, the old face multi-dimensional disadvantages including lack of assets, isolation and physical infirmity. They are associated with the institutional arrangements and the aspects that exclude them from full participation in the economic, social, and political life of their communities. Such discriminatory aspects include biased laws and practices of Governments and attitude changes and negative perceptions for aged among the family members. This often leads to denial of support system and services in terms of age. The aged are at high risk of deprivation and insecurity in different aspects. This problem is very prominent in the metro areas where life is so fast and materialistic with high cost of living standard but in some hinterlands the support system of aged is still prevalent.

Thus the above discussed fountainheads account to gradual but severe change in patterns of relationships and ways of living.

Various Thespians Responsible for bouleversement fostering Social Exclusion

Social exclusion being the dynamic process that precludes full engagement in normatively prescribed activities of a given society and denies access to information, resources, sociability, recognition and identity, eroding self respect and reducing capabilities to attain personal goals.[10] The various drivers of social exclusion that make the relevance possible in spite of several strategies and policies for support of aged people.

The Thespians Responsible for the Pertinence of Social Exclusion for Old Age People (Figure 2)

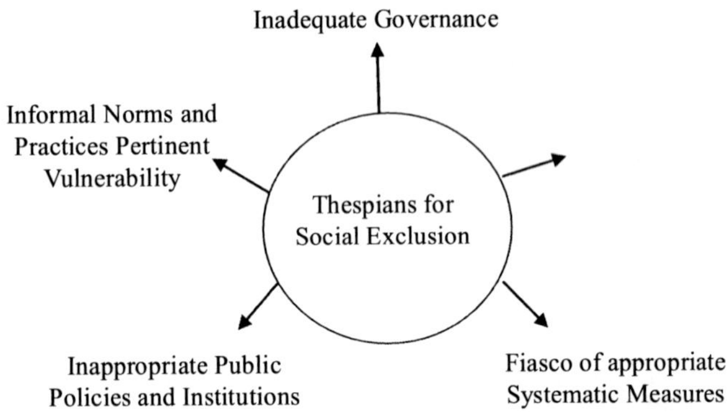

(a) **Inadequate Governance:** The ability on the part of government and societal institutions which uphold and enforce the traits of good governance i.e. rule of law, equity, transparency and accountability, counteract corrupt practices, red tapism, minimise the illegitimate bureaucratic affairs, clientelism and promotion of political participation.

(b) **Pertinent vulnerability:** Deprivation, social insecurity, physical inability to be a part of productive activities, disability, illness and a hard course of living being dependent and taking life as a compromise at the twilight facet of life and not being blithesome in the real terms.

(c) **Informal Norms and Practices:** Inappropriate rights to safeguards, unfair ways of living, hedonism, more attachment to economic pursuits, busy life and changing patterns of living due to several alien factors. The changing scenarios of societal setup and inability to cope up with them pronto due to inadequate system of support is quiet problematic and make them feel out of the place. Discrimination against aged on the basis of their age, their participation in earning the livelihood and certain social as well as personal characteristics

(d) **Inappropriate Public Policies and Institutions:** The inability of public policies and institutions to promote equity and precise access to opportunities, resources and all the benedictions which are made available to them via various institutional arrangements and public strategies.

(e) **Fiasco of Appropriate Systematic Measures:** The prominent factor which defines the inability on the part of Government to bridge the gap between De Jure and De Facto. The failure to provide adequate human capabilities of living that prevents them from accessing adequate and sustainable income resources.

Impact of such bouleversement on elderly and society

The elder abuse has a deep but negative impact on the aged themselves as well as on society. The aged persons are disorganised further leading to suicide and deteriorate condition to demise. The present young generation is kept aloof of the experiences, teachings and valuable thoughts of elders. The society also penalize for this kind of treatment towards aged. The individual disorganisation leads social disorganisation, upheaval in the relationships. Thus, the abuse of elders by unscrupulous caregivers is a gleaming issue high and dry. Responsibility of nurturing as well as protecting them earlier was vested in the hands of families and community which are the fountainhead of abuse in the 21st century.

Strategical measures for ageing Population by Government: There are certain provisions, strategies, policies and support system which have been made available to elderly population by the Government such as:

(a) Universal Declaration of Human Rights (1948): There are certain Articles available for dignified living, protection from discrimination, privacy, social security, right to marriage, love and family and adequate standard of living.

(b) International Covenant on Economic, Social and Cultural Rights (1966): It provides for Right for progressive realisation, living in just and favourable conditions, healthy living, secured and better living.

(c) International Covenant of Civil and Political Rights (1966), Convention on the Elimination of All forms of Discrimination Against Women (1979), International Plan of Action for Ageing (1982) etc.

(d) The various Acts and Plans of Government: Section 25(1) (d) of code of Criminal Procedure Act (1973), NHRC (1993), NPOP (1999), Article 14, 15 and 16 ensuring equality, freedom from discrimination, equal opportunities and equality before law.

(e) Article 41 and 46 of Directive Principles of State Policy ensuring secured living in all economic and social terms.

(f) The Maintenance and Welfare of Parents and Senior Citizens Bills, 2007: where by clause 5 (1), clause 4, clause 14 and clause 42 of the Act provides for protection and a peaceful living by effective support system from the relatives.

Even though there is a crystal clear dark side of their living. Therefore, the aged indeed face troubles, disregard and exclusion from the various institutions and lead a life with compromise towards situations and circumstances. They are the real sufferers at the golden period of their life.

Dire need for Strategic Innovations for the well being of Aged: The need of the hour calls for certain changes in the institutional arrangements to provide a dignified living to the aged. The problems need to be recognised and medicated at the strategic level.

(a) **Investment in geriatric health care services:** Government should strive hard to provide the effective health services to the aged. The nurses, doctors and medical personages are to be sensitized regarding elder abuse. Hospital should have adequate provisions and facilities for aged as well as precise in number. Government should provide proper funding to the hospitals and medical clinics. Hospital staff must not take them for granted and feel themselves responsible to support the elders willingly and in a better way.

(b) **Updating the pension policies and security programmes for elders:** Government must update the pension programmes for the elders. They must have appropriate source of income after retirement from active employment such as income should be in time and with standard of living of country of which the aged is a members. There should be improvement in systematic aspects; the elders must not harass due to lengthy, time and energy consuming methods. Those living in old age homes must be given timely old age pension without long run exertion. Pension amount should be updated time to time to give them a quality life.

(c) **Awareness programmes for young generation in education system:** Education develops the character of a human being but we have to maintain that character by all fair means. Young generation must be aware of their responsibilities towards the elderly. Camps, workshops, seminars must be conducted along with the teaching aspect in schools and colleges so that the young generation is filled with broad and new outlook towards their elders. This would break the orthodox stereotypes for the aged and help in remodelling the new aesthetic and relevant societal framework.

(d) **Sensitizing the agencies of justice for elderly population:** Education and training those who are in criminal justice systems such as police, prosecutors and judiciary an older abuse as well as increase legislation to protect the elders. This helps to minimise elder abuse and also provides improves assistance to victims of elder abuse.

(e) **Awareness programmes for NGOs, society and the aged:** The Government should aim to aware the aged of their rights, health and hygiene. They must be aware of their importance and need in the society. They must be updated regarding the rules, laws and schemes of the Government for their better living. The familial institutions and communities should be awarded of their value, need and sensitize to respect the aged.

This is needed for maintaining harmony in the society and preventing all from disorganisation. The NGOs must be funded only by enquiring into its prospects if it is really working for the well being of aged or not. We need a proper remedy and synchronization among Government, NGOs and people living in the society.

(f) **Provisions for re-employment:** Government must provide them opportunity to seek re-employment. Proper and pliable employment options are to be made available so that they can use their primal knowledge, capacities and capabilities. This could liberate them from feel of dependency and enable them to have ample source of income to live as they wish. Moreover, it would keep them bust and divert their mind from all troubles that may put a halt on their mental, physical and social well being. Their productive potential is utilized in the community services. It also enhances their longevity.

(g) **Revamping the institutional means:** it is essential to focus on the protection of already existing social support systems/ traditional social institutions such as family and kinship, neighbourhood bonding, community bonding and community participation and some institutions fit for the elderly social interactions. They must be made free to choose their spouses if they need, peers and friends and set free to spend time with them. There is a need to revitalise the institutional means to provide them civic, cultural and recreational satisfaction. The Government must support the establishment of more day care centres, adequate old age homes so that they could go there and lead their twilight years as they want to be.

(h) **Stronger mechanism to prevent older abuse:** There should be single point of access to all ageing information and services in the community and the strategic expansion of services that would help the aged is essential. All the agencies and institutions must be educated and taught to work in a fair legal manner. Those who try to violate the existing mechanisms must be penalised to make justice to the victims. The Acts and provisions which serve the aged must be changed with the dynamic circumstances for the benediction of the aged and society as a whole.

(i) **Sustainable human rights community for aged:** It means a community in which all the members from policy makers to ordinary citizens learn about and adhere to human rights obligations. All organisations-public or private join to monitor violations and implementation of human rights at all levels of society. They would develop the methodology to ensure all decisions, laws , policies, resource allocation and relationships are bound by human rights norms and standards at all levels of decision making and problem sorting aspects. This would bring about economic and social change necessary for sustainable development.

(j) **Empowering the elderly population in real practical sense:** Elders must be empowered for their own exigencies and get them fulfilled within the human rights framework. The elders must be given a proper opportunity in practical sense to build a supportive society for them. This would give them opportunity to live with freedom, dignity and celebrating their golden phase of life. They must be supported by Government to use the mechanisms for their own well being. All must contribute to act as active thespians for prolonging the weal of aged.

(k) **Need for professional care givers:** It is essential so that the family members who cannot spare time due to their work load but could support the elders with monetary aspects; can have the opportunity to hire the care givers for their elders. The caregivers must be professional and have emotional setup which is substantial for the better look after of aged. There should be provisions and support for care giver support groups so that they could nurture the dependent elderly. It is also essential to prevent the elders from being harassed and abused.

(l) **Strengthening the role of electronic media and print media:** In the present time, electronic as well as print media play a prominent role in guiding the public. Most of the time of children as well as elders is spent watching the channels catering to their desires. So, Government should make efforts to promote the initiatives on their part. Moreover, the media should use its strength and contribute positively by ushering the right aspects so as to serve as an active guide for the different generations. It could help a lot in synchronizing and harmonising the different aspects of society.

(m) **Strengthening the Voluntary initiatives:** Community involvement to prevent the elder abuse is must. Communities can develop programmes that are structured around meeting the needs of elder persons. Government should initiate the reward and support system adequately for those who come forth to serve the valuable segment of the society. The various multidisciplinary groups which consist of public and private professionals who promote advocacy programmes for the vulnerable elders must be supported financially so as to boost their efforts to solve the problems of elders.

(n) **Counselling services to aged:** Counselling services have paved the path for well being of the family, aged as well as the society. **It is the mid path to bridge the gap between the aspirations as well as the expectations**. Both specialised personages as well as family members could serve as the active agent to resolve the misunderstandings between old and young generations. It is the open environment where the neglected, depressed, annihilated as well as abused elders revamp their energy and sort out their issues and grudges. It enables the elders to adjust the changed circumstances and cooperate with young generation. **It serves as an important component of family therapy.**

Conclusion

There is a need to take pronto action to address such issues on aged living. Aged being the vulnerable segment of society should be provided with awareness involving education in social, cultural, political rights and also precise retirement and widowhood pension schemes should be provided to their betterment. They must be kept away from upheavals and corrupt and delayed practices of Government. Aged are the diamonds and they can be preserved only if the society really provides them effective support system like hard gold foundation. Human rights issues relating to elderly population in India can be tackled by creating a network of support system within or outside the family as a whole because golden agers being the most imperative segment of the society must be protected as they are the source of transformation of values, store of knowledge and experiences. It is to be clearly understood that the problem once created cannot be eliminated, but can be curbed to a large extent by synchronising and guiding efforts in a right way.

References

1. Social Exclusion in the UK.
2. Dr Shakuntala C. Shettar, "Problems of Aged in Changing Indian Scenario", in *Yojana,* April 2015.
3. A Report by United Nations Population Fund and Help Age International.
4. http://www.grhgraph.wordprss.com
5. Diilin A, Gottschling DE, Nystrom T; Gottschling; Nystrom (2014), "The good and The Bad of Being Connected :The Integrons of Aging", *Curr Opin Cell Biol* 26: 107-12 Doi:10.1016/j.ceb.2013.12.003.
6. Syam Prasad, "Deprivation and Vulnerability among Elderly in India" in *Indira Gandhi Institute of Development Research,* Mumbai, July 2011 http:// www.igidr.ac.in/pdf/publicayion/WP-2011-013.pdf
7. Hilary Silver, "Social Exclusion: Comparative Analysis of Europe and Middle East youth", in *Middle East Youth Initiative Working Paper (September 2007),* p. 15.
8. Alder School of Professional Psychology.
9. www.ilcuk.org.uk.
10. Babken Babajanian and Jessica Hagen-Zanker, "Social Protection and Social Exclusion:

    An Analytical Framework to Access the Links", in *Background Note of The Overseas Development Institution,* UK, October 2012.

23

Land Acquisition for SEZs: An Issue of Socio-Economic Exclusion

—***Manish Kumar***

Abstract

The process of land acquisition for special economic zones has given rise to widespread protest around the length and breadth of the country. In the absence of concrete measures for rehabilitation of displaced people, the future of most of the affected, especially of small farmers and dependents, remained uncertain. SEZs in this context had been seen as symbol of growth redden with social and economic exclusion. It was promised by the government that 'humane' displacement for the establishment of special economic zones would be followed by relief and rehabilitation. However, the historical evidences were contrary in this regard. Fecundity of the new law to address the concerns is still to be ascertained.

Implementation of the policy of establishing special economic zones has roused a nation-wide debate as the economic changes are necessarily followed by some social ramification. Resultantly in several states there existed a widespread attitude of pessimism about the process of establishment of special economic zones. Since the independence very few policies were subject to such political opposition from the affected public and faced such fierce intellectual criticism from across the spectrum of commentators including those in international multilateral organisation. The Parliamentary Standing Committee on Commerce even recommended that there should be freeze on SEZ approvals (Seminar 2008, 12, 22).

It was resented that through the policy of special economic zones, the country was going to set up 'inequalities enclaves' of development which would result in exclusive growth. Some critics were of the view that the SEZ policy could lead to a dehumanised progress 'where wealth accumulates and men decay (Vombbatkere 2006). On some quarters they went as far as declaring the SEZ policy unconstitutional (Citizen Research Collective 2008). Special economic zones faced resistance around the length and breadth of the country. From Amritsar in Punjab and Jhajjar in Haryana in the north to Kakinada in Andhra Pradesh and Nandagudi in Karnataka in the south; from Nandigram in West Bengal and Jagatsinghpur in Orissa in the East to Raigadh, Mangalore and Goa in the west coast of India. Farmers, landless workers, fishermen, and artisans had expressed their anger against the loss of their livelihood and habitat due to establishment of special economic zones (Seminar 2008, 14). These zones were described as an official tool used by big industrialists and real estate developers to grab land from farmers for making money (Levien 2011; Palit and Bhattachargee 2007). A Report of Expert Group released by the Planning Commission expressed its doubt regarding the benefits of SEZs (Government of India 2008):

> Land acquisition for Special Economic Zones (SEZ) has given rise to widespread protest in various parts of the country. Large tracts of land are being acquired across the country for this purpose. Already, questions have been raised on two counts. One is the loss of revenue in the form of taxes and the other is the effect on agricultural production.

The Committee on State Agrarian Relations and Unfinished Task in Land Reforms set up in 2008 made a strong case for reassessment of the Special Economic Zones Act, 2005 and put a ban on the transfer of common property resource and agricultural land for its implementation (Government of India 2009). The New York Times (2006) expressed its concerns about Shenzhen, a role model for special economic zones all over the world:

> Few cities anywhere have created wealth faster than Shenzhen, but the cost of its phenomenal success stare out from every corner: environmental destruction, soaring crime rates and disillusionment and degradation of its vast force of migrant workers.

The main issue that unnerved the process of setting up of SEZs in India was displacement and loss of livelihood of the people due to land acquisition. Land acquisition for special economic zones became a serious problem. Earlier the state governments were legally acquiring land for private zones without seeking consent of the local people under Land Acquisition Act, 1894. The Act allowed the government to acquire land for 'public purpose' that was defined for an age when the government used to carry out many development activities which were now in the domain of the private sector (Mukhergi 2008). This triggered off protest in a number of special economic zones located in India, where people refused to give up their residence and traditional sources of livelihood easily. People of Nandigram in West Bengal fought at great personal cost to retain their land (Kasturi 2008). Table 1is a specimen of multiple resistances those had gained prominence across the country.

Table 1: Some Social Movements against SEZs across India

State	*Key Facts*
West Bengal	* Agitation led to the death of at least 14 villagers on 14 March, and severe government crackdown in November 2007. * SEZ in Nandigram was withdrawn.
Goa (various parts)	* Village resistance under the umbrella organization 'SEZ Virodh Manch' (People's Movement against SEZs). * Strong, nonpartisan support from church. * All 15 SEZs scrapped in the state on 31 December 2007
Karnatka (Nandagudi)	* Under the umbrella organization 'Nandagaudi Raitha Hitarakshana Samithi', 21000 farmers from 36 villages were resisting land acquisition for a 12,000+acre SEZ. * Land has high real estate value due to close proximity to upcoming international Airport.
Karnatka(Mangalore)	* Under the umbrella organization 'Krishi Bhoomi Smrakshana a Vedike', affected residents were protesting the proposed 2000+ acre SEZ that

(*Contd...*)

	would engulf 4 villages and displace over 2000 residents. * In October 2007, protesters managed to send back an SEZ survey team.
Maharashtra (Raigad)	* protesting farmers from at least 24 villages being supported by multiple partisan and non-partisan and non partisan umbrella organizations. * 1000 protesters burnt land acquisition notices in June of 2007 and 5000 farmers blocked a high-way.
Orissa (Jagatsinghpur)	* Farmers were resisting an SEZ project by Posco Steel Company (considered to be India's largest FDI project).
	* 22,000 villagers potentially affected by land ac-quisition.

Source: Jones, Jonathan (2008).

In the absence of concrete measures for rehabilitation and displaced people, the future of most of the affected, especially of small farmers and dependents, remained uncertain. Sensing the potential of further eruptions, the Central Government put on hold the all pending proposals to establish special economic zone (Dohrmann 2008). It was promised by the government that 'humane' displacement for the establishment of special economic zones would be followed by relief and rehabilitation. However, the historical evidences were contrary in that regard. According to an estimate, since 1950 nearly 40 million people (of which about 40 per cent are tribal and 25 per cent are *dalits*) lost their land on account of displacement due to large development projects. As far as rehabilitation is concerned at least 75 per cent of them were still awaiting competition (Citizen Research Collective 2008).

Though farmers were given price value or compensation for their land but the procedure of fixing value, based on current use of the land (which did not recognize the converted use) was denounced as completely colonial and most unfair (Ranganathan 2007). Market price roughly reflected the discounted sum of the expected value of output produced by land in future, net of material and labour cost. To an owner-farmer, however, ownership of land gives an opportunity to work, given widespread underemployment in the rural sector. If the farmer did not have land of his own, probably he would have remained unemployed for a longer period of year than he was then. This particular advantage that land gives him would not be reflected in the market price. The value of land for small farmer is even higher than what is determined by the market. A small farmer owning a piece of land usually markets a very small part of the produce and keeps larger part for self-consumption. Now if farmer sells the land, he will have to procure food grains for his self-consumption from the market at higher market price. The market price of food-grain is much higher than the price at which farmer sells his produce. Thus the market price cannot properly compensate that probable loss of the owner-farmer. Questions were also raised about the practice of evaluating land on the basis of what land could earn in future, if put to an alternative use. Evidently, the value of land would be higher if it was used for industry, compared to its present value when it was engaged in agriculture sector. Social justice required that the present owner of land should also get share of that increased valuation (Sarkar 2007).

Millions of jobs would be created but one could not expect much rise in opportunities for the non-skilled displaced persons. It was contended that losers of livelihoods were not gainers of employment (Asher 2007). There might be some jobs for labourers during construction of infrastructure but that too would be for limited period only. After that, jobs available would require expertise and experience and hence could not be offered to farmers who knew nothing other than farming. Thus, one could not expect that the SEZs, which would create plenty of jobs, would benefit those agriculturists and dependent people, who parted with their resources of livelihood and future security. There was an imperative need to recognize rehabilitation and resettlement issues as intrinsic to the development process. Conditions should be formulated with the active participation of the affected persons, rather than externally-imposed requirements. The Parliamentary Committee on SEZs recommended a freeze on special economic zones. It recommended that (Government of India 2007):

(a) The maximum size of a multi-product SEZ should be 5000 hectares of fallow land or 2000 hectares of one crop land. There should be no SEZs on multi-crop land.

(b) Land should be taken on lease from farmers and farmers should be paid periodic rentals.

(c) That the state government should set a benchmark price for land and farmers should be paid a price higher than that price.

(d) Processing area in a zone should be raised from 35 per cent to 50 per cent of the total area.

(e) The committee noted the lack of representation from the Ministry of Agriculture in the process of implementation of special economic zones

The government resorted to form an Empowered Group of Ministers to devise a way out for resuming the policy. Though various measures were introduced during that period, those were mostly technical in nature. The government was aware that there was an absence of a national law to provide for the rehabilitation and resettlement and compensation for loss of livelihoods. The ministry of rural development initiated work on policy of Relief and Rehabilitation to address the heightened public concern on issue of land acquisition

The National Rehabilitation and Resettlement Policy, 2007

The National Rehabilitation and Resettlement Policy, 2007 calls for a broader concerted effort on the part of planners to include in the displacement, rehabilitation and resettlement process framework, not only those who directly lose land and other assets but also those who are affected by such acquisition of land. The policy necessitates the careful assessment of the economic disadvantages and social impact of displacement. The aim is to minimize large-scale displacement. It also provides that as far as possible, projects may be set up on wasteland, degraded land, or un-irrigated land. Prior to initiating the acquisition of land for a project the appropriate government should, *inter-alia* take into consideration the alternatives that will:

1. Minimise the displacement of people due to the acquisition of land for the project;
2. Minimise the total area of land to be acquired for the project;
3. Minimise the acquisition of agricultural land for non-agricultural use in the project.

Land Acquisition and Rehabilitation and Resettlement Bill (LARR), 2011

The undergoing efforts of the Ministry later culminated into Land Acquisition and Rehabilitation and Resettlement Bill (LARR), 2011. Though multiple amendments have been made to the Land Acquisition Act, 1894, the principal law continued to be the same. The Bill seeks to address the concerns of displaced persons, farmers as well as those who whose livelihood is lost due to their dependence on the land being acquired. At the same time it facilitates land acquisition for industrialisation, infrastructure and urbanisation. A welcome change is that it recognises the intrinsic relationship between land acquisition and rehabilitation and resettlement. It provides that in a case where the government is involved in the process of land acquisition including partial acquisition for public purpose, the process must be accompanied by rehabilitation and resettlement.

The Bill requires that if government acquires land for the use of private companies for stated public purpose or for immediate and declared use by private companies for public purpose, the prior consent of 80 per cent of project affected families for proposed acquisition is necessary. Rehabilitation and resettlement provisions will also apply when a private company buy more than 100 acres of land in a rural area and more than 50 acres of land in urban area for a project. Along with land owners, the Bill also extends benefit of rehabilitation and resettlement to livelihood losers who are without any ownership of land. Only those families shall be considered in this context whose livelihood is primarily dependent on the land being acquired and resources therein for last three years. Thus, agricultural labourers, tenants or sharecroppers, forest gatherers, hunters, fisher folk, boatmen etc. are also brought under the umbrella of benefits. Similar condition will apply to non-owners dependent primarily on the land being acquired in the urban areas.

The Bill defines land as "benefits to arise out of land, and things attached to earth or permanently fastened to anything attached to the earth." It prohibits the acquisition of multi-crop irrigated land except as a demonstrably last resort, in that case too; the acquisition should not be more than 5 per cent of the total multi-crop irrigated area in a district. It further provides that if a private company wants to purchase land for a project more than the area limit stipulated in the Bill, it can pursue only after the Collector pass individual awards covering rehabilitation and resettlement entitlements. The Bill devises some safeguards against indiscriminate acquisition:

- Mandatory social impact assessment.
- Approval of 'public purpose' and social impact assessment report by Chief Secretary Committee/Delegated Committee.
- Summary of rehabilitation and resettlement package to be included in draft Declaration.
- The purposes specified in the land use plan submitted at the time of land acquisition cannot be changed afterward.
- No change of ownership is allowed without due permission.
- Land shall be transferred to state government's land bank if it is not used in accordance with the specified purpose within 10 years.
- Upon every transfer of land without development, 20 per cent of the appreciated land value shall be mandatorily shared with the original owner whose land has been acquired.

Several measures have been adopted to bring in transparency in the process such as Gram Sabha is to be consulted for social impact assessment, social impact assessment report to be made available for public scrutiny, rehabilitation and resettlement scheme to made available for public scrutiny besides, all documents are to made available in the public domain. In addition to these, timeframe has also been stipulated; compensation will be given within a period of 3 months from the date of award; monetary rehabilitation and resettlement entitlements will be provided within a period of 6 months from the date of award; infrastructure entitlements will be provided within a period of 18 months from the date of award; no involuntary displacement shall take place without completion of rehabilitation and resettlement. On the whole, an attempt has been made in the Bill to bring the interests of land owners in tune with process of infrastructural and industrial development. Besides resettlement, displacement causes various other difficulties such as problem of social cohesion at new place, no knowledge of new area, cooperation, and problems related to education of children and health facilities. Fecundity of the new law to address these concerns is still to be ascertained.

References

Asher, Manshi and Patrik Oskarsson. "Se(i)zing the coast and the countryside." *Seminar*, February 2008.

Citizen Research Collective. "SEZs and Land Acquisition: Factsheet for an Unconstitutional Economic Policy." *Seminar*, 2008: 15-19.

Dohrmann, Jona Arvind. "Special Economic Zones in India- An Introduction." August 26-September 2, 2008. http://www.asienkunde.de/articles/a106_asien_aktuell_dohrmann.pdf (accessed January 3, 2013).

Government of India. *Development Challanges in Extremist Affected Areas*. Report of an Expert Group , New Delhi: Planning Commission, 2008.

Government of India. *Draft Report of the Committee on State Agrarian Relations and Unfinished Task in Land Reforms*. New Delhi: Ministry of Rural Development, 2009.

Government of India. "Parliamentry Standing Committee Report." Parliamentry Report, 2007: cited in Mukhergi 2008.

Jones, Jonathan. "India's democracy has a heartbeat." *Seminar*, February 2008: 65-68.

Kasturi, Kannan. "Of public purpose and private profit." *Seminar*, February 2008: 32-35

Levien, Michael. "Rationalising Dispossession: the Land Acquisition and Resettlement Bills." *Economic and Political Weekly* 46, no. 11 (March 2011): 66-71.

Mukhergi, Rahul. "Special Economic Zones in India: Recent Developments and Future Prospects." Working Paper, Institute of South Asian Studies, National University of Singapore, Singapore, 2008.

Palit, A., and S. Bhattachargee. *Special Economic Zones in India- Myths and Realities*. Delhi: Anthem Press, 2007.

Ranganathan, V. "Special Economic Zones: Rationale and Prospects." *The Hindu Survey of Indian Industry*, 2007: 24-26.

Sarkar, Abhirup. "Development and Displacement." *Economic and Political Weekly* 42, no. 16 (April 2007): 1435-1442.

Seminar. February 2008.

The New York Times. December 19, 2006.

Vombatkere, S.G. "Neo-zmidari Zones." *Mainstreame* 44, no. 51 (December 2006): 9-10.

Index